READING
and
UNDERSTANDING
the BIBLE

READING
and
UNDERSTANDING
the BIBLE

BEN WITHERINGTON III

Oxford   New York
Oxford University Press

Oxford University Press is a department of the University of Oxford.
It furthers the University's objective of excellence in research, scholarship,
and education by publishing worldwide.

Oxford   New York
Auckland   Cape Town   Dar es Salaam   Hong Kong   Karachi
Kuala Lumpur   Madrid   Melbourne   Mexico City   Nairobi
New Delhi   Shanghai   Taipei   Toronto

With offices in
Argentina   Austria   Brazil   Chile   Czech Republic   France   Greece
Guatemala   Hungary   Italy   Japan   Poland   Portugal   Singapore
South Korea   Switzerland   Thailand   Turkey   Ukraine   Vietnam

For titles covered by Section 112 of the US Higher Education
Opportunity Act, please visit www.oup.com/us/he for the
latest information about pricing and alternate formats.

Published in the United States of America by
Oxford University Press
198 Madison Avenue, New York, NY 10016
http://www.oup.com

Library of Congress Cataloging-in-Publication Data
Witherington, Ben, III, 1951-
    Reading and understanding the Bible / Ben Witherington, III.
       pages cm
    Includes bibliographical references.
    ISBN 978-0-19-934057-6
    1. Bible--Hermeneutics. 2. Bible--Criticism, interpretation, etc. 3. Bible--
Introductions. I. Title.
    BS476.W588 2014
    220.601--dc23
                                                            2014014137

The Bible is the greatest of all books; to study it is the noblest of all pursuits; to understand it, the highest of all goals.

—Charles C. Ryrie

CONTENTS

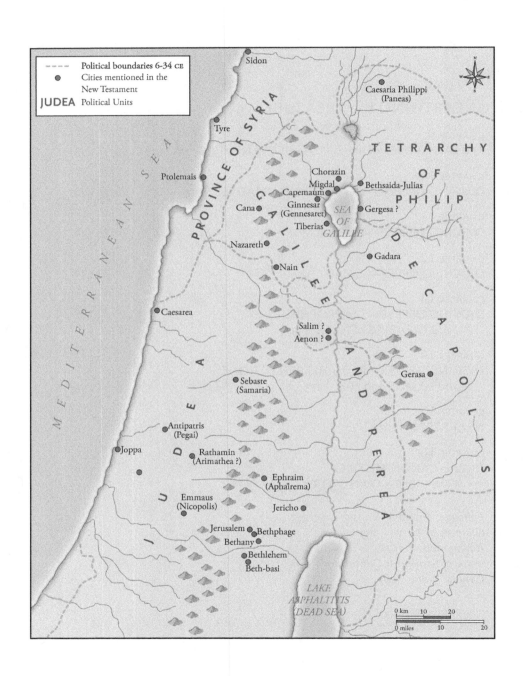

Political boundaries 6–34 CE
Cities mentioned in the
New Testament
JUDEA Political Units

Sidon

Caesaria Philippi
(Paneas)

Tyre

PROVINCE OF SYRIA

T E T R A R C H Y

O F

P H I L I P

Chorazin
Migdal
Capemaum
Ginnesar
(Gennesaret)
Tiberias

Bethsaida-Julias

Gergesa ?

Ptolemais

G A L I L E E

MEDITERRANEAN SEA

Cana

SEA
OF
GALILEE

Nazareth

Nain

Gadara

D E C A P O L I S

Caesarea

Salim ?
Aenon ?

J U D E A

Sebaste
(Samaria)

Gerasa

Antipatris
(Pegai)

Joppa

Rathamin
(Arimathea ?)

Ephraim
(Aphaîrema)

Emmaus
(Nicopolis)

Jericho

P E R E A

Jerusalem
Bethphage
Bethany
Bethlehem
Beth-basi

I D U M E A

LAKE
ASPHALTITIS
(DEAD SEA)

0 km   10   20
0 miles   10   20

ABBREVIATIONS

ANE Short for the ancient Near East, referring to the lands east, south, and north of Israel (not including the western Mediterranean world of Greece, Rome, etc.).

L The material found only in Luke's Gospel.

LXX The Greek number 70, but this is the abbreviation for the Greek translation of the Old Testament, supposed to have been accomplished by 70 translators (presumably in Alexandria).

M The material found only in Matthew's Gospel.

NT New Testament.

OT Old Testament.

Q From the German *Quelle*, it refers to the sayings material shared in common by Matthew and Luke but not derived from Mark.

TRANSLITERATIONS

Transliterations are italicized in the text and glossary terms are in bold at first mention.

almah Hebrew word for a sexually mature young woman of marriageable age. It is not a technical term for "virgin," but in that culture "virginity" would be assumed and implied; otherwise, this positive or neutral term would not be used in an honor-and-shame culture.

apocalypsis Greek word meaning the unveiling of secrets.

běreshit bara The first two words of the OT meaning "in the beginning God created" or "when God began to create."

bios "Life" in Greek; it came to mean a story about a life, hence a "biography."

chreia A rhetorical form of composition that involves a compact narrative which is a true story, usually ending with a memorable saying or deed of a well-known person.

děrakhim The Hebrew word *derek* means a road or a way, but it came to be used in a moral sense as a chosen course or path in life, a "way." *Děrakhim* is the plural, often referring to the ways or behaviors of a person. This language continues in early Judaism, which refers to the "two ways": one to blessing, the other to destruction.

dia pisteōs Christou A highly debated Greek phrase which literally reads "through the faith/faithfulness of Christ." The debate centers on whether the phrase refers to faith in Christ (an objective genitive phrase) or the faith/faithfulness of Christ himself (a subjective genitive phrase), which seems more likely in the view of the contexts where this phrase and similar ones occur in Paul's letters.

doulos Greek word for "slave" or "servant."

ehyeh asher ehyeh   Hebrew phrase whose translation is debated—either "I am that I am" or, more probably, "I will be what I will be," referring to a future action where God reveals his name and nature.

eikōn   Greek word for "image." It is closer in meaning to **schēma** than to **morphē**, but when used in the "image of God" phrase it says something about the character or capacity of the person, not his nature or appearance. Humans do not have the "appearance" of God, nor do they bear "the divine nature" (**morphē**).

ekklēsia   Greek word for "assembly," which is used in the Greek OT to refer to the assembling of God's people and in the NT, especially in Paul's letters, to refer to a religious assembly of people.

encomium   A carefully composed rhetorical oration used usually at funerals to laud the deceased.

ethos   The authority and presence of the speaker, something that an orator must establish at the beginning of a discourse, securing a favorable hearing and making clear the person's right to speak. It involved the appeal to the more surface emotions.

euthys   Literally "immediately" in Greek, but the term usually is used to mean something like "and then."

eved   Hebrew word for "servant." The term could sometimes be used in a more specific and religious sense to refer to "servants" of God such as the prophets or Israel's leaders, rather than in the normal mundane sense.

gnōsis   Greek term for "know"; like the Hebrew term **yada**, it usually refers to more than "knowing about something." It means something close to "understanding due to personal experience."

golem   Hebrew for "embryo" or the curled-up "fetus," for the verbal form of the word means "wind up."

harpagmos   Greek word meaning in Phil. 2 "taking advantage of" something one already has, rather than "grasping" for something or even "stealing" something one does not have.

hayah   Hebrew intransitive verb meaning "to be."

hesed Hebrew word sometimes translated "mercy" or "loving kindness," but many scholars think it refers to a specific kind of love—covenant love and loyalty.

hokmah Hebrew word for wisdom, of whatever sort.

koinōnia Greek word, which means sharing in common or participating in common with someone in something. It should not be translated as "fellowship," though "fellowship" can be the result of sharing or participating in something in common with fellow believers.

Kyrios Greek word for "Lord," whether a human one or a divine one. It is the word used in the Greek OT (the LXX) for Yahweh, but in the NT it is almost exclusively used of Jesus as the risen Lord.

lĕ David A debated Hebrew phrase which could mean "to," "for," or "by" David, referring to King David.

logos Greek word for "word," but in a rhetorical context it refers to the substance of the discourse, the series of arguments introduced after the initial establishing of **ethos** by the speaker.

macrothymia Greek word regularly translated "patience," but what it literally means is going a long time before blowing up or, as we would say, having a long fuse. *Thymos* refers to anger or rage.

malak YHWH This Hebrew phrase refers to a special messenger of God, in this case an angel, hence the frequent translation "the angel of the Lord."

mashal Hebrew term for figurative or metaphorical speech including proverbs, aphorisms, riddles, one-liners, parables, and even allegories.

mizmor Hebrew word for "song."

morphē Greek word for "form," but it does not refer to mere outward appearance. It refers to an outward manifestation of what the person or thing really is.

nefesh Hebrew word for "life" or even "life-breath."

paga Hebrew term for "make intervention for," "make entreaty for."

pais Greek word for "son," though in some contexts it can also mean "servant."

parabolē	Same definition as **mashal**, only this is the equivalent Greek term. It is the term from which the English word "parable" comes, which confuses the issue since we think of a parable as a short story. In fact, in the Bible, *parabolē* can refer to any and all the forms of wisdom speech—proverb, riddle, aphorism, one-liner, short fictional narrative, allegory.
parthenos	Greek term for "virgin." It is a more specific term than **almah** as it focuses on the virginity of the person in question, whereas **almah**, in a positive context like Isa. 7.14, implies virginity.
pathos	The deeper emotions, such as love or hate, which were to be appealed to at the end of a discourse to conclude and convince the audience by the act of persuasion.
pesakh	Hebrew word first rendered into English by William Tyndale as "passover," which in turn became the English term used to refer to the annual feast that celebrated the deliverance from Egypt.
pistoi	Greek term which in a rhetorical context refers to "proofs" or "warrants," not "faiths" or "believers."
progymnasmata	Elementary school exercises, most of them of a rhetorical nature.
psalmos	Greek word for "song," from which the book of Psalms gets its name.
qadosh	Hebrew word for "holy," which has as its root sense "set apart," as does the Greek equivalent **hagios**.
schēma	The outward and changeable appearance of something.
sefer tĕhillim	Hebrew for "book of praises."
selah	Hebrew word found in the Psalms from time to time. It probably is a liturgical direction meaning "pause here."
Shĕma	Hebrew word which begins the great Israelite confession "Hear O Israel, the Lord our God, the Lord is one" (Deut. 6.4).
skopos	Greek word referring to the finish line marker or pole that a runner would aim for as he ran a race.

skubalon   Greek word referring to spoiled food, garbage, or even dung—in short, anything that is refuse or to be thrown out, always with a negative connotation of something that stinks.

sophia   Greek word for "wisdom," of whatever sort.

synkrisis   Greek term referring to a rhetorical comparison, often a comparison by contrast. See, for example, Romans 5:12–21, where Adam and Christ are compared but largely contrasted.

telos/teleios   Greek words. The former refers to a goal or an end which one reaches and the latter, to completion or maturity or even "perfection" in some sense, when used of human beings.

tohu vavohu   Hebrew phrase from Genesis 1, often translated "formless and void," but this translation loses the rhyme involved.

tsalmavet   Hebrew term for "deep shadow" or "deep darkness." It probably does not mean "shadow of death."

tselem   "Image" in Hebrew.

yada   "Knowledge" in Hebrew, often with the sense of intimate knowledge and, thus, "experience."

YHWH   The personal name in Hebrew for the biblical God, possibly derived from the "to be" verb **hayah** or even the expanded phrase **ehyeh asher ehyeh**.

PREFACE

This book is divided into two major parts entitled "Surveying the Terrain, Studying the Map" and "Unearthing the Treasure." Readers are invited to go on a journey of exploration in a step-by-step fashion so that they may become adept at both reading and understanding the Bible. The first half of the book works through the major types of literature found in the Bible (narrative, history, law, prophecy, parables, apocalypse) and carefully explains how to best interpret each genre or type of literature. Special attention is paid to the oral, rhetorical, and social character of these ancient documents and how that affects interpretation. The first half of the book closes with a guide to how to deal with the theological content of the Bible.

The second half of the book, after an explanation of the basic hermeneutical rules for interpretation, invites the student or reader to go deeper, providing core samples of how to do in-depth interpretation of the various kinds of literature we find in both the Old Testament (OT) and the New Testament (NT). This is followed by a discussion of how to take the next steps in interpreting the Bible once one has mastered the skills discussed in this book, and the final chapter provides an explanation of where exactly the Bible came from and how it was formed in the first place, answering the usual questions the Bible raises on this topic for modern readers.

ACKNOWLEDGMENTS

Thanks must be given to Mark Fairchild for his wonderful photographs, which make this a much more user-friendly and appealing textbook. Kudos also go to the various readers of the two major drafts of this document who went through it meticulously and provided useful suggestions as to how to make it a better textbook: Margaret English de Alminana, Southeastern University; Michael F. Bird, Crossway College; Cherice Bock, George Fox University; Samuel A. Dawson, Detroit Baptist Theological Seminary; Craig Evans, Acadia University; Kyle Greenwood, Colorado Christian University; David Howle, Wayland Baptist University; Scot McKnight, North Park

University; Edward Meadors, Taylor University; G. Vincent Medina, Evangel University; Jon Mark Robertson, Multnomah Biblical Seminary; Steve Rodeheaver, Point Loma Nazarene University; Kenneth Schenck, Wesley Seminary, Indiana Wesleyan University; Brent Schlittenhart, Wayland Baptist University; Robert B. Stewart, New Orleans Baptist Theological Seminary; Josh Strahan, Lipscomb University; Duane F. Watson, Malone University; Mark Wessner, American Public University; T. Scott Womble, St. Louis Christian College; and David L. Woodall, Moody Theological Seminary. Finally, a special thanks to Kaitlin Coats and Robert Miller at Oxford University Press for helping this book to see the light of day and be properly promoted in good time and in good order.

An INVITATION to EXPLORE the BIBLE

Pick up a Bible today and you may be tempted to think it's just another book, with a really lackluster cover and too few illustrations. Were you to look at an ancient manuscript of the Bible it would have even less visual appeal. In fact, it would look like a piece of ancient paper with a lot of letters run together.

The Bible is in fact not just *a* book but a whole library of books, sixty-six to be exact, if you go with the usual OT and NT canon list. These various books were

Figure 1 A fragment of one of the famous Dead Sea Scrolls. (© Mark R. Fairchild, PhD)

written over a huge time span, more than a thousand years, and involved many people—from prophets to priests to kings to scribes to apostles to final editors. Some of these books are compilations of the work of several people, even several generations of people. In addition, the Bible includes a huge variety of types of literature, both prose and poetry, ranging from narratives to laws to songs to prayers to prophecies to apocalyptic visions to proverbs to parables to letters to biographies and more. Each different type of literature communicates its meaning in slightly different ways and requires different ways of interpreting to get at that meaning. The Bible is easily one of the most diverse compendiums of literature ever assembled.

You may be tempted to think of the Bible as just another big book from remote antiquity that seems to be of little relevance to the twenty-first-century world in which we live. Before you draw such a conclusion, you should pause to remember a few facts. In any given year, the Bible is the best-selling book in the entire world, hands down, despite the fact that it never appears on any best-seller lists. It is also the most owned and read book in any given year, all over the world. Indeed, it is the most copied and printed and owned book in all of human history.

If you recall the story of the first printing press of Johannes Gutenberg, you will remember that the Bible was the first book off that press in about 1440, over fifty years before Columbus ever sailed to America. Obviously, someone thought it was the most important book ever written if it was the first book ever printed. Ever since then, the Bible has been the most published book in the world and published in the most versions and editions as well.

But even before 1440, the Bible was the most hand-copied document all over the world. It is thus not a surprise that while we have some five thousand ancient manuscripts of the Greek NT (some even dating to the second century AD, just after the NT was written), the number of ancient manuscripts of Julius Caesar's *Gallic Wars*, Homer's *Odyssey*, Virgil's *Aeneid*, or other ancient classics pales by comparison, with only a handful of each one still extant. The Bible is not just a classic; it's the most important classic book of all time, and the way it has been copied, translated, bound, and presented since the second century AD demonstrates this fact.

Furthermore, the Bible has been and is the foundation of much of Middle Eastern and Western culture, and indeed, it has had an enormous impact on the English language itself, not to mention classical music and art. There would have been no Dante's *Divine Comedy*, Milton's *Paradise Lost*, Bunyan's *Pilgrim's Progress*, Shakespeare's sonnets, Hawthorne's *Scarlet Letter*, and more great literature if there had been no Bible. There would be no Handel's *Messiah* or *Amazing Grace* or Bach's *St. Matthew's Passion* if there had never been a Bible. Even if you only have some interest in understanding

Western culture and its development, you would need to know the Bible well to understand that culture's growth and development.

One of the most amazing features of the Bible is that despite the many human hands and writers involved in its composition and the fact that it was composed in many different places at many different times, there is in fact a unity to the Bible. It does not read, for example, like a random selection of the best short stories of 2014. It has major ideas, themes, and characters that can be traced from Genesis 1 to Revelation 22; and this in itself produces a certain unity to the whole. It tells a consistent story about the one God of the Bible and God's relationship with both his chosen people and the world, a story involving creation, falling into sin, redemption, judgment, and beyond. It is a story that has the largest possible arc a human story can have—from creation to death to new creation.

Furthermore, there is a unity to these documents when it comes to truth claims. It is always telling the same story about the same God and his same plan of salvation for the world. The word *God* does not refer to one deity in the OT and some other deity in the NT. The Bible is *monotheistic* from start to finish, by which is meant it affirms the reality of only one God and only one savior and mediator between God and humanity, Jesus the Christ, and only one Holy Spirit, the Spirit of the one true God.[1] In the very pluralistic world out of which the Bible came and into which the Bible now speaks, this fact stands out. Early Jews and early Christians believed in only the God that the Bible and their experience revealed to them, and this profoundly shaped the way they wrote about their God.

Indeed, these same early monotheists profoundly believed that this one God had inspired them to say and write what they did about him. They believed that what they were saying and writing about their God was not merely the opinions of human beings but God-whispered words. Consider, for example, what Paul says about his own preaching in one of the earliest NT documents: "We constantly give thanks to God for this—that when you received the Word of God that you heard from us, you accepted it not as a mere human word, but as what it really is, God's Word which is at work in you believers" (1 Thess. 2:13). In other words, at least some, if not all, of the writers of the Bible believed they were speaking and writing sacred words, words that came from God.

If you survey the world at the time when the OT and NT was written, you discover that, apart from Jews and Christians, the religious peoples of the ancient

---

1 The point I am making here is that the OT, while it does not mention Jesus by name, also does not mention any other savior sent by God from heaven to take on flesh and redeem the race. In other words, the OT does not contradict the NT assertions on this point.

Near East and the Greco–Roman world did not really have a singular and very particular sacred book like the Bible. They were not "the people of the book." This was something that set apart the original composers and copiers of the Bible. Jews and Christians believed that God spoke clearly to a surprisingly wide variety of people over a huge expanse of time and the message was the same—people needed to be redeemed and to have a positive relationship with God and God loved people so much that he both involved himself in human affairs in order to redeem them and inspired holy persons to speak his Word and to write sacred texts. Often, those texts were no more than a record of the orally spoken Word, especially when we are talking about prophecies or letters that were surrogates for a discourse given in person.

There is much more to be said about this remarkable book called the Bible, but let this suffice to be your invitation to go on a journey of reading and learning about this Bible with the aid of this book. Let this book be your guide and GPS device pointing you in the right way to navigate this book of books and understand its content. The journey will involve many twists and turns. I promise it will not be boring, and it will lead somewhere you may discover you always wanted to go, with the joys of discovery coming at many points along the way.

READING
and
UNDERSTANDING
the BIBLE

PART I

SURVEYING the TERRAIN, STUDYING the MAP

CHAPTER

1

"LET the READER UNDERSTAND"

Some books are to be tasted, others to be swallowed, and some few to be chewed and digested.
—Francis Bacon

I consider as lovers of books not those who keep their books hidden in their store-chests and never handle them, but those who, by nightly as well as daily use thumb them, batter them, wear them out, who fill out all the margins with annotations of many kinds, and who prefer the marks of a fault they have erased to a neat copy full of faults.
—Desiderius Erasmus

WHERE ARE WE GOING?

In this initial chapter we will discuss how to begin to read the Bible properly (carefully, prayerfully, intensely) so that it makes sense and can be understood today. We will ask and answer the question, Where should I start in reading the Bible?

Figure 1.1 An illuminated first page of a gospel. (© Mark R. Fairchild, PhD)

HOW TO READ THE BIBLE

On first blush, it may seem silly to try and tell a person that he or she needs a little help in learning how to read the Bible. After all, reading is reading—or is it? Suppose, however, you are reading a translation of an ancient text, and your own culture and language is so different from the biblical culture and language that it is inevitable that you will unconsciously but mistakenly read your own culture, ideas, concepts, and preferences into the text, rather than reading the original meaning out of the text? Suppose you are as likely to misread the Bible as to properly read it, due to ignorance of the original languages and of the historical, literary, social, and rhetorical contexts of the Bible that are so different from our modern contexts? Suppose reading the Bible, even in English, is rather like reading *Beowulf*, the great ancient epic, without any notes or aids? Suppose you don't even enjoy reading and would much rather play sports or video games or some other kind of activity? If any of these things are true of you, then you need help in reading the Bible. The truth is we all need help in reading and understanding the Bible, even those who know and have studied the Bible for a long time. The problem is where to start.

A very long time ago, in 1940, Mortimer Adler wrote a classic best-selling book entitled *How to Read a Book*, which went through numerous reprintings and a second revised edition in 1972. One of the key things Adler points out is that there is a difference between reading for pleasure and reading for discovery or even reading analytically. There is also a major difference between remembering something someone said or something you read and understanding it.

Think for a minute about the famous story in Acts 8 of the Ethiopian eunuch riding south in a chariot down the road by the sea from Israel into Egypt. As he is riding along he is reading an Isaiah scroll, reading the words aloud but not understanding. Notice what he says when Philip the Evangelist, coming alongside the chariot, asks him "do you understand what you are reading?"

The reply is worth repeating: "How can I, unless someone explains it to me?" Some things, especially some complex things, require guidance to understand them; and frankly, there are many things in the Bible like that. This is why some readers of the Bible get frustrated and give up. This has far more to do with the perceptiveness of the reader than the perspicuity of the text.

Adler suggests that elementary reading involves learning what the text says. This, of course, is the beginning of being familiar with a text but hardly the end or aim of reading a book like the Bible. In the case of the Bible, many persons over the years have memorized huge portions of what it says, and this is a good thing. But knowing what the text says is only the prelude to understanding what it means, much less applying the text to your own life. The Bible requires what Adler calls *analytical* reading. He describes it this way: "Analytical reading is thorough reading, complete reading, or good reading—the best reading you can do. . . . The analytical reader must ask many, and organized, questions of what he is reading. . . . Reading a book analytically is chewing and digesting it."[1]

But if one is going to try to apply or practice what a book instructs a person to do, this requires something beyond understanding. It requires knowing how to take an ancient text and apply it to a very different time and cultural situation. There is, in short, a very significant journey from knowing what is said to understanding what is said, to knowing how to use or apply the text. The Bible does not simply call people to learn or understand theoretical truths; it calls a person to embrace them, apply them, live them.

---

1 Mortimer J. Adler and Charles Van Doren, *How to Read a Book: The Classic Guide to Intelligent Reading* (New York: Touchstone, 1972), 19.

THE STARTING POINT

Some guides to reading the Bible take the inchworm approach—you start by learning key words, key phrases, key sentences, and key paragraphs and build from the bottom up.[2] The problem with this whole approach is that it is you who is doing the heavy lifting of assembling a context for understanding the text using theoretical principles of approach, instead of following the cues in the text itself.

I would suggest just the opposite approach. You need to begin by having a sense of the *grand narrative* of the text of the Bible. What is the big story that it tells from Genesis to Revelation? What is the plot, and who are the major characters in the story? Where does the story begin, come to a climax, and finally conclude? In other words, you need to have a narrative framework in which to understand all the particulars of the text, all the different sorts of literature in the Bible.

For example, the book of Leviticus is likely to appear to you as a gigantic rule manual if you don't understand the sacrificial system used in ancient Israel and the covenantal nature of God's relationship with his people. Leviticus, taken out of its narrative context, will seem like a handbook for ancient priests that tells us next to nothing of relevance about being a Christian or following Christ. Are we all really supposed to avoid wearing clothes that involve a mixture of cotton and polyester if we believe in a "priesthood of all believers" (see Lev. 19:19)?

This reaction of bewilderment is understandable, until one reads Leviticus in light of the stories in Genesis and Exodus about covenant and sacrifice, the beginnings of the priesthood, and why sacrifices to God and rules for the priesthood were needed. Furthermore, for the Christian, Leviticus needs to be read in light of the way Hebrews talk about the sacrificial system and Christ as high priest. Sometimes when you begin to read the Bible with Genesis, you never get beyond Exodus. Or you stumble over, or simply get bored with, Leviticus, reading one rule after another after another.

Even if you glide through Leviticus and then move on to the continuation of the story in Numbers, Deuteronomy, Joshua, Judges, Ruth, and Esther, you may have problems with the fact that books like 1–2 Chronicles seem to be edited down reruns of 1–2 Samuel and 1–2 Kings. Then you can't figure out why there is a hymnbook in the middle of the story in the OT (the Psalms). Then you get

---

2 A very good example of this sort of more inductive approach to the text can be found in J. Scott Duvall and J. Daniel Hays, *Grasping God's Word: A Hands-On Approach to Reading, Interpreting, and Applying the Bible*, 2nd ed. (Grand Rapids, MI: Zondervan, 2005).

bogged down in prophecy after prophecy after prophecy because prophecies often have very little narrative context to provide clues for interpretation and understanding.

Then you come to the NT and immediately have to wade through a genealogy in Matthew, which seems very odd. When was the last time you saw a descending genealogy of men into which is squeezed four strange women and then the wife of the primary person at the end of the genealogy (Joseph's wife Mary), and then you learn that in fact Jesus is not the physical descendent of Joseph but only of Mary—yet this is Joseph's genealogy? Having gotten past the genealogy in Matthew, you discover that this gospel and the two that follow it seem like variations on a theme, but the Fourth Gospel comes out of left field and is very different from the first three.

Next, after reading through Acts and beginning to get a handle on reading biblical narrative, you suddenly discover that almost the entire rest of the Bible is composed of letters or sermons or discourses—not narratives at all. To top that, the Bible concludes with a bang, a book of apocalyptic or visionary prophecies that prove to be the most difficult part of the whole book to properly interpret. Even the most diligent of students is bound to be somewhat confused by the array and arrangement of materials found in the Bible. The Bible's table of contents seems, on first glance, rather like a catalog of new books available on Amazon, with very little indication of any connection between the books listed and what that connection might be.

It is for these and other reasons, having done this ground-clearing exercise, that we will start our journey of trying to understand the Bible by looking first at the grand sweep of the story. We will have occasion later to talk about the story of the Bible, how it was assembled, and how we came to have it in 900 English translations. But it is to the story in the Bible that we must turn first. Before we do, a word about what can go wrong if we don't study the Bible in its original contexts is in order.

There was a young man who liked to have a "verse for the day to live by." The way he arrived at the verse was by a method he considered pious, sort of like casting lots. He would close his eyes, thumb through the pages, put his finger down, open his eyes, and read the verse where his finger landed. On this particular day, when he first tried this method the verse he landed on was "and Judas went out and hanged himself." The young man found this troubling and said, "Surely this is not what you want me to do today, Lord." So he decided he had better try again. Maybe he had put his finger down too quickly or carelessly. The second time he closed his eyes, thumbed through the pages, and put his finger down, the verse he found himself reading was "Go and do likewise." Now the young man was really sweating. "Something's not right here. Well, perhaps third time lucky." So the young man tried this approach once more. This time the text read, "What you are about to do, do quickly."

Obviously, this is not how to apply the Bible to your own life, and what it illustrates is the method by which you study and apply the text matters; it matters enormously. Indeed, any kind of approach that takes words or phrases or verses or paragraphs out of context and tries to apply them is a recipe for disaster. Better to start big, with the grand narrative of the Bible, and work your way to the small. We will follow that dictum beginning in the next chapter.

FOR FURTHER READING

For a proper introduction to the nature of the Bible, rules for interpreting it, how to pick a translation, and related subjects, see my *The Living Word of God: Rethinking the Theology of the Bible* (Waco, TX: Baylor University Press, 2008). A classic and helpful guide to reading the Bible is Gordon D. Fee and Douglas Stuart's *How to Read the Bible for All Its Worth* (Grand Rapids, MI: Zondervan, 2014).

2

The GRAND NARRATIVE of the BIBLE

The BIBLE shows how the world progresses. It begins with a garden, but ends with a holy city.
—Phillips Brooks

The BIBLE—banned, burned, beloved. More widely read, more frequently attacked than any other book in history. Generations of intellectuals have attempted to discredit it, dictators of every age have outlawed it and executed those who read it. Yet soldiers carry it into battle believing it more powerful than their weapons. Fragments of it smuggled into solitary prison cells have transformed ruthless killers into gentle saints.
—Charles Colson

WHERE ARE WE GOING?

After a brief discussion of what the Bible is and is not and what it is and is not about, we will survey the basic story line of the Bible from creation to fall, to the beginnings of redemption, to the coming of the Redeemer, to the return of Christ, final judgment, and finally to new creation.

The Bible is a book about many things. It is about God, it is about human beings, and it is about the relationship, or lack thereof, between God and humankind. Most of the Bible is in fact about the divine attempt to restore the broken relationship between God and human beings. This means that the Bible is mainly about history, theology, and ethics. Because the story is mainly about God's various attempts to redeem or save his people, the main story in the Bible has rightly been called **salvation history**. There are also many things this story is not about, and there are many things the Bible itself is not.

WHAT THE BIBLE IS AND WHAT THE BIBLE IS NOT ABOUT

Many arguments about the Bible could have been avoided had someone who really knew the character of the Bible stepped in and said, "the Bible is not about that." For example, the Bible is not a scientific textbook written in a prescientific era for people who knew nothing about modern science. It does not teach us geology, cosmology, chemistry, biology, anthropology, or physics. Attempts to force the Bible to teach us about such subjects always lead to mistakes—and to pseudoscience, for that matter. We have to be able to distinguish between the subjects the Bible *teaches* us about and subjects that the Bible merely *touches*, or refers to in passing. Let's take a few examples.

In various places in the Bible we hear about "the sun rising and setting." Of course, we talk this way as well, even though we know perfectly well that the earth revolves around the sun and that what appears to be a sunset is not something happening to the sun, which is at the center of our solar system, but rather something that the earth is doing—revolving. In other words, we, like the ancient persons who wrote the Bible, can use *phenomenological* language, the language of how things appear to the naked eye, to describe things. Such a description is not meant to be a scientifically precise analysis of what is actually the case. It's just how things appear to the human eye.

Or take another example. Bishop James Ussher (1581–1656) famously came up with the conclusion that the world began on a nice spring morning about 4004 BC.

How did he reach this conclusion? He reached it by combining and adding up, as it were, all the genealogies of the OT with a few fixed points in the chronology. The problems with this were multiple: (1) few of the biblical genealogies are exhaustive or complete; (2) in fact, some of them are royal genealogies which deliberately leave out individuals who are skeletons in the closet, sometimes omitting whole generations (as does the genealogy in Matt. 1); (3) if Bishop Ussher had been correct, this in turn would make God into a deceiver. What I mean by this is that we have all these fossils that make clear that the earth is far more ancient than 6,000 years old; indeed, it is more accurate to talk about it being millions of years old. These fossils do not merely give "the appearance of great age"; they are genuinely very old. Ask yourself this question: would God create fossils and rock formations which merely *appeared* to be very ancient but really weren't? That doesn't comport with the biblical idea that God is light and that in God there is no darkness, no deception at all.

One more example will have to suffice. The Bible talks frequently about the human heart as if it were the control center of the human personality—the center of thought, feelings, and will. So, for example, we hear a prayer "cleanse the thoughts of my heart." From a scientific point of view, hearts do not have thoughts—brains do. A heart is simply a blood pump. Most ancient peoples did indeed see the heart as the control center of the person. For example, you find many pictures from ancient Egypt of a person's final judgment in which the heart is being weighed in a scale. The heart was mummified, as were the other internal organs, and then placed in small jars, called *canopic jars*. In Figure 2.1, the person on the left is being led to the place of judgment (the scales) by Osiris the god with the bird-like head, and in the hand of the god is the *ankh*, the key to the afterlife. Usually, the human in the picture holds a feather, the symbol of truth. The idea is that the person is telling the truth about his life and his heart, in the small jar on the left-hand scale pan, is being weighed, tested.

The Egyptians were in many ways the most advanced of ANE civilizations, but even they did not realize that the human brain was the real center of human thought, feeling, and will. In fact, the priests who mummified the deceased person would pickle the internal organs but draw out the gray matter from the head and throw it away, presumably thinking it was no more than congestion in the head. You might say that Egyptian ideas about anthropology and the afterlife were a no-brainer! The biblical writers spoke in these same kinds of ways as well about the heart and other internal organs.

Let me be clear that I am not saying that the Bible teaches us wrongly about such subjects. I am simply saying it doesn't intend to teach us anything about such

Figure 2.1 A pharaoh is informed about the afterlife. (© Mark R. Fairchild, PhD)

subjects. We have ancient persons speaking in normal colloquial ways, common in their day and in their universe of discourse. Once again, the subjects the biblical authors intend to teach us about are (1) history, and not just any kind of history but salvation history; (2) theology (about God and his relationship with humankind); and (3) ethics. The sooner we accept these facts, the fewer arguments we will have with modern and postmodern people about the Bible.

Within the realm of history even a cursory reading shows us that the Bible does not provide a historical account about all of humanity. Did you ever wonder where the spouses of Cain and Abel came from? The Bible is primarily interested in telling the story of God's people from Creation to Fall, to various acts of redemption, to new creation. Other peoples come into the story only tangentially when they interact with God's people, whether the OT or the NT people of God.

For example, the Bible does not tell us the story of the rise and development of the Babylonian people, the Assyrian people, the Hittites, the Egyptians, the Greeks, or the Romans. These other peoples come into the story only when they interact with God's people. And God's people are the Hebrews or, as they were later known, the Jews. Indeed, almost every single book of the Bible was written by Jews. The only exceptions to this rule may be Luke–Acts and possibly 2 Peter. It should go without saying that Jesus, Paul, the Twelve, and all the very earliest followers of Jesus were Jews. The Bible is a thoroughly Jewish book, from cover to cover. The people of God only expand to include many Gentiles once Jesus comes into the picture to redeem not only Israel but the nations.

Perhaps here is also a good place to say something about the issue of objectivity. The only being in the universe who is and can be perfectly objective about any and all things is God. Only God is omniscient. All human beings have only a limited capacity for objectivity. We all see things through our own eyes, from our own points of view. This is no less true of the writers of the Bible than it is of us. This is why you may encounter the word *tendentious* when scholars talk about the character of the biblical narrative. What they mean by that is that the Bible was written by convinced believers in God. It is written, in other words, by people of faith and from their point of view. They are not pretending to be objective observers of reality. Having said that, the fact that the Bible is also the Word of the living God means that the point of view of these inspired writers is assumed to also be God's viewpoint. In other words, their interpretations of the facts and events recorded in the Bible are the true ones because they reflect God's view of things. Bearing these things in mind, let us consider the biblical narrative itself.

THE GREATEST STORY EVER TOLD

The story of the Bible begins with the story about the origin of all things, the entire universe and most especially humankind. The story in Genesis 1 is told in poetic prose, a sort of celebration or rhapsody about the Creator God and what he did in making all things. While the author uses the seven-day framework to discuss Creation, the alert reader notices immediately that the sun of our solar system is neither mentioned nor created until the fourth day of creation (Gen. 1:14–19). It is thus impossible to take the "evening and morning" structure of the account of the acts of

Figure 2.2 The Edenic story of a tree and forbidden fruit does not tell us what sort of tree or fruit. (© Mark R. Fairchild, PhD)

creation as a guide to exactly how long it took God to create the universe. The point is that nothing was too difficult for this Creator. We might say that it was all in a week's work for this God. But the real focus of the beginning of the story is not on inanimate matter, whether sea or land, nor on the animals but on the creation of humankind, both male and female created in God's image.

Adam, whose name derives from the Hebrew word for "earth" and, thus, "the Earthling" because of how the story says he was formed, is different from all the lesser creatures in that he (and later Eve) bears "the image of God." But Adam has a problem. He needs a mate in order to fulfill the mandate to "be fruitful and multiply." So it is that Eve is created as a suitable companion and helper for Adam. Nothing in this language implies Eve's subordination to Adam. Indeed, the word for "helper" here is also used of God various times in the OT when it is said that God is the helper of his people. Indeed, Eve proves to be the crown of creation, after which God "ceases" to create (see Gen. 1–2).

In other words, Adam and Eve are created for relationship with both God and other human beings. And only human beings, apparently, have a unique capacity for an intimate relationship with God. The Hebrew word *tselem*, translated as "image" here, can also mean "idol." There is then a sense in which human beings are God's idol or image or representation on earth, and this is why images of lesser creatures should never be turned into idols or representations of God. God is not a mere creature. God is the Creator of all things.

This concept of creation by the one God sets the biblical story apart from many other ANE stories of origins in two ways: (1) it indicates there is only one God who made it all and (2) it makes clear that God did indeed create something out of nothing. God did not need preexisting matter to create either the universe or his creatures that populate the world.

Adam and Eve are also given tasks or a mission in life. They are to tend the garden, to fill the earth and subdue it, and to avoid the fruit of one particular tree in the garden, the fruit of the tree of the *knowledge* of good and evil. The Hebrew word for "knowledge" here, **yada**, probably means "experience." If they partake of the forbidden fruit, they will experience the gamut of good and evil, not merely know about it. The careful reader of Genesis 1–3 notices that it is only Adam who receives the commandment to avoid the tree in question. We are to assume that Eve learns about it secondhand, from Adam. And it appears she was poorly taught because she assumes that God had even said not to touch the fruit in question, which is not true. While Eve is the first to eat of the tree, apparently Adam is right there with her, for it says she hands him the fruit and he eats. Since it is Adam who was first given the prohibition, it is also Adam who is mainly blamed for the sin and its horrific consequences not only here in Genesis but in the NT as well (see Rom. 5:12–21).

Whenever God is disobeyed in the Bible, there are negative consequences. In this case the consequences involve labor pains: (1) Adam will have to work the land "by the sweat of his brow" (that is, the work will be hard, back-breaking, and even dangerous) and (2) Eve will also experience dangerous pains in labor as she bears children and becomes "the mother of all living." But the worst consequence of the original sin was that "your desire will be for your husband, and he will lord it over you." That is, the original *curse* was that an equitable relationship that involved "to love and to cherish" would degenerate into "to desire and to dominate." In other words, it is not just the grim reaper (death) which enters the picture because of the original sin but also gender hierarchy and **patriarchy** in which men subordinate and dominate women in various ways (see Gen. 3).

The rest of the story of the OT chronicles God's various acts of redemption, attempting to restore the now warped or bent image of God in humanity and, thus, the primeval relationship between God and humankind. And this brings us to the whole business of ancient religion. As soon as we get to the story of Cain and Abel, we note immediately that the story is about making sacrifices to God, something that is nowhere in evidence in the story about humanity in the garden before the Fall.

Sacrifices are, in fact, human attempts to assuage the anger of God against human sin, attempts to restore a right relationship between the sacrificer and his or her deity.

The essence of most ANE religion was sacrifices, priests, high places, and then eventually temples. The presupposition of such sacrifices was that humans were estranged from God and needed reconciliation, with animal and food sacrifices assumed to be the means to accomplish that end. Only humans offer such sacrifices because only humans were created in the image of God, created with a capacity for intimate relationship with God, and only humans disobeyed the one commandment God gave Adam.

This, in a nutshell, is the story of the Creation and the Fall as it is told in Genesis 1–3. From Genesis 4 onward, what we hear about is God's various efforts to restore his relationship with humankind, whether we are talking about the story of Noah, whose family was the sole family rescued from the catastrophic flood; the story of Abraham, who was promised descendents and so a people but did not live to see a full-fledged people emerge; the patriarchs, during which time the people called the Hebrews emerged; Moses, whose onerous task was to free Hebrew slaves from bondage in Egypt and set up a covenantal relationship between God and the Hebrews at Mt. Sinai; Joshua, who with other Hebrews took possession of the Promised Land in which Abraham had once dwelt; or the period of the judges, the monarchy, the exile, and finally the return from exile.

All of the literature in the OT presupposes this basic story of Creation, Fall, and redemption and can be said to characterize God's people and their relationship with God in some stage of the process of redemption after the initial story of the Creation and Fall. In a sense then, the vast majority of the OT is about recovery, restoration, and redemption, though there is some foreshadowing of the final new creation in Isaiah 40–66 and in some of the more apocalyptic prophecy in Ezekiel, Daniel, and Zechariah.

The story takes a decisive turn for the better when one progresses from Malachi to Matthew. Here, we learn not merely about a human mediator between God and his people—a prophet, a priest, a king, a Moses, a David, a Solomon—but of God sending his people a final Anointed One, his own Son to accomplish a redemption that previous mediators had only been able to give a foreshadowing or a foretaste of, at best.

The differences between this mediator and previous ones are that (1) this one is without sin and resists all temptation, unlike even the best of the previous mediators; (2) this one is God's only begotten Son, not merely another anointed one but the final Anointed One; and (3) this one is not merely a human representative to God but God's representative to humans—a double mediator. This is why, for example, we hear in 1 Timothy 2:5–6 that "there is one God and one mediator between God and human beings, Christ Jesus, himself human, who gave himself as a ransom for all people."

Jesus is both priest and sacrifice, as well as temple (the locus where God dwells on earth), and by offering himself, he is the one, necessary and sufficient, once-for-all sacrifice for sin that makes all further sacrifices or human attempts at reconciling with God both obsolete and unnecessary. In other words, Jesus's action on the cross *changed* the nature of God's relationship with humankind. Going forward it would be about a new covenant in which there were only two priesthoods, the priesthood of all believers and the heavenly high priesthood of Christ. The only sacrifices would be of praise and self as living sacrifice to God (Rom. 12). The only temple would be the human body, where God's Spirit now dwells, as it dwelt in Jesus when he walked the earth.

The NT was written by people who were convinced that the final act of redemption had transpired in and through Christ and, therefore, that God's people are living in the eschatological or final age, the age when the kingdoms of this world become the kingdom of God and God reigns fully and finally in his creation. But interestingly enough, that is not the end of the story. The story does not end with an offer of spiritual redemption and a free pass into the living presence of God in heaven.

The story is brought to an end only by a return performance by the Son, who comes again, returning to raise the dead, judge the world, and usher in once and for all the new creation here on earth. All the writers of the New Testament stand on tiptoe awaiting the return of the King, God's Son. They affirm that what happened to Jesus one Easter Sunday morning will happen for those in Christ when he returns—namely, bodily resurrection. In a sense, this brings the story back to Genesis 1. It stands to reason that the Creator God would not be satisfied with exchanging all his beautiful creation for the redemption of some human souls in heaven. After all, there is much more to creation than just humankind.

Paul in a dramatic passage talks about how all of creation has something to look forward to, a redemption and restoration yet to come. He puts it this way: "The creation waits in eager expectation for the children of God to be revealed [by resurrection]. For the creation was subjected to futility, not by its own choice, but by the will of the one who subjected it, in hope that the creation itself will be liberated from the bondage to decay and brought into the freedom and glory of the children of God" (Rom. 8:19–21). In other words, new human creatures in Christ here and now foreshadow the final redemption of all creatures great and small and of the earth itself. This is also the vision of John of Patmos, who tells us that the end of the story (told at the very end of the Bible in Rev. 21–22) entails a corporate merger between heaven and earth. The Son, the bridegroom, returns from heaven for the church, his bride; and all of creation puts on its wedding attire and is made new.

Salvation, as it turns out, involves the redemption of the whole self—body and spirit. It involves the restoration of the whole of creation by the Creator God who is alpha and omega (the first and last letters of the Greek alphabet), the God who creates at the beginning and at the end so that he may dwell with his people Immanuel (which means "God with us") not just at the beginning but in the end too.

This all too brief synopsis of the story in the Bible covers the major events of Creation, Fall, acts of redemption, and then final judgment and restoration. This is the narrative thought world that all the writers of the NT worked with and, with the exception of some parts of the final picture being omitted or opaque, the narrative thought world that the writers of the OT worked with as well. They all believed in a God whose saving reign would one day come on earth, as in heaven; and for this they fervently prayed epoch after epoch and still do today. Isaiah 2:3–4 puts it this way:

> And many peoples will come and say, "Come, let us go up to the mountain of the LORD, To the house of the God of Jacob; That He may teach us concerning His ways And that we may walk in His paths." For the law will go forth from Zion and the word of the LORD from Jerusalem. And He will judge between the nations, and will render decisions for many peoples; and they will hammer their swords into plowshares and their spears into pruning hooks. Nation will not lift up sword against nation, and never again will they learn war.

What you have just read is a love story. A story about a God who so loved the world, that this is the length that he was prepared to go to redeem human beings and have an everlasting relationship with them that would prompt them to fulfill the great commandment—"you shall love the Lord your God with all your heart, soul, mind and strength, and your neighbor as yourself" (Deut. 6.5/Mark 12.30).

WHAT JUST HAPPENED?

In this chapter we reviewed the major storyline of the Bible as a whole, a story of creation, fall, redemption, judgment, and re-creation. The story stretches from the creation of the universe to the re-creation of heaven and earth. The focus of the story is not on cosmology but on God's relationship with humankind and, more particularly, with his chosen people, the Jews and then later the Jews and Gentiles united in Christ. It is not a story about everyone and everything; indeed, its subject matter can be said to be three things: theology, ethics, and history. It does not tell us everything we always wanted to know about God or ourselves but were afraid to ask. Furthermore, the whole story is told in an antique way, speaking in ancient languages, reflecting the conventions of ancient cultures, and assuming conventions and values that modern people know little or nothing about, unless they have actually studied the ANE or the Greco–Roman world. So, how does a beginner weave his or her way through such a book?

As we close this chapter, a practical suggestion is in order. Start your Bible reading by working through the narrative portions of Genesis through Esther. Then read Daniel and Jonah. Follow that by reading the Gospels and Acts, and then finally read Revelation. Read in this order, and in this way you will be able to see the narrative arc we have been discussing in the second half of this chapter.

Having gotten the story straight and made evident the narrative thought world of the Bible, it is time for us to press on. We must turn to a discussion of the historical framework and substance of the Bible in our next chapter.

FOR FURTHER READING

A very fine survey of the story of the Bible and of its theology and ethics can be found in Sandra Richter's very engaging and readable *The Epic of Eden: A Christian Entry into the Old Testament* (Downers Grove, IL: InterVarsity Press, 2008). If you would like to see how one particular biblical writer, Paul, tells the story, see my *Paul's Narrative Thought World: The Tapestry of Tragedy and Triumph* (Louisville, KY: Westminster/John Knox Press, 1994).

3

The HISTORY in the BIBLE

*I am an historian, I am not a believer, but I must confess
as a historian that this penniless preacher from Nazareth
is irrevocably the very center of history. Jesus Christ is easily
the most dominant figure in all history.*
                    —H. G. WELLS

*There are more sure marks of authenticity in the Bible than
in any profane history.*
                    —SIR ISAAC NEWTON

WHERE ARE WE GOING?

*In this chapter we consider the nature of history, more particularly that of the history in
the Bible, and discuss the differences between ancient and modern history writing. We
also discuss the differences between ancient history writing and ancient biographical
writings, which are two different, though related, types of ancient literature.*

Figure 3.1 The hippodrome at Jerash, biblical Gerasha. (© Mark R. Fairchild, PhD)

Now that you have a sense of the overall story the Bible presents to the reader, it is time to ask the question, What kind of story is this? After all, stories can be either fictional or based in fact, either mythical or historical or some combination of the two (we've become fond lately of the term *faction*, fiction with facts in it, as applied to novels and films). The truth about God and humankind can be conveyed in a huge array of different types of literature—narrative, poetry, songs, laws, parables, biographies, histories, proverbs, genealogies, prophecies, and apocalyptic visions. Upon close examination we actually have all these types of literature in the Bible. Some of these ways of conveying the truth are more metaphorical and figurative, and some are more literal and factual. This is why when someone asks the age-old question, Do you take the Bible literally or figuratively?, the appropriate answer should be, Yes. It depends on which part of the Bible we are discussing and what type of literature that part of the Bible is.

Let's be clear then from the outset that the truth about God and his relationship with his people can be conveyed in a wide variety of literature, including fiction. In fact, this is exactly what the parables of Jesus are, literary fictions telling us the truth about God's kingdom. So the question of what kind of storytelling we have in the Bible is both appropriate and necessary. Let's start with a discussion about how to read the historical narratives in the Bible.

IS HISTORY HIS STORY?

Whether we are talking about the OT or the NT, there is a lot of narrative in the Bible that most scholars take to be some sort of history writing even if the oldest parts involve saga, epic, or legend. The question is, What sort of history writing? It is true to say that most modern historians do not talk about God's activity in history, miracles in history, angels and their role in history, or the Devil and his role in history. Sometimes you even have modern secular historians suggest that if you talk about such subjects in your writing of history, you are not a "critical scholar." This is unfortunate and reflects not merely the skepticism of modern academia about such things but really a form of closed-mindedness not shared by most ancient historians.

For example, the father of history writing in general is usually said to be the Greek writer Herodotus (ca. 484–ca. 425 BC). If you read his work, you discover that he frequently talks about the role of the divine in human history. The ancient historians, whether we think of Herodotus or Thucydides or Polybius or Tacitus or Livy or Josephus (the first three being Greeks, the second two Romans, the last a Jew), were certainly capable of critical thinking about history; but the vast majority of them also believed and talked about the role of the divine in human history.

The biblical history writers, whether we are thinking of the persons who wrote 1–2 Samuel, 1–2 Kings, or Luke–Acts, in some ways wrote very much like other historians, ancient or modern. They used sources, they edited their material, and they focused on specific subjects. As we have already stressed, the Bible is not the story of all peoples but of a particular people, the Jews, and then, in the NT, of their messiah, who is also the savior of the world and of his people. The writers of the Bible were not attempting to write the history of the world but the history of a people and their God. It is thus neither fair nor reasonable to fault them for things they are not trying to do.

When we study the characteristics of ancient history writing, a few important things stand out. Firstly, ancient people did not walk around with sundials on their wrists, nor did they carry hourglasses with sand in them. They were much less concerned about chronological precision than modern persons, including modern historians, are. Most time references in the Bible are of a general, not a specific, sort. Take, for example, the use of the Greek word *euthys* by Mark. It is one of his favorite adverbs, and a literal translation of the word would be "immediately." Actually, however, what Mark means by the word is something like "next" or "and then." The word very seldom means what we might mean by the term *immediately*.

Figure 3.2 The father of history writing, Herodotus. (Shutterstock/Renata Sedmakova)

Or take, for example, the phrase "after three days" used in the gospels to talk about the time lapse between Jesus's death and his resurrection. The phrase seldom means "three twenty-four hour days." In fact, it can be as general as the phrase "after a while" or, more specifically, "after parts of three days"; but it is a major mistake to read the time references in the Bible as if they had the same meaning as they might today. Ancient historians wrote according to ancient conventions of history writing, not modern ones.

Secondly, ancient historians had a good deal of freedom in how they arranged their material. It was by no means always done in chronological order. Sometimes the ordering was more logical than chronological, and in the gospels sometimes it is more theological than chronological.

Let's take two examples. Thucydides, in his history of the Greek wars known as the Peloponnesian wars, writes his account region by region. This becomes confusing for those looking for strict chronology because it means that he invariably backtracks whenever he talks about a new region where hostilities took place. Or consider the gospel accounts of Jesus's cleansing of the Temple. All four gospels mention this event and tell this story only once. Matthew, Mark, and Luke tell this story as part of their account of the last week of Jesus's life. John, by contrast, tells this story very early in his gospel, in chapter 2. The placement of the story in John is theological, not chronological. The Evangelist is trying to make clear from the outset of his narrative that Jesus fulfills the institutions of Judaism in himself—he is the sacrificial lamb of God who takes away sin, he is the locus of God's presence on earth, and thus his body is God's temple, and so on. The author of the Gospel of John is not particularly concerned about when Jesus cleansed the Temple. He is concerned with making clear what the event's theological significance is.

Thirdly, all history writing, whether ancient or modern, involves more than just reporting facts. *History writing is always facts plus an interpretation of the facts.* Even just the decision of which facts to report involves a decision about which are historically significant in the writer's mind and, thus, ought to be recorded. The fact that the biblical historians interpret the history they present does not distinguish them from most modern historians. What distinguishes them is that the biblical historians are interpreting the events theologically, like various other ancient historians.

For example, any historian in any age could report that Jesus died on a Roman cross in Jerusalem in about AD 30. But when a biblical historian writes "Jesus died on a cross *for our sins*" this is clearly a theological interpretation of Jesus's death, meant to bring out its deeper significance. What you have to ask about any piece of interpretive history writing is, Is the interpretation true or false? Does it obscure or illuminate the meaning or significance of the fact in question?

THE DIFFERENCE BETWEEN HISTORY AND BIOGRAPHY

In antiquity, as well as today, most people can readily distinguish history from biography. *Bios* is the Greek word for "life," and a *biography*, therefore, is a writing about someone's life. A *history*, by contrast, is a story that focuses on historic or significant events. Put this way, we don't really have much in the OT that could be called biography. Interestingly, the exceptions in the OT seem to be mostly about women, Ruth and Esther, although the book of Jonah could be placed in the category of some sort of brief biography.

The other historically substantive books in the OT focus on events, in particular events that involved God's people, the Hebrews. Notice, for example, how the book of Judges deals with a series of judges and events and does not tell in any full way the story of any one of them. This is history writing, not biography. It could be said, of course, that God is the main character of the OT, the one character who appears in all of the books in one way or another; but none of them seek to tell the story of "the life and times of Yahweh." God is present in all generations, but the stories focus on salvation history, on God's mighty acts for his people.

In the NT, we have something different. Suddenly, in three of the first four books of the NT, we have biographies of Jesus, ancient biographies to be sure but, nonetheless, biographies. Jesus dominates the landscape of Matthew, Mark, John, and, to some extent, Luke. Indeed, in one way or another, Jesus is the focus of the whole NT, or at least he is the presupposition and reason for all that is said.

Here, it will be helpful to list some of the traits of ancient biographies. (1) Unlike ancient histories, biographies, while they do relate real events, do not necessarily recount "historic" events. What biographies are about is telling any stories which best reveal the character of the person being chronicled. So, for example, you might have an anecdote about how Socrates liked olives. This is not the stuff of salvation history or even a fact of historic significance, but it does tell us something about Socrates's personality and preferences. (2) Ancient biographies, unlike modern ones, were not womb-to-tomb accounts of someone's life. Ancient writers did not have computers and could not afford to write endlessly about someone's life. Papyrus was not cheap, nor was ink; and scribes could be costly as well. Ancient scrolls had certain lengths, and if one went on too long, the scroll became too unwieldy as one glued one roll to another to another. Therefore, ancient biographies tended to be more selective than modern ones, and the gospels follow this practice. (3) Ancient peoples knew nothing of modern theories of human psychology or early childhood development. They did not necessarily believe that what happened to a person in childhood could mark or mar that person for life. In fact, they didn't think the childhood or young adulthood of important persons was all that important or revealing, usually. It is thus not surprising that the gospels include only one story about Jesus as a young man—Luke 2:41–52. Otherwise, the entire focus is on the adult Jesus (Mark) or his origins and then the adulthood of Jesus (the other gospels). Ancient biographers focused on the adult figure and his or her character as revealed by his or her words and deeds. (4) Ancient writers do not tend to psychoanalyze their subjects. They simply let the words and the deeds of the person reveal the character. We would call this a form of *indirect* portraiture. Editorial analysis or comments or asides tend to be few and far between as the author doesn't much try to intrude into the recounting of a life. Finally, (5) we must try to avoid reading the Bible from a modern individualist point of view. By this I mean that ancient peoples believed that your group identity was more important and formative than your individual identity.

Did you notice that people in the gospels do not have last names? Geography, gender, and generation were assumed to determine who people were and what their personality would be like. So, for example, Jesus is Jesus of Nazareth, Saul is Saul of Tarsus, one of the Simons is called Simon the Pharisee, Peter is called Simon bar-Jonah (which means Simon son of Jonah or John), Joanna is called Joanna of Chuza (i.e., the wife of a man named Chuza, Herod's estate agent), from the OT Ruth is called the Moabitess, and Uriah is called the Hittite. This is because what was assumed to distinguish people was where they came from, what gender they were, what tribe they were a part of, and more specifically who their father was. It was not what made a person stand out from the crowd but, rather, what crowd a person was part of which was assumed to shape or even determine who that person was. Of course, ancient persons were individuals, but they were not usually individualists like we are.

You may have noticed several odd things about the NT. Apart from some of the things said from time to time in prophetic utterances, the NT is very different from other ancient history chronicles in that nothing is said about wars or fighting. This material is not like Julius Caesar's *Gallic Wars*, Tacitus's *Annals*, or even parts of the OT. Most ancient historical chronicles did focus on wars and their outcomes. This is not the case in the NT. In some ways this is not surprising since what we have in the NT is salvation history, the story of the redemption of humankind, not the story of their battles, destruction, displacements.

You may have also noticed that I did not suggest that Luke's Gospel is an example of an ancient biography. It is not. Listen for a moment to its preface:

> Inasmuch as many have undertaken to compile an account of the things accomplished among us, just as they were handed down to us by those who from the beginning were eyewitnesses and servants of the word, it seemed fitting for me as well, having investigated everything carefully from the beginning, to write it out for you in consecutive order, most excellent Theophilus; so that you may know the exact truth about the things you have been taught. (Luke 1:1–4)

Notice that Luke speaks of "the *things* that have happened among us." His account will focus on events, things, not persons. He will write a two-volume work, Luke–Acts, as an ancient historian, not as a biographer of Jesus; and it comprises about one-third of the whole NT. Notice as well the stress on writing an orderly account. This might mean chronological order since this is history writing and chronology was much less of a concern in ancient biographical writing. It also means, however, a logical ordering of things. Notice as well that Luke relies on eyewitnesses and sources. He has done his homework, investigating things closely.

Sometimes devout readers of the Bible assume that the biblical writers simply sat in their studies and were inspired by God's Spirit to write what they wrote, without any research or consulting of sources or normal human processes. Luke's preface makes clear this is not true. While unmediated revelation can be said to be the case when it comes to some of the prophecies in the Bible, it is mostly not the case if we are talking about other sorts of literature in the Bible. A document can be inspired whether the words in it come directly through a vision or auditory revelation from God or indirectly through normal human processes of inquiry and study with the providence of God overseeing those processes.

What we have done in this chapter is begun to discuss the issue of **genre**, a word which refers to the type or kind of literature a particular document falls into. We have been focusing on biblical narratives because they are the carriers and conveyors of the essential story in the Bible. Therefore, we have addressed the characteristics of ancient historical and biographical narratives. In our next chapter we will focus on how to read other sorts or genres of material in the Bible.

WHAT JUST HAPPENED?

In this chapter we began to study the various types of ancient literature we find in the Bible, focusing on the two major categories of history and biography. It was important to approach things this way because it is the Bible narrative that provides the framework for understanding the meaning of the Bible, and other kinds of literature supplement, or explicate, or apply the meaning of the story.

For review it would be a good thing to look up the meaning of the word *genre* (see the glossary at the end of this book) and begin to think how and to what degree the kind of literature you are reading dictates what you can expect to find in it and to get out of it. You would not expect to get the same kind of material out of a rule book (like much of Leviticus) as you would out of a song book (like the Psalms) or out of an ad hoc letter written to a particular audience (like Paul's letters). Thus, we must bring different expectations to different kinds of literature. We would not go to a phone book looking for the definition of a word. That's a category mistake. Thus, if a book is trying to teach us history, theology, and ethics and we come to it expecting it to teach us geology, cosmology, and anthropology, we are bound to misunderstand and misuse the book or to simply get frustrated with its failure to answer our burning questions. The sooner we learn how to recognize the type of literature we are dealing with and then to ask the right kinds of questions of that literature, the sooner we will be on our journey to understanding a complex book like the Bible, which is made up of all different kinds of material, as will become even more apparent in our next chapter.

One final guideline is in order. As you read through the Bible, always bearing in mind the overall arc to the story of Creation, Fall, judgment by flood, redemption, final judgment, re-creation, you need to regularly ask the question, Where am I in the telling of this story? For example, when reading the Psalms, when you ask this question you realize the Psalter presupposes an existing temple, a monarchy, a time when Israel is in the Promised Land and can worship together in Jerusalem or when Israel is back in the land after exile and still sings some songs from exile as well as earlier songs.

Perhaps one more example will help. When reading Leviticus, you have to realize that this book is part of the stipulations of a covenant God has between himself and his people. It reflects a time when God's people are already in a covenantal relationship with their God, a time, that is, after Moses and the Sinai covenant has been set up. If you read Leviticus in light of the Exodus–Sinai events and events thereafter, you will begin to understand that God was setting up rules to try and protect his people from being totally assimilated by the other surrounding larger groups, to keep them distinct, not least because they bore a particular belief in a singular God. So then the questions What time is it? and Where are we in the story? are major keys to understanding whatever part of the Bible we are currently reading.

FOR FURTHER READING

For a useful guide to OT history, see Iain Provan, V. Philips Long, and Tremper Longman III, *A Biblical History of Israel* (Louisville, KY: Westminster/John Knox Press, 2003). On NT history, see my *New Testament History: A Narrative Account* (Grand Rapids, MI: Baker Academic, 2003). On the use of ancient biographical forms in the NT, see Richard A. Burridge, *What Are the Gospels?*, 2nd ed. (Grand Rapids, MI: Eerdmans, 2004).

On FIGURING OUT WHAT'S FIGURATIVE and on LEARNING ABOUT the LETTER of the LAW

The first qualification for judging any piece of workmanship from a corkscrew to a cathedral is to know what it is—what it was intended to do and how it is meant to be used.
—C. S. LEWIS, PREFACE TO *PARADISE LOST*

*If the object of poetry is to make human beings, then poetry
is the heir of prophecy.*
—MUHAMMAD IQBAL

WHERE ARE WE GOING?

This chapter will explore the issue of figurative and literal language. We will stress that figurative language is still referential language, just as literal language is; and we will explore the use of exact or legal language in the context of ancient covenants, a crucial way God relates to his people. We will also point out that both figurative and literal language can be found in a variety of types of literature.

The Bible is one of the greatest works of literature in any language, not least because of its remarkable diversity and range of material and the sterling quality of all the different types of literature found in the Bible. By no means is the Bible all simply prose narrative. To the reader unfamiliar with the Bible, it will appear to be a confusing array of different types of materials. Who could figure out which shelf to put this book on in a bookstore? Is it poetry or prose? Is it history or fiction? Is its subject law or gospel? And we could go on. The Bible is more of a compendium than one particular kind of literature. And the very variety makes it more interesting to read, more appealing in various ways. Lawyers may enjoy studying the laws. Poets may enjoy studying the poetry. Musicians may enjoy studying the psalms. Prophecy buffs may immerse themselves in the prophecies. Historians will want to ponder the history and biography in the Bible.

The Bible has something for almost every kind of literary and subject matter interest. In this chapter and the next one, we discuss some of the nonnarrative material in the Bible and discover how knowing what kind of literature it is helps guide the proper interpretation of that literature. For example, as we said at the end of the last chapter, you would not go to a dictionary to look up a phone number. Why not? Because it would be a category mistake. And when you make a category mistake about a type of literature, you are bound to misinterpret that piece of literature. Let me illustrate.

Back in the late 1960s, after Neil Armstrong had walked on the moon, my friend Doug Harris and I took a ride on the Blue Ridge Parkway in the mountains of North Carolina. We were driving my Dad's old '55 Chevy. We were having a great time on a beautiful day, until the clutch blew out; and then, as the Bible might say, "my countenance fell." There were no gas stations on the Blue Ridge Parkway, and no help would be forthcoming. Picture us being pushed down an exit ramp by another car to get off the Parkway and then coasting into a gas station on a secondary road.

We realized our joyriding and picnic were spoiled, and we decided to hitchhike back to High Point in the middle of the state, where we lived. So we stuck out our thumbs, and the very first persons who picked us up were a very elderly mountain couple, dressed in black. My friend Doug, now a lawyer, was always a big talker; and he tried to strike up a conversation with the gentleman who was driving.

Doug said, "What did you think of Neil Armstrong walking on the moon, and all those beautiful pictures of the round earth revolving and revolving?" The response he got was not what he expected.

"That's all fake," said the man, "just a Hollywood stunt. Anyone who knows the Bible knows that the world is not round or revolving around the sun."

Doug, not recognizing invincible ignorance when he saw it, was inclined to argue. I whispered to him, "Shut up Doug, we need this ride."

Still, Doug persisted, "But why do you think the world is not round?"

The old man cleared his throat, glanced back at Doug, and said, "It says in the book of Revelations that the angels will stand on the four corners of the earth. Can't be round if it's got four corners, now can it?"

Beware of a person who begins a sentence "It says in the Book of Revelations. . . ." That's actually not the name of the last book in the Bible, though it certainly involves revelations (plural). But the real problem with the old man's statement is not that he took the Bible seriously but that he took an apocalyptic and figurative statement literally. The statement was not meant to teach cosmology but, rather, theology. The verse he cited means no more than that God will send all his angels to the four points of the compass to gather his people. In other words, the old man had made a category or genre mistake in his reading of Revelation 7:1. Obviously, especially when we are dealing with poetic and figurative language, like we have in poems and songs and prophecy and parables, some literary sensitivity is necessary lest we misunderstand that literature. Let me give illustrations from a variety of kinds of biblical literature, showing the use of figurative or metaphorical language. Before we can survey more types of literature, we need to broach the subject of figurative versus literal ways of expression that occur in all kinds of literature. We also need to consider the use of literal language, for example, in laws.

THE USE OF FIGURATIVE LANGUAGE

While almost any kind of literature can include figurative language, certain kinds more regularly do so. Take, for example, the songs we find in the OT hymnbook Psalms (*psalmos* being the Greek word for "song"). While some of the Psalms are sung prayers, some are simply songs that use beautiful poetic language. Consider the following examples:

> The mountains skipped like rams, the hills like lambs. Why was it, O sea, that you fled, O Jordan, that you turned back? (Ps. 114:4–5)

Here, we have the use of the poetic device known as *personification*, in which inanimate matter is given personal traits. Mountains can't literally skip, and they don't have legs. Seas can't literally flee, and they also don't have legs. The point of any kind of poetic analogy is to compare two unlike things that in some particular way are alike. In this case the psalmist is talking about what happens when God comes down to earth in a **theophany** cloud and the earth responds with a whole lot of shaking or tsunamis or the like.

> The Lord sent Nathan to David. When he came to him, he said, "There were two men in a certain town, one rich and the other poor. The rich man had a very large number of sheep and cattle, but the poor man had nothing except one little ewe lamb he had bought. He raised it, and it grew up with him and his children. It shared his food, drank from his cup and even slept in his arms. It was like a daughter to him. Now a traveler came to the rich man, but the rich man refrained from taking one of his own sheep or cattle to prepare a meal for the traveler who had come to him. Instead, he took the ewe lamb that belonged to the poor man and prepared it for the one who had come to him." David burned with anger against the man and said to Nathan, "As surely as the Lord lives, the man who did this must die! He must pay for that lamb four times over, because he did such a thing and had no pity." Then Nathan said to David, "You are the man! This is what the Lord, the God of Israel, says: 'I anointed you king over Israel, and I delivered you from the hand of Saul.'" (2 Sam. 12:1–7)

This familiar parable of the prophet Nathan draws an analogy between David's theft of Uriah's wife Bathsheba and the stealing of a much beloved ewe lamb. Obviously, this is a metaphorical analogy, and parables themselves, whether in the OT or the NT, use lots of metaphorical analogies, even when they take story form, as this one does. Bathsheba is no mere lamb; she is a beautiful woman, much beloved by her husband. And so the analogy works. But if you don't realize that this is figurative or metaphorical language, you might think Nathan was accusing David of literal sheep stealing!

> At once I was in the Spirit, and there before me was a throne in heaven with someone sitting on it. And the one who sat there had the *appearance* of jasper

and ruby. A rainbow that shone *like* an emerald encircled the throne. Surrounding the throne were twenty-four other thrones, and seated on them were twenty-four elders. They were dressed in white and had crowns of gold on their heads. From the throne came flashes of lightning, rumblings and peals of thunder. In front of the throne, seven lamps were blazing. These are the seven spirits of God. Also in front of the throne there was what looked *like* a sea of glass, clear as crystal. In the center, around the throne, were four living creatures, and they were covered with eyes, in front and in back. The first living creature was *like* a lion, the second was *like* an ox, the third had a face *like* a man, the fourth was *like* a flying eagle. (Rev. 4:2–7)

I have highlighted the use of the language of analogy in this visionary prophecy. Were you to compare it to Ezekiel 1, which recounts a similar vision, you would discover many more examples of the use of the word *like* to compare two unlike things. In the case of the living creatures, they were not literally a lion, an ox, a man, or a flying eagle. They simply looked like such creatures. John is using analogies and similes, groping for language big enough to describe what he saw in heaven. Prophecies often involve metaphorical language that was never meant to be taken literally but was meant to be referential and to be taken seriously. On other occasions it involves a mixture of figurative and literal language. Sometimes prophecies are in poetic rather than prose form. Take, for example, the following passage:

Who has believed our message
and to whom has the arm of the Lord been revealed?

He grew up before him *like* a tender shoot,
and *like* a root out of dry ground.

He had no beauty or majesty to attract us to him,
nothing in his appearance that we should desire him.

He was despised and rejected by mankind,
a man of suffering, and familiar with pain.

Like one from whom people hide their faces
he was despised, and we held him in low esteem.

Surely he took up our pain
and bore our suffering,
yet we considered him punished by God,
stricken by him, and afflicted.

But he was pierced for our transgressions,
he was crushed for our iniquities;
the punishment that brought us peace was on him,
and by his wounds we are healed.

We all, *like* sheep, have gone astray,
each of us has turned to our own way;
and the LORD has laid on him
the iniquity of us all.

He was oppressed and afflicted,
yet he did not open his mouth;
he was led *like* a lamb to the slaughter,
and as a sheep before its shearers is silent,
so he did not open his mouth. (Isa. 53:1–7)

Fortunately, this particular translation of this prophecy (the NIV) makes clear by the way it presents the form of the lines that we are dealing with poetry, not straight prose. I have once again highlighted the word *like* to show the use of metaphorical analogy. Obviously, God's people are not literally sheep; and equally obviously, the suffering servant referred to is not literally a lamb, a tender shoot, or a root. While it may be less obvious that this is metaphorical, God, who is spirit, also does not have a literal arm (see verse 1).

As we have already said, the point of a metaphor, simile, or analogy is to compare two unlike things which in some particular ways are alike; for example, the silence of the lamb just before slaughter is said to be like the silence of the sufferer before he is executed. In short, whether we are talking about songs, parables, or prophecies, all of them use metaphorical or figurative language. In some cases both figurative language and literal language are used (for example, in prophecy, especially apocalyptic prophecy). But unless we take into account how language is used, we cannot begin to properly interpret the language.

LAYING DOWN THE LAW

While we may tend to think of laws as nothing but part of a law code, that is not how laws worked when it came to God's people. Laws tend to be more precise and, indeed, literal ways of speaking. Laws, or as we might prefer to call them "commandments," were part of a covenantal arrangement between God and his people. **Covenants**, or treaties, took various forms in antiquity; but the kind that is of relevance for our discussion is lord–vassal covenants. These were not negotiated settlements between equals but, rather, covenants between a superior and an inferior or inferiors, a king, for example, and his people. Scholars have shown repeatedly that the covenants of the OT look most like ancient suzerainty (or lord–vassal) treaties between a conquering nation and a sublimated nation. The conqueror dictates all the terms but, interestingly, also binds himself to do certain things for the vassal or vassal state. Here is the basic form such a covenant would take:

HISTORICAL PREAMBLE (e.g., "I am the one who brought you out of bondage . . . and you became my people . . .")

LAWS (e.g., "Accordingly, you shall have no other gods [or rulers] before me, you shall not commit murder . . .")

WITNESSES, READING, AND STORAGE—The agreement must be witnessed (in Jewish tradition the testimony of two witnesses was required for something to be validated or verified), and provision must be made for safe storage of the covenant. It must be read from time to time.

PROMISES OR BLESSINGS (e.g., "If you keep the stipulations of this covenant, then I will make sure you live long in the land and no one will

Figure 4.1 Ancient Hittite treaty or covenant document. (Shutterstock/zebra0209)

trouble you. . . ." Notice the conditional nature of the promises; many of the promises, and even the prophecies, in the Bible are conditional in character.)

SANCTIONS OR CURSES (e.g., "If, on the other hand, you violate my laws and break this covenant, then I will cut you off and destroy your land . . .")

You can find a covenant or treaty document of this sort in Exodus 20–24, as follows: (1) title (20:1); (2) historical prologue or preamble (20:2); (3) requirements, basic (20:3–26) and detailed (ch. 21–23); (4) provisions for reading and storage of the text (24:4, storage; 24:7, reading); (5) witnesses (24:9–11); and (6) consequences (i.e., blessings and curses; cf. Deut. 28).[1]

Some of these curse sanctions will sound rather harsh, but it is typical of the rhetoric of such treaties or covenants. The sanctions and penalties for violating the agreement had to be stiff enough to provide a real deterrent against doing so. *And not only were they literally expressed, but they were literally enforced as well.* There are two more features we need to note about these agreements. They were always sealed with a sacrifice, signifying the new bond between the two parties and the seriousness of the matter; and there was also regularly a covenant sign. For example, in the case of the Mosaic covenant, circumcision was the covenant sign. It was, in fact, a symbol of the sanction or oath curse. Just as the foreskin of the male Israelite was cut off, so this symbolic act was meant to remind the Israelites that if they did not "keep" the covenant and "obey" the laws, they themselves would ruin their relationship with God and so be "cut off" from God. By contrast, baptism, a much more gender-inclusive sign, is the sign of the new covenant. The changing of the sign of the covenant signals that we are dealing with a different covenant, not just the renewal of a previous covenant.

In short, the laws were not given arbitrarily or in isolation; they were given as stipulations meant to keep an ongoing relationship on track and the subordinate persons in line. Different covenants would have different laws. Indeed, in the Bible, the Mosaic covenant was far more elaborate and detailed in regard to laws than was the Abrahamic covenant discussed in Genesis 12–15. Similarly, the new covenant was not simply a reiteration or renewal of the old covenant, and accordingly it had some different laws and commandments, as well as reiterating some of the commandments that were in earlier covenants between God and his people. Furthermore there was a change of covenantal sign—the sign of the new covenant

---

1 For still the most helpful discussion of these parallels, see Meredith G. Kline, *The Treaty of the Great King* (Eugene, OR: Wipf and Stock, 2012). For an online discussion of the parallels, see http://trivialcontemplations.wordpress.com/page/2/.

is baptism, not circumcision. Notice that Jesus and Paul explicitly reaffirm all of the Ten Commandments of Moses in one way or another, with one exception—the Sabbath commandment. The followers of Jesus were to observe a different day of worship, the Lord's Day, celebrating the resurrection of Jesus and the inauguration of the new covenant.

Then, too, Jesus in the Sermon on the Mount adds some new requirements for his followers, requirements not found in any form of the old covenant—for example, loving one's enemies, never retaliating, always forgiving. At the same time, Jesus declared all food clean and suitable for eating (Mark 7:15–20), though various of his disciples apparently did not get the memo for a while. In general, Jesus did not reinstitute the laws of clean and unclean that we find in the OT. The new covenant was genuinely a new covenant.

Here, we can mention that a proper understanding of how ancient covenants work can prevent a whole host of mistakes in interpreting the Bible, especially the NT. For example, only those portions of previous covenants that are reaffirmed continue to be binding on God's people in a new covenantal situation. Those portions that are either annulled or not reaffirmed are not still binding on God's people. However, any new commandments given by Jesus or the earliest Christian leaders, for example, the apostles, are also binding on Christians and have the force of law. The commandments of God are not suggestions or optional ethical advice for God's people. They, in fact, have the force of laws. All covenants have laws including the new covenant, and they were meant to be obeyed.

The surprise may be that obedience to God is not optional in the new covenant, even though conversion or the new birth happens purely by grace through faith. Salvation, however, is not just about conversion. It also involves sanctification; as Paul urges the believing community, "work out your salvation with fear and trembling, for it is God who works in your midst to will and to do" (Phil. 2.12–13). Law and grace are not seen as being at odds with one another in the Bible. The OT covenants are not purely law codes with no grace or promises, and the NT covenant is not purely grace with no laws or commandments. It is the grace of God that enables one to obey the laws of God. And this brings up another important point.

Obviously, it is impossible to love God with one's whole heart, love one's neighbor as oneself, and even love one's enemies apart from the dramatic help of God's grace and the working of God's Spirit within the believer. When it comes especially to the new covenant, God does not require of us more than he will enable us to do. And this applies also when it comes to prohibitions or the "thou shalt not . . ." kind of commandments. In fact, we even have promises in the new covenant about dealing with temptations. Paul puts it this way in 1 Corinthians 10:13, "no temptation has overcome you that is not common to humanity, such that with the temptation, God will provide an adequate means of escape."

The Bible is an ethically serious book, and obedience to God is never seen as an optional matter. Scholars will debate what the precise relationship is between obedience and ongoing salvation or sanctification, but clearly both the promises and the prohibitions in the new covenant, as in the old covenant, are seriously, indeed literally, meant and are not optional extras. But here I must stress that laws anywhere in the Bible are not meant to be applied to just anyone, anywhere, at any time. They are rather part of specific requirements for the ongoing special covenantal relationship between God and his people. They are not intended, for example, to be part of secular law codes, the subjects of which are citizens of a particular nation who may or may not be Jews or Christians.

Furthermore, as a comparison of the Mosaic and new covenants will show, God is free to change the stipulations or laws from one covenant to the next as God sees fit. They are only binding (1) on the people who have such a covenant with God and (2) only for the period of time that that particular covenantal agreement is still valid. In the case of the new covenant, which is intended as the last, eschatological, and permanent covenant between God and his people, there is no expiration date.

WHAT JUST HAPPENED?

In this chapter we covered the issue of figurative versus literal language and in that context raised the issue of literal laws, and obedience to them, in terms of covenants between God and his people. As we said, figurative and literal language can be found in a variety of kinds of literature; but generally speaking, poetry or poetic prophecy or songs tend to use more figurative language, while laws tend to be much more literal in character. In the next chapter we will explore more types of literature that tend to use a good deal of figurative speech.

FOR FURTHER READING

On the issue of imagery and figurative language in the Bible, see G. B. Caird's classic study *The Language and Imagery of the Bible* (Bristol, UK: Bristol Classical Press, 1988) and especially Leland Ryken, James C. Wilhoit, and Tremper Longman III, eds., *Dictionary of Biblical Imagery* (Downers Grove, IL: InterVarsity Press, 1998).

5

OF PARABLES, PROMISES, and PROPHECIES

God does not give us everything we want, but He does fulfill His promises . . . leading us along the best and straightest paths to Himself.
—DIETRICH BONHOEFFER

Every happening, great and small, is a parable whereby God speaks to us, and the art of life is to get the message.
—MALCOLM MUGGERIDGE

WHERE ARE WE GOING?

In this chapter we will examine wisdom literature, a highly figurative form of discourse and teaching found in both the OT and the NT. We will focus especially on Jesus's form of wisdom discourse, particularly his parables. This will be followed by a discussion of promises and prophecies, including the use of figurative language in those forms of literature.

WISDOM LITERATURE—
PARABLES, PROVERBS, APHORISMS

One of the least well-known types of literature in the Bible is wisdom literature, yet we have three entire books of wisdom literature in the OT (Proverbs, Ecclesiastes, Job) and plenty of examples of wisdom speech in various places in the NT. So this literature and the clues to how to interpret it deserve considerable attention at this juncture.

Studying wisdom literature requires both patience and time. This is because so much of it involves indirect speech (metaphors, similes, figures, images, aphorisms, riddles) rather than straightforward propositions, discourses, or narratives. Wisdom literature then requires not merely reading but rumination. It is meant to tease the mind into active thought, not merely command or demand assent to some particular point of view. Confusing the issue somewhat is the fact that the word *wisdom* in the Bible (*hokmah* in Hebrew, *sophia* in Greek) can refer to knowing what is the politically astute thing to do (and so being worldly wise; 1 Kgs. 5:21); to having encyclopedic knowledge of nature (1 Kgs. 4:33); to the gift of discernment or how to evaluate various options (1 Kgs. 3:16–28); to a saying, riddle, or proverb that reveals a secret about life that gives one true insight into how things actually are; and to skill, expertise, or even artisanship (and so a wise person is one who has such skills; 1 Chron. 22:15, 2 Chron. 2:7).

Perhaps most frequently, the wise person is the one who knows how to read the ways and moral structure of the world and live according to them so that one not merely survives but, rather, thrives and lives well and in an upright manner. Wisdom literature, if not mainly produced in royal courts, was certainly collected by the scribes who worked in royal courts; and certain royal figures, such as Solomon and later Jesus, became famous for their wisdom, Solomon being famous for coining some proverbs and Jesus, for his parables. Scribes could sometimes be sages, and so counselors to kings; but they were also those who recorded the wisdom of the ages.

What is a **proverb**? One definition I like, from one of my instructors at Duke, is that it is a short saying founded on long experience containing a truth.[1] It is meant to be pithy, sometimes provocative, and always to provoke careful thought. Were we to study proverbs in the original Hebrew we would also discover that they are often put in a memorable and memorizable form, involving rhythm, rhyme,

---

1 James L. Crenshaw, *Old Testament Wisdom: An Introduction* (Louisville, KY: Westminster/John Knox Press, 2010), 67.

assonance, alliteration. This is also true of some of Jesus's aphorisms, beatitudes, one-liners. Proverbs tend to summarize popular wisdom based on studying nature or human nature; and as such, *they are generalizations.* They are often true but not always true. For example, it is often true that if a parent trains up a child in the morally right way to go, that child will not depart from it in his or her old age (Prov. 22:6). This is not, however, always or universally true; and many of us could give examples where this does not happen.

There is something else about most proverbs we need to understand: they presuppose that the times and world are not out of joint. By this I mean that they presuppose that society is not at war or totally in chaos or dysfunctional. For example, it is not always true that hard work pays off and leads to prosperity. This is especially not the case in a bad economy where people can't even get work. It is for this reason that we actually find two different kinds of wisdom in the Bible— wisdom for when the culture is functioning rather normally and there is not a lot of social upheaval and then wisdom of a counterorder sort that reflects a different and difficult social setting. The book of Proverbs would be an example of the former, whereas Ecclesiastes would be an example of the latter.

Listen, for example, to what the author of Ecclesiastes says about what he has seen in life—rather than wisdom making a person healthy, wealthy, and happy, the author says "for with much wisdom comes much sorrow, the more knowledge the more grief" (Eccl. 1:18). While traditional wisdom would say that having children is a great joy and birth is a good thing to celebrate, the writer of Ecclesiastes says that the day of death is as good as the day of birth. He also says, "so I hated life, because the work that is done under the sun was grievous to me. All of it was meaningless" (Eccl. 2:17).

What is most interesting is that we find both traditional and counterorder wisdom in the OT and in the teachings of Jesus and James and other early followers of Jesus. On the one hand, Jesus will say things like honoring parents is a good and necessary and wise thing to do. On the other hand, Jesus will say things the writer of proverbs would never have said—for instance, "it is easier for a camel to go through the eye of a needle than for a rich man to enter the kingdom of God" (Mark 10.25). This could only be deemed as bad news for someone as rich as Solomon.

Furthermore, Jesus even offers what can be called eschatological wisdom, the wisdom of reversal, counterintuitive wisdom. He says things like the first shall be last, and the last first. The lowly will be lifted high, and the exalted brought down. This, of course, is not normally how life works. But Jesus is envisioning intervention by God in the eschatological age on behalf of the least, last, and lost so that they might become the most, the first, and the found. This is wisdom based not on the analysis of nature or human nature but on the basis of the knowledge of God and his salvific work.

Proverbs tended to have a couple of lines of pithy thought, but aphorisms or riddles tended to be like zingers, memorable one-liners. And then there is the more extended form of wisdom speech that we call parables. The problem, however, is that the Hebrew word **mashal** and the Greek word **parabolē** both can be used to refer to the whole gamut of wisdom speech, whether proverbs, aphorisms, riddles, or parables. What is most important to remember is that all of this sort of speech is metaphorical in character and, therefore, indirect in nature. In one sense, a parable is just an extended analogy or metaphor. The Kingdom of God is *like* a seed growing secretly. Here, what we have already said about figurative speech applies.

Jesus's wisdom speech overwhelmingly had one subject of discussion, the kingdom of God, or, put another way, the in-breaking final eschatological saving activity of God. Here too we have a problem with English translation, for the Greek and Hebrew terms we tend to render as "kingdom" are just as apt to have a verbal sense as a noun sense. They can refer to a place, an activity, a realm, or a reign. When Jesus tells parables of the realm or reign of God sometimes he is talking about the current saving activity of God, changing lives, and sometimes he is talking about the future realm and reign of God that will finally come fully to earth. Only the context helps us grasp which is meant in particular cases.

The wisdom speech of Jesus that we call parables can be as brief as a quick analogy or as long as a short narrative. But in every case we are talking about a comparison of the kingdom/reign/realm of God to something in this world—whether it be agriculture or human behavior. Jesus even warns at one point that while he is prepared to explain his teachings to his inner circle of disciples, to everyone else, all outsiders, it is all things in wisdom speech, which is to say all things in proverbs, aphorisms, riddles, and parables.

Jesus even goes so far as to say, quoting Isaiah 6:9–10, that the point of speaking to Israel in general in parables is to make clear to them that they do not understand God or their situation and will not do so or understand Jesus's parables unless they repent and turn back to God. In other words, parables were as likely to conceal as reveal the truth, depending on the spiritual condition of the listeners. They were as likely to make clear to the audience that they don't understand as to enlighten them, and this is because Jesus believed they were mostly spiritually lost. It is not a compliment to call people "the lost sheep of Israel" (Mt. 15.24). Sheep are not notably bright. In other words, Jesus's wisdom speech was not made up of nice little sermon illustrations or examples of moralizing. On the contrary, it was confrontational in character and admonitory, having an ominous and warning tone to it. "Repent, for the in-breaking final activity of God is at hand" was the implied message of all the parables.

Sometimes you will hear commentators say that Jesus's parables are true to life in his day and time. This is often not the case. Shepherds don't abandon ninety-nine sheep to go and find one straggly lost one, women don't put a whole bakery full of yeast into one loaf of bread, farmers do not carelessly scatter seed on a road, and so on. The parables are true to the surprising, remarkable, and compassionate character of God and his kingdom but not necessarily to daily life in ancient Israel. One more thing: Jesus didn't invent the parable. As we already saw in the last chapter, even an ancient prophet like Nathan could tell a parable. But Jesus's ministry was characterized by telling lots of parables to listening audiences. Here is a famous list, made by T. W. Manson, of the 45 or so parables of Jesus.

LISTS OF THE PARABLES[2]

Notations: *—indicates that the word *parable* is used by the Evangelist
+—indicates that it is so designated by Jesus himself
1—also in Q
2—also in Mark
3—from Luke's Sermon on the Plain
4—also in L
5—also in M
( )—some doubt as to whether saying is actually a parable

MARK

2:17	(The whole and the sick)
2:19f.	Children of the bride chamber[a]
2:21	New patch on old garment*
2:22	New wine in old wineskins
3:22–26	Divided kingdom or house*[a]
3:27	Strong man armed*[a]

---

2 T. W. Manson, *The Teaching of Jesus* (Cambridge: Cambridge University Press, 1959), 66–68.

4:3–9	The sower*+
4:21	Light under a bushel[a]
4:24	(Measure for measure)[a]
4:26–29	Seed growing of itself
4:30–32	Mustard seed[+a]
7:14f.	What defiles a man*
7:27	(Children's bread to dogs)
8:15	(Leaven of Pharisees and Herod)
9:49f.	Fire and salt[a]
12:1–11	Vineyard*
13:28f.	Fig tree[+]
13:34–37	Absent householder

Q

Luke 6:38	(Measure for measure)[b,c]
6:39	Blind leading blind*[c]
6:41f.	Mote and beam[c]
6:43–45	Tree and fruit[c]
6:47–49	Wise and foolish builders[c]
7:31–35	Children in the marketplace
9:58	(Foxes have holes)
10:2	Harvest and laborers
11:11f.	Stone for bread, etc.
11:17	Divided kingdom or house[b]
11:21f.	Strong man armed[b]
11:33	Light under a bushel[b]
11:39–41	Cleansing outside of cup
12:35–38	Lord returning from marriage feast
12:39	Householder whose house is broken into*
12:42–46	Faithful and unfaithful stewards
12:47f.	(Servants who know or do not know)
13:18f.	Mustard seed*
13:20f.	Leaven*
13:24–30	The shut door
14:34f.	Salt[b]
16:13	(Servant and two masters)
19:11–27	Pounds* (= talents in Matt.)

M

Matt. 5:14	City on a hill
7:5	(Holy things and pearls)
12:11f.	(Sheep fallen into a pit)
13:24–30	Wheat and tares*
13:44	Hidden treasure (cf. Matt. 13:53)
13:45f.	Pearl of great price (cf. Matt. 13:53)
13:47–50	Dragnet (cf. Matt. 13:53)
13:52	Householder with new and old things (cf. Matt. 13:53)
15:13	(Tree not rightly planted)
17:25	(Tribute of earthly kings)
18:12–14	Lost sheep[d]
18:23–35	Unmerciful steward
20:1–16	Laborers in the vineyard
21:28–31	The two sons[+] (cf. 21:33)
22:1–10	Marriage feast, I*[d]
22:11–14	Marriage feast, II*
25:1–12	Ten virgins

L

Luke 4:23	"Physician, heal thyself"[+]
7:40–43	Two debtors
10:30–37	Good Samaritan
11:5–9	Importunate householder
12:16–21	The rich fool*
13:6–9	Unfruitful fig tree*
14:7–11	Places at table*
14:16–24	Great feast[e]
15:3–7	Lost sheep*[e]
15:8–10	Lost coin
15:11–32	Lost son
16:1–8	Unjust steward
16:19–31	Dives and Lazarus
17:7–10	From field to kitchen
18:1–8	Unjust judge and importunate widow*
18:9–14	Pharisee and publican*

PROMISES AND PROPHECIES

God's promises, as we have already seen, were given in the context of his on-going covenantal relationship with Israel. Many of those promises were conditional in character. Consider, for example, the famous saying in 2 Chronicles 7:14—"if my people who are called by my name will humble themselves and pray and seek my face and turn from their wicked ways, then I will hear from heaven and forgive their sin and will heal their land." Notice the conditional nature of this promise. God's people have to repent and turn to God, and then forgiveness and healing are possible. Otherwise, it's not likely to happen. Of course, there are unconditional promises as well, namely, that God will never completely forsake his people. But we need to bear in mind that these promises are part of the interactive nature of the relationship and that they depend on the state of the relationship as to their force. And this brings us to the prophecies in the Bible.

Prophecy is, of course, a "late word from God." And in the Bible we basically only have prophecies directed to God's people, not to everyone, even though there were plenty of prophets in other cultures in both the ANE and the Greco–Roman world. Jewish prophets have been called God's prosecuting attorneys of the covenantal lawsuit. That is, their main job was to remind Israel of how and when they were falling short of the mark, failing in keeping the covenant, and what the consequences would be if they didn't keep it. They were not always prophets of doom and gloom, but often they had to be. And prophets did not just address the nation; they also often spoke truth to power, warning kings like Saul and David when they had gone awry.

If we are asked to define biblical **prophecy**, it involves inspired speech intended to speak God's truth into some situation where it is needed. Sometimes it involves revealing the truth about the past or, more often, the present; and sometimes it involves foretelling some things about the future. It would be a mistake, however, to think of a prophet as always a prognosticator or predictor of the future. A prophet was a soothsayer, which is to say a truth-teller.

There tended to be two different kinds of prophets: auditory prophets and visionary prophets. The auditory prophets would listen to a late word from God and then relate it to the proper audience verbatim. Often, they would use the formula "thus says Yahweh . . ." to make clear they were quoting what they heard from God verbatim. The visionary prophets, like Ezekiel, Daniel, and Zechariah, had revelations involving both seeing and hearing. The problem, of course, with a vision is that you have to describe what you see; and much of it is so overwhelming that you have to resort to the language of analogy, saying "it was like . . . it was like." Prophecy that is basically visionary in character tends to be more metaphorical and figurative than merely auditory prophecy.

Interestingly, visionary prophecy tended to speak more about the other world and the afterlife, not just the here and now. So Daniel 12 can talk about the future resurrection of God's people, or John of Patmos in the book of Revelation can talk about both what is happening in heaven and what will happen at the end of human history. The only full book of prophecy we have in the NT is Revelation, and it is apocalyptic prophecy.

The OT, however, has many more books of prophecy, both auditory and visionary, so many that they are divided into the major prophets, like Jeremiah and Isaiah, and the minor prophets, like Amos, Hosea, and Joel. The terms *major* and *minor* are not meant as evaluations of their importance but, rather, refer to the lengths of the books. Minor prophets are those who provided shorter collections of prophecies. A few basic guidelines about how to read prophecy are now in order.

1. One of the major things that characterizes the writers of the NT is that they believed they lived in the age of the fulfillment of prophecies. More specifically, they believed that the prophecies and promises of God began to come fully and finally true when Jesus stepped on the stage of human history. As such, they did not see a lot of need for more new prophets and prophecies, though there were some (see 1 Cor. 14). This helps explain the orientation of the NT, focused as it is on fulfillment and lacking more than one book of prophecy (only Revelation counts, and some individual passages in other books, e.g., Mark 13). The writers of the OT, however, were all too painfully aware that God's final promises and prophecies were mainly not coming true in their own age. They lived in an age of expectation more than fulfillment, so it is not surprising that we have so many prophetic works and passages in the OT.

2. For the most part, prophets spoke to their own immediate age and situation. When they did venture to comment on the more distant horizon, they tended to do so in general or highly metaphorical ways (e.g., the lion will lie down with the lamb, presumably without longing for lamb chops). This is precisely why the future prophecies of the Bible have been thought to speak to any and all the ages of church history. They are generic enough in character to do so. In every age of human history there are wars, rumors of wars, earthquakes, famines, cosmic marvels, God's saving activities, human infidelity to God and

others, tyrants and evil empires, economic woes—and we could go on. It is precisely the generic character of most future biblical prophecy that makes it relevant to any age, including our own. This generic character is also why so much of the wisdom literature is still a word on target.

3. When, on occasion, a future prophecy is more specific (e.g., Christ will return accompanied by cosmic signs), there is a deliberate avoidance of speculating about the timing of such an event. Rather, the event is characterized by analogical language like "he will come *like* a thief in the night," which completely discourages any attempts to predict the timing of the event, for the metaphor suggests a surprising and unexpected time for the event, a time which could not be guessed. It is worth adding that there has been a 100% failure rate every single time someone in human history has attempted to predict the timing of the return of Christ. That should have discouraged theological weather forecasting. God only reveals enough about the future to give us hope but not so much that we do not have to live by faith every single day.

4. Sometimes, prophecies have a partial fulfillment in the time of the prophet himself but then a more complete and final fulfillment in a later age. This is particularly true of the so-called messianic prophecies in the OT. For example, Isaiah 7:14, in the first instance and read in its immediate literary context seems to be speaking about a situation during the lifetime of Isaiah, possibly the birth of Hezekiah. But clearly enough, the author of Matt. 1–2 sees it as being completely brought to pass in the events surrounding the birth of Jesus.

5. If you wish to become a wise student of prophecy, then begin with classical prophecy, such as we find in Amos or Hosea. Do not begin with the largely visionary prophecy of Daniel or Revelation, which is complex and proves to be some of the most difficult material in all of the Bible to figure out.

6. As a basic rule, what the text meant in its original setting is still what it means today, and what it never could have meant in its original setting when spoken by an ancient inspired prophet it cannot mean today. For example, John of Patmos's audience could not have understood John to be speaking specifically and in detail about the twentieth or twenty-first century or about America, Iran, etc. These things did not exist in the time of the first century AD, and the basic principle is that everything written in the book of Revelation was intended to be a word on target for the seven churches in Asia Minor that the book addresses. It was the

word of God for them in the first place. It did not suddenly become intelligible and applicable in our own day. All the prophetic books of the Bible address their own time or speak only elliptically about the more distant horizon. Before we draw this chapter to a close we need to say a bit more about apocalyptic prophecy.

APOCALYPSE NOW

Here is a basic definition of **apocalyptic** prophecy, to help us understand books like Daniel, Zechariah, and Revelation:

- "A genre of revelatory prophetic literature with a narrative framework in which revelation is mediated by an otherworldly being [i.e., an angel] to a human recipient." It "discloses a transcendent reality which is both temporal, insofar as it envisages eschatological salvation and spatial insofar as it involves another, supernatural world."
- It is usually "intended for a group in crisis with the intent of exhortation or consolation by means of divine authority."[3]

This is the basic definition given by scholars for this complex literature. The very word *apocalypse* refers to the unveiling of something hidden that otherwise would not be known. This then is revelation with a capital *R*. It is in some ways the opposite of some kinds of wisdom literature that derive from close human observation of nature and human nature. Apocalyptic literature arose in a Jewish context in the first place due to the experience of exile. Justice was not being done, and God's people were being oppressed for generations. This led to a belief that God would rectify things in another world or in an afterlife. Since this is minority literature, it is not surprising that a good deal of coded and symbolic language is used to convey the message. Many of these symbols are deliberately **multivalent**, by which I mean they are referential but could refer to a variety of persons or things because they are so generic in character.

If one compares the throne chariot vision in Ezekiel 1 and the similar vision in Revelation 4, it is perfectly clear that these images are plastic and flexible and can be modified. They are not literal descriptions of anything. We are dealing with analogical language ("it was like") and metaphorical language. It is more like political cartoons than literal descriptions of things. For example, the descriptions

---

3 This definition originated in the Society of Biblical Literature Seminar on Apocalyptic Literature and was further refined by D. Helmholm.

of Christ as lion, lamb, alpha, and omega are character descriptions rather than physical descriptions. The same can be said of the Nero-like figure Mr. 666. There is, not surprisingly, a great fascination with numbers since the saints are counting the days until something better happens.

Gematria is the term used for symbolic numbers. Some are what we would call biblically significant numbers—3, 7, 10, 12, and multiples thereof. If 7 is the number of perfection, then 666 is the number of imperfection, incompletion, chaos. These numbers represent definite things but seldom are given as literal numbers of years. For example, the millennium probably does not mean exactly 1,000 years. It means a very long time but with a terminus.

Finally, one of the major themes of John's revelation is the need for the audience to be prepared to suffer for their faith, even unto death, coupled with the promise that if they do so, they will overcome and find their names are written in the book of eternal life. This is part of the consolation offered.

WHAT JUST HAPPENED?

In these last two chapters we have covered a great deal of ground; indeed, we have covered other basic types of literature we find in the Bible, other than historical or biographical literature, which were covered two chapters ago. From a literary point of view, you are now ready to read all the different sorts of literature in the Bible with some awareness of both the character and nature of these different types of literature. You've thus far learned the basic story the Bible tells and the different literary forms in which the story is told, explained, amplified, or used to teach theology, ethics, or history. But there is more to the character of the Bible than just its narrative or literary dimensions. It also partakes of the oral, rhetorical, and social character of the cultures in which it was written, as we will see in the next two chapters.

FOR FURTHER READING

If you would like to study the development of wisdom and of prophetic literature in the Bible, see my *Jesus the Sage: The Pilgrimage of Wisdom* (Minneapolis, MN: Fortress Press 2000) and *Jesus the Seer: The Progress of Prophecy* (Peabody, MA: Hendrickson, 1999).

6

The ORAL and RHETORICAL CHARACTER of the ANCIENT BIBLICAL WORLD

So was I speaking and weeping in the most bitter contrition of my heart, when, lo! I heard from a neighboring house a voice, as of boy or girl, I know not, chanting, and oft repeating. "Take up and read; Take up and read." ["Tolle, lege! Tolle, lege!"*] Instantly, my countenance altered, I began to think most intently whether children were wont in any kind of play to sing such words: nor could I remember ever to have heard the like. So checking the torrent of my tears, I arose; interpreting it to be*

no other than a command from God to open the book, and read
the first chapter I should find. . . .

   Eagerly then I returned to the place where Alypius was
sitting; for there had I laid the volume of the Apostle when
I arose thence. I seized, opened, and in silence read that section
on which my eyes first fell: "Not in rioting and drunkenness, not
in chambering and wantonness, not in strife and envying; but
put ye on the Lord Jesus Christ, and make not provision for the
flesh, in concupiscence" [Romans 13:14–15]. No further would
I read; nor needed I: for instantly at the end of this sentence, by
a light as it were of serenity infused into my heart, all the
darkness of doubt vanished away.
                                        —AUGUSTINE[1]

WHERE ARE WE GOING?

In this chapter we consider the oral and rhetorical character of the biblical world,
where only a small minority of persons (perhaps as little as 10–15%) could read
or write. What was the function of texts, especially sacred texts, in a largely oral
culture?

Having examined the Bible's story and its literary characteristics, the careful student will have already gotten the impression that the Bible is a very different book from most any modern book one could read. Its story is different, its literary conventions are different, and in this chapter we will discover that its basic oral and rhetorical contexts are different. Documents were different in character and served many different functions in antiquity compared to today. If we do not study documents in their original contexts, we are bound to misread them. The dictum I offer to my students when it comes to reading the Bible is as follows: *a text without a context is just a pretext for whatever you want it to mean.*

   Surely, if a person believes the Bible is God's inspired word, written by inspired persons, we ought to have the courtesy of reading their work in the ways they intended for it to be read; and this requires that we have knowledge of the contexts out of which and into which these documents were written. This chapter will help us to begin to have a sense of that oral and rhetorical context.

---

1 Aurelius Augustine, *The Confessions of St. Augustine*, trans. Edward Pusey, vol. 7, pt. 1, bk. 8, chap 12, The Harvard Classics. (New York: P. F. Collier & Son, 1909–1914).

Figure 6.1 Prophets shared divine words with their people. (Shutterstock/Only Fabrizio)

ORAL EXAMINATION

All of the ancient cultures of the biblical world were oral cultures, not cultures based on texts. Whereas, in our culture we tend to think of texts as primary sources of information and oral conversations or proclamation as secondary, it was just the opposite of this in the world of the Bible. The oral word was primary, and documents were entirely secondary. There is a reason that Jesus said to his disciples "let those with two good ears hear." Most eyes could not read. The oral word was given pride of place, not least because of the low literacy rates in most parts of the ANE and the Greco–Roman world. Not only was the oral word the dominant form of ancient communication but the oral nature of the culture shaped the way people wrote and read documents—they were oral documents, meant to be read out loud.

By this I mean that the biblical documents, like so many other ancient documents, reflect oral speech—they have rhythm, rhyme, alliteration, assonance, and various aural devices. Especially when people wanted to persuade others about something, they would seek to make what they said pleasing, interesting, intriguing to the ear, and not merely memorable but even memorizable. And there was a whole class of persons who did most of the writing—scribes.

Figure 6.2 A scribe holding his stylus and a piece of papyrus. (Shutterstock/Jose Ignacio Soto)

Scribes were used not least because the materials were expensive, and there was really little margin for error (doing erasures was very difficult with ink on papyrus, though sometimes wax tablets and a stylus were used for a first draft). They were also used in part because the historical evidence suggests that only 10–20% of the ancient world could read or write, and actually those were two different skills. More people could read than could write a document with accurately formed letters in straight lines. The document shown in Figure 6.3 was copied by a professional scribe in a

Figure 6.3 Ancient Greek manuscripts were written in scriptio continua, that is, a continuous flow of Greek letters without separation of words. (Shutterstock/Rafal Redelowski)

"fair hand." If you are getting the impression that writing was a specialized skill in antiquity, and reading was largely the provenance of the rich who could afford a decent education and even to buy manuscripts or "books", you would be right.

It took skill in writing, skill obtained by training and education, which only a minority of people had access to; and that minority was usually from the elite and wealthy members of society. The copier of the document in Figure 6.3 was not merely literate; he was skilled. Look carefully at this picture of an ancient document. Notice the continuous flow of letters. It would be difficult to read this document unless (1) you already knew its content and/or (2) you read it out loud to figure out where the divisions between words, sentences, and paragraphs were meant to go. The Bible was not divided into chapters and verses until an archbishop named Stephen Langton (1150–1228), who clearly had too much time on his hands, provided us with our modern form of the Bible. Indeed, it was apparently not divided into separate words for several centuries after the original writing of the NT documents.

There was a very good reason that ancient documents almost always had a continuous flow of letters—economics. The less papyrus used, the cheaper the document was to produce. There was another reason as well. Ancient documents were not normally produced for the general public; they were produced for patrons, clients, or libraries of and for the wealthy. The general public could not afford to buy such documents and could not read them (they had enough trouble just reading short inscriptions on tombstones and public proclamations of the emperor), and reading and writing, indeed most education, had been the provenance of the wealthy, in particular of royal courts and temples since time immemorial. There was no concept in antiquity of the general public's right to know—or to be educated, for that matter. The very use of a continuous flow of letters suggests an insider talking to another literate insider, and this brings up an interesting point.

Early Christianity (unlike most forms of Judaism in any age) was an exuberantly evangelistic religion, so the early Christians produced documents that could be proclaimed or used for the persuasion of nonbelievers, documents which were meant to be heard in the original Greek, not primarily silently read in private. The documents of the OT are insider literature as well and often are meant to be read out loud, but they do not really promote sharing their religion with the world. Even a document like Esther or Daniel simply promotes having Jews in high places in pagan courts in order to protect the lives of fellow Jews, not to convert pagans.

In other words, the rhetorical character of the documents of the OT and NT is somewhat different. While both testaments are forms of preaching to the choir (that is, they are addressing those who are already part of their religion), the NT documents also have one eye on evangelizing the whole world. Convincing the outsider required more rhetorical skill, more substantive acts of persuasion; and accordingly, many of the writers of the NT used Greco–Roman **rhetoric**, the ancient art of persuasion familiar to Gentiles all over the Roman Empire, to accomplish such aims. You will not find Greco–Roman rhetoric in the OT, though certainly you find some Jewish means of persuasion.

There is a famous anecdote about two very famous early Christian thinkers named Ambrose and Augustine. Augustine once said that he found Ambrose to be the most remarkable man he had ever met because *he could read a document without moving his lips or making a sound.* This was highly unusual in Augustine's view. Most ancient reading was done out loud, even if you were only reading to yourself. Libraries in antiquity must have been very noisy places. Precisely because both the earliest Jews and the earliest Christians were part of such an oral culture and precisely because Christians so deeply wanted others to believe in Jesus, they took care to compose their documents in ways that would be aurally effective and, indeed, persuasive. As it turns out, the phrase *oral text* is not an oxymoron, a self-contradictory phrase. The documents of the Bible were by and large meant to be read or, in the case of the Psalms, sung out loud; and some, like the Psalms or Paul's letters, were even intended to be orally shared in worship events.

Since Christians believed it was their job to share the good news of Jesus Christ with all and sundry, from the least, last, and lost to the foremost, first, and found, they did not shape or direct their message just to the cultured, wealthy, and literate. Many of their documents were written to whole groups of people—the church in Corinth or Philippi, for example. They were "public" communications in ways that many ancient documents were not, and they were public communications for the whole spectrum of society, from the elites right down to the slaves and children. These were ethnic and gender-inclusive documents as well, not written just for literate males. But how did Christians with their evangelistic zeal make these documents accessible to the widest possible audience including the illiterate?

The answer is they used literate readers, who already knew the document and would read it out to a whole congregation. Today we might call such a person a **lector**, a literate person trained to read an important manuscript (a sacred text, a public proclamation) out to an audience with appropriate feeling, pauses, and insight. Two examples from the NT will make my point.

In the last document in the NT, the Revelation of John of Patmos, we find the following at Revelation 1:3: "Blessed is the one who reads aloud the words of this prophecy, and blessed are those who hear it and take to heart what is written in it."

John of Patmos is the author of the document, but he is in exile on the island of Patmos, off the west coast of modern Turkey. He will not be the person who reads out loud these words to the churches in Ephesus, Smyrna, and elsewhere. That will be the job of the lector, who, with scroll in hand and with an advance knowledge of its contents, will be able to read the continuous flow of letters and perhaps explain some things along the way. The hearers in Revelation 1:3 are clearly distinguished from the reader of the document. And notice the reader is singular here: "the one who reads."

We find the very same Greek phrase and phenomenon in the Gospel of Mark 13:14. In the midst of a discussion about the defiling of the Temple in Jerusalem by what is called "an abomination which makes desolate" (using a phrase from the OT prophetic book Daniel), the author inserts the parenthetical remark "let the reader understand." Notice again that the word *reader* is in the singular. This is because while Mark's audience is a group of people, they are merely the hearers of the document. The singular reader of the document is the lector sent to undertake the job of reading it out loud, and perhaps explaining it, to the many hearers who could not read it themselves. Indeed, the world of the Bible was a world of oral cultures; and where texts existed, they were mainly oral texts, most of them intended to be read out loud (even if written to only one or a few people, like a family).

"ALMOST THOU PERSUADEST ME"

Besides the oral context in which the Bible was written, there is also the matter of the rhetorical context. By "rhetoric" I do not mean political hyperbole; I mean the ancient art of persuasion. Rhetoric had been a part of formal education, even elementary education, all over the biblical world from at least the time of Alexander the Great (356–323 BC). Aristotle had been his tutor, and Alexander resolved to spread the Greek language, Greek culture, and Greek education all over the then known world; and he largely succeeded. Part of that education was learning what Aristotle himself had taught, and he taught extensively about rhetoric, the art of persuasion. Aristotle taught this to Alexander as a part of statecraft. It was better to convince an audience to do the right thing than to force them to do so, and in an oral culture speech, convincing speech, was at a premium. Rulers had to persuade their generals, generals had to persuade their troops, lawyers had to persuade judges, and leaders of all sorts had to persuade their people. And if you were starting a new religion, it would require an enormous amount of persuasion to get the unconvinced and unconverted on board. Why?

For one thing, ancient people were not enamored with the "new." They had not swallowed the myth that the "newest is the truest and the latest is the greatest," particularly when it came to religion. In fact, one could say that the ANE and the Greco–Roman world had a bias in favor of what was old, what was tried and true, what was well established and many times tested. This was especially true when it came to beliefs about one's god or gods. If you read Josephus's (37–100 AD) famous book *Antiquities of the Jews*, you will find him mounting an argument not just for how ancient the Jewish religion is but also for how other religions, including Greek ones, had learned their best ideas from Moses! Obviously, this is apologetics, and it is historically unlikely as well; but the point is that the more ancient a religion, the more likely it was credible and trustworthy.

Unlike modern persons living in the twenty-first century, the people of the world of the Bible were not enamored with youth, youth culture, the ideas of the young, or anything absolutely "new," especially when it came to religion. Indeed, during the time of the Roman Empire "new" religions were often labeled as "super-stitions" and banned. This caused problems for Christianity when it became clear to political officials that Christians were not simply part of the Jewish religion, which had a long pedigree and was accepted in the empire as a legitimate religion (a *religio licita*, or "licit religion," they called it) mainly for a specific ethnic group— the Jews. Paul himself was dragged before the Areopagus court in Athens because he was accused of introducing new deities and, thus, suspect or even illegal religious ideas into Athens (see Acts 17).

So what was ancient rhetoric like? How did it persuade? You can see from what I have already said that what might convince ancient peoples about religion would not likely convince a lot of modern ones. Indeed, if an evangelist today were to use the argument "You ought to believe Christianity because it is an ancient religion," that would likely be counterproductive. The modern response could well be, "Old religions are out of date, out of touch, no longer relevant. Besides I'm spiritual not religious, and not interested in organized religion. Why should I listen to you?" This is not how most ancient persons would have reacted to claims that a religion was ancient. Accordingly, Christians couched their message as "good news" not as "new" news. They also sought at length to show how belief in Jesus was the logical fulfillment, extension, and conclusion of OT religion, of Jewish religion. In other words, they avoided suggesting that they were preaching something totally new.

A further thing that made Christian proclamation persuasive was and is a certain inherent persuasiveness to eloquent speech full of lofty ideas, well spoken with nice turns of phrase and memorable lines—or, as we would call them, sound bites. This seems always to have been true, whether in antiquity or in modernity.

The whole Bible is full of this sort of rhetoric, which involves assonance, alliteration, rhythm, sometimes even rhyme. Take, for instance, the very first chapter of Genesis. Two brief illustrations will do: (1) The Bible begins with alliteration, *běreshit bara* (emphasis on the *B* sound). We translate this "in the beginning [God] created. . . ." And look what happened. All the poetic and rhetorical finesse of the original is lost in translation. In general, it is the poetry (the alliteration, assonance, rhythm, rhyme) that is lost in translation. It is one of the reasons many moderns have not recognized that we are dealing with poetry or poetic prose in Genesis 1. (2) A little farther into Genesis 1 we hear that things were "formless and void." While that is an accurate translation, the Hebrew original says *tohu vavohu*—it rhymes. But you would never know this by reading most English translations. It is lost in translation.

You can begin to see now why I am stressing not only that things get lost in translation, especially the poetry and therefore some of the persuasive or rhetorical force of the material, but that every translation is already an interpretation of the original. This is why original language reading of the Bible is so preferable to reading it in a translation into another language, including English.

In the second place, part of the learned skill of rhetoric involves the use of literary devices like personification, dramatic metaphors, figures of speech that are memorable and stick in the minds of the listeners. We find these sorts of things all over the Bible. For example, in Proverbs 8–9 we have personifications of folly and wisdom, both as women, presumably because the word *hokmah*, "wisdom" in Hebrew, is a noun of the feminine gender. Yes, nouns in Hebrew and Greek have genders, unlike English nouns. In our earlier discussion of figurative language we pointed to the use of colorful metaphorical phrases like "and God's nose burned," which of course meant that he was angry. Or in the NT we could point to the use of a word like *macrothymia*, which literally means "having a long fuse before blowing up with anger," though it is regularly translated as "patience."

Consider for a moment the use of rhetorical questions, questions that do not expect an answer from the listener. For example, in Hosea 11:8 Yahweh asks, "How can I give you up Ephraim? How can I hand you over Israel?" Or at the end of 1 Corinthians 12 Paul asks, "Not all are apostles, are they? Not all are prophets are they? Not all are teachers, are they? Not all work miracles, do they? Not all have gifts of healing, do they? Not all speak in tongues, do they?" The answer to rhetorical questions that begin with the word "not" is always no. The examples I have given thus far are examples of what I would call *micro-rhetoric*, the use of small rhetorical devices. But there are uses of much larger and more complicated rhetorical devices in the Bible as well.

For example, the famous Psalm 119 is what can be called an *alphabet acrostic*, that is, a psalm which has one stanza for each letter of the Hebrew alphabet—aleph, beth, gimel, daleth, etc. So the first stanza begins with the letter aleph, the second with the letter beth, and so on. One could say the psalmist is telling you everything you need to know about Torah or the Law from *A* to *Z* or, to use the Hebrew, from aleph to taw. Unless the English translation tells you that an alphabet acrostic is what is going on by labeling stanzas with the letters of the Hebrew alphabet, as the New International Version does, you would never have guessed this sort of elaborate rhetorical structuring of things was happening. This took no little skill for the psalmist to do in a convincing and persuasive way.

There are a multitude of elaborate rhetorical devices and forms of discourse in the NT itself, and a little background will help us understand why. We must go into a little more detail about ancient education and rhetoric to better interpret the rhetoric in and of the NT. Rhetoric was a popular spectator sport in the first century AD. Most persons were either producers or consumers of some kind of rhetoric, and Greco–Roman rhetoric had long been a staple of education before any NT document was written, at all levels, beginning with elementary education.

In elementary education, children would learn how to do rhetorical comparisons (called *synkrisis*) for the sake of the formation of their values, so they would know the difference between being a virtuous person and being a wicked one. They would also learn how to compose *chreia*, short pithy stories which usually would have a memorable saying at or near the end, for instance, the story of Jesus's discussion with the wealthy young man, which culminates with the famous "it is easier for a camel to go through the eye of a needle than for a rich person to enter the Kingdom of God" (Mark 10:25). Rhetorical education would continue as the child got older, and it was even made a staple item of higher education in Roman times. In fact, the rhetorician came to be the person who dictated what was taught in higher education during the period of the empire.[2] Rhetoricians were found in all the great cities of the Roman Empire, many of which also had schools of rhetoric or at least schools which made rhetoric one of the dominant subjects studied.

Education was, of course, by and large the privilege of the more elite members of society; and it tells us something about the leaders of early Christianity that they could read and write, and various of them had rhetorical skills as well. Generally

---

2 See my discussion in *Conflict and Community in Corinth: A Socio-Rhetorical Commentary on 1 and 2 Corinthians* (Grand Rapids, MI: Eerdmans, 1995), 39–43, and all the reference there. See especially Donald Lemen Clark, *Rhetoric in Greco–Roman Education* (New York: Columbia University Press, 1957).

Figure 6.4 Cicero, the most famous Roman orator, giving a speech. (Shutterstock/Renata Sedmakova)

speaking, rhetoric was part of the training of wealthy males seeking to enter the *cursus honorum*, a Latin phrase referring to climbing up the ladder of public offices and pursuing a career in public life in one way or another, as a lawyer, a senator, an ambassador, a government employee, or the like.

While there were a few examples of rhetorically trained and skilled women in antiquity, such as Hortensia, the daughter of the famous rhetorician Q. Hortensius Hortalus, who delivered a public oration to the triumvirs in 42 BC arguing her own legal case, she was surely an exception to the rule and probably gained her training in the home. Women were not, in general, either encouraged or, in some cases, allowed to pursue "higher" education, which means that even wealthy women tended to lack rhetorical training beyond the *progymnasmata*, by which I mean the rhetorical exercises offered at the elementary level of education (see Quintilian's *Institutio Oratoria*, 1.1.6).[3]

But the *progymnasmata* exercises were actually extensive. One learned how to deal with the following literary forms and verbally form them in interesting and persuasive manners:

Fable

Narrative

Chreia

Proverb

Refutation

Confirmation

Commonplace

Encomium

Vituperation

Comparison

Impersonation

Description

Thesis or Theme

Defend/Attack a Law

Some of these exercises were quite complicated and corresponded to specific elements in a speech of any of the three species of rhetoric. In addition, even early in Greco–Roman education there was training in public speaking. One would be set a topic, sometimes trivial ("in praise of a flea" or "the shame of male baldness") and sometimes serious ("proposition—that the emperor deserves to be worshipped"), and one would produce a speech to an imaginary audience about the matter. As I have said, most ancient peoples used rhetoric and were avid consumers and critics

---

3 Eva Cantarella, *Pandora's Daughters: The Role and Status of Women in Greek and Roman Antiquity* (Baltimore: Johns Hopkins University Press, 1987), 141, 214.

of its more skilled practitioners. The more showy styles with lots of verbal pyrotech-nics were in vogue, the more one was likely to hear **epideictic** rhetoric in the market-place and elsewhere, the rhetoric of praise and blame. It could be the most frivolous form of rhetoric but also the most eloquent and aesthetically pleasing. Epideictic rhetoric was to be especially associated with the rise of the so-called second Sophistic period in the second century AD, a movement of orators given to mere verbal elo-quence; but those tendencies were already in evidence in the first century.

In an oral culture, orators might well make a considerable living; and some, like Herodes Atticus, who helped build the theater in the shadow of the Parthenon in Athens, became very wealthy indeed because of their gift of eloquence. Consider, for example, a papyrus fragment dating from about AD 110 which reads in part, "Pay to Licinius . . . the rhetor the amount due to him for the speeches [in] which Aur[elius . . .] was honored . . . in the gymnasium in the Great Serapeion, four hundred drachmas of silver."[4] This was more than a Roman soldier's annual wages, according to the Roman historian Tacitus (*Annals* 1.17). The broad acceptance and indeed great popularity of rhetorical oratory are attested by important literary works that lionize orators, such as Athenaeus's *Deiphnosophists* and Philostratus's *Lives of the Sophists*. Not only did the popular orators have many fans, but they were widely imitated.

Notice it was the Sophists or "flatterers"/"entertainers" who were famous for their verbal pyrotechnics that made "news." This proved to be problematic for those who wanted to persuade audiences on some serious subject and who were unwilling to entertain or thrill the crowd with their verbal artistry. The alternative, however, was not to eschew rhetoric altogether but rather to use it in a more sub-stantive and sober manner, all the while castigating those "Sophists" who were not philosophically (or theologically) serious about what they were doing.

The art of persuasion had a multitude of rules and forms involved in its praxis, and it will be well if we lay them out in some detail here. There were three different species of ancient rhetoric—**forensic**, **deliberative**, and epideictic. Each originally was used to address a particular social setting and had distinctive purposes. *Foren-sic rhetoric*, as the name suggests, was the rhetoric of the law court, the rhetoric of attack and defense; and it focused on things done in the past. This was the type of rhetoric most frequently practiced in the NT era, and we hear samplings of it in the trials of Paul in Acts 22 and 26. *Deliberative rhetoric* was the rhetoric of the assem-bly, originally of the democratic assemblies in Greece, and the rhetoric of advice

---

4 Robert K. Sherk, *The Roman Empire: Augustus to Hadrian* (Cambridge: Cambridge University Press, 1988), 195.

and consent, trying to get one course of action or another, one policy or another, voted on in an affirmative manner. The temporal focus of this rhetoric was the future as change was sought in some policy or action in the near future. Finally, there was *epideictic rhetoric*, the rhetoric of display. Its social venues included the agora (for entertainment), the funeral for encomiums or eulogies, or celebrations, like the proconsul's birthday. This was the rhetoric of praise and blame, more praise than blame especially at funerals; and its temporal focus was the present. It did not seek to change beliefs or behavior or opinions or attitudes, but rather it sought to reinforce the existing ones. It was possible to mix things up in a rhetorical discourse, say, to have an epideictic digression in the midst of an otherwise forensic discourse; but there was a certain way of doing this, where one made clear one was digressing. We see this practice in 1 Corinthians 13, which is an epideictic showpiece in praise of love in the midst of an otherwise deliberative discourse.

During the period of the Roman Empire, epideictic rhetoric came to the fore as flattery could get you advancement or patrons or at least noticed in a positive way. In a society that had a set, even rigid, authority structure involving patrons and clients, with the emperor being the biggest patron of all, the art of sucking up was the order of the day, not speaking truth to power. Rulers liked rhetoricians—prophets, not so much, unless they were saying nice things about the ruler and his future.

In such a setting it is no surprise that the rhetorical handbooks of the first century AD, such as Quintilian's *Institutio Oratoria* which wanted rhetoric to be taken seriously, focused on forensic rhetoric since it was the form of substantive rhetoric most frequently practiced in that era. What is especially interesting about the NT is that it more frequently exhibits deliberative rhetoric as it seeks to persuade people to change their beliefs and behaviors. It should be added that deliberative rhetoric was still in play in the Roman Empire, not in democratic assemblies but in ambassadorial missions when one group or country was negotiating with others to conclude some kind of pact or treaty.

What is revealing about the preference for deliberative rhetoric in the NT is that it suggests that the orator believes the audience is free to respond positively or not and therefore needs to be persuaded. In other words, good evangelism and good preaching involved persuasion, not manipulation and strong-arm tactics. It may well be very revealing that Paul repeatedly called the house meetings of Christians meetings of the *ekklēsia*—formerly the term for the democratic assembly and now the term for the assembling of Christians. Was this because Paul believed that the church was now the place where dialogue, discussion, and debate could still be carried on and should lead to important conclusions about belief and behavior? I think so.

In the NT era style often prevailed over substance when it came to rhetoric, and much emphasis was placed on stylistic devices, figures of speech, colorful metaphors, exclamation, apostrophes, wordplay, epigrams. These sorts of rhetorical devices are not lacking in the NT, but they are used to serve serious purposes about matters theological and ethical.

In regard to verbal style, there were two major styles of rhetoric—the more reserved and formal Attic style and the more florid and luxurious Asiatic style. In general, Asiatic style tended to be more emotional, involving more colorful and longer sentences, lots of hyperbole, and metaphors and the like. Attic style was seen as more appropriate in some quarters, but even Cicero preferred the Asiatic style for his Roman trials as it did a better job of stirring the emotions.

A normal rhetorical discourse had three basic emotional phases, dealing first with the issue of *ethos*, then *logos*, and finally *pathos*. At the opening of the discourse there was an appeal to the simpler and more surface emotions, such as a feeling of being hospitable or friendly, or the capacity for laughter as the rhetorician sought to establish rapport and his authority with his audience. *Ethos* was all about establishing the speaker's character and making clear he was trustworthy and believable. Lots of things could affect one's ethos. When the toupee of the rhetorician blew off in the agora in the middle of an otherwise compelling discourse, he was having a bad ethos day, and his speech lost credibility. *Logos* refers to the real meat of the discourse, its emotion-charged arguments. In Greek, arguments were called *pistoi*, interestingly enough, "proofs"; but this is also a variant on the word for beliefs. At the end of the discourse the rhetorician needed to appeal to the deep emotions—love or hate, grief or joy, anger or pity—and so create *pathos* in the audience so that they would embrace the arguments not merely intellectually but affectively as well. When that happened, the act of persuasion had achieved its aim of winning the whole person or group over, body and soul.

There was a normal structural outline to a rhetorical discourse, though certain elements could be rearranged or omitted in some cases. The outline is as follows:

The *exordium* is the beginning of the discourse, attempting to make the audience open and well disposed to what follows.

The *narratio* then explains the nature of the disputed matter or the facts that are relevant to the discussion. This element could be omitted on occasion.

The *propositio* or thesis statement, is crucial and normally follows the *narratio* though sometimes it comes before the narration. In a forensic discourse the essential proposition of the prosecutor and the defendant might both be laid out by way of contrast.

The *probatio* then enumerates the arguments for the proposition, supporting the speaker's case. This might be, but would not necessarily be, followed by the *refutatio*, the refutation of the opponent's arguments. It is interesting that Paul tends to follow this taxonomy with some rigor. Thus, in Galatians the real bone of contention is delayed until the allegory is presented in Galatians 4 to create animus against the Judaizers, and in Romans Paul saves the refutation until Romans 9–11, where he refutes the suggestion that God has abandoned his first chosen people.

Finally, the *peroratio* sums up or amplifies some major argument and/or makes a final appeal to the deeper emotions to make sure the argument persuaded.

Let me illustrate how all this applies to a couple of NT books. The first thing to say is that some of the documents which have a letter form, at their beginning and end, are basically not much like letters, either ancient or modern. They owe far more of their structure to the rhetorical outline presented here and to rhetorical devices than they do to epistolary forms and practices. Some of these documents can be called "homilies" or "sermons," for example, 1 John, which has no epistolary features at all, even at the beginning or end; Hebrews, which has epistolary features only at the end because the document has been sent from a distance; or James, which has some epistolary features of a circular letter at the outset but for the rest of the document we are looking at an exhortation of some sort. And then there are the more elaborate rhetorical discourses of a person like Paul.

Before we begin to examine in more detail the rhetoric we find in the NT, one final point should be made. One of the keys to understanding any rhetorical discourse, whether it is a full discourse like Romans or 1 John or a speech summary like in Acts, is that one needs to not only determine the species of rhetoric in play (forensic, deliberative, or epideictic) but find the proposition and peroration of the discourse to figure out what it is about and where the argument is going.

One of the real benefits of rhetorical analysis of the so-called epistolary literature of the NT is that if one can find the proposition and peroration of a discourse, understanding the many and sometimes convoluted arguments that follow the proposition becomes much easier as we know the point and purpose of the discourse. Of course, it is true that an epideictic discourse seldom has a proposition statement since it is not trying to argue a particular case but rather to praise an already approved and embraced matter or subject. Nevertheless, as we shall see, finding the opening thesis statement and closing summary is crucial when a document has such features, becoming a key to interpreting the document. Bearing these caveats, conditions, and suggestions in mind, we are ready to do more detailed rhetorical analysis of a sample or two from the NT itself.

One of the rhetorical forms used in the gospels, in this case in Mark, is the *chreia*. A *chreia* is a concise, compact narrative taken from the memoirs of some famous historical person and shaped so that it builds to a climax with the mention of some famous saying or famous deed of the great person or both. One example will have to suffice, though most of the controversy stories in Mark are shaped into the form of a *chreia*. Mark 2:23–28 presents a brief vignette that climaxes with the famous saying of Jesus in verse 27 about humans not being made for the Sabbath but rather vice versa, followed by a brief conclusion in verse 28. The famous saying of Jesus does not stand in isolation but brings the controversy at hand to a close, by means of an authoritative utterance. In other words, the saying is integral to the telling of the story and precipitates its climax and conclusion. These are precisely the sorts of historical anecdotes schoolchildren were taught to form and memorize as part of their education in rhetoric.

Our second example of rhetoric in the NT is much more elaborate and not surprisingly comes from one of the two or three most well educated of the writers of the NT, Paul (the other two being Luke and the author of Hebrews, plus perhaps the composer of 1 Peter). Here is a rhetorical outline of Paul's discourse to the Galatians, certainly one of his most polemical discourses.

EPISTOLARY PRESCRIPT—1:1–5

EXORDIUM/INTRODUCTION—1:6–10—TWO GOSPELS?

NARRATIO/NARRATION OF FACTS—1:11–2:14—A NARRATIVE OF SURPRISING EVENTS

PROPOSITIO/THESIS STATEMENT—2:15–21—SAVED BY THE FAITHFULNESS OF CHRIST, NOT BY WORKS OF THE MOSAIC LAW

PROBATIO AND *REFUTATIO*—ARGUMENTS PRO AND CON— SEVEN ARGUMENTS TO SUPPORT THE THESIS—3:1–6:10

PAUL'S AUTOGRAPH—6:11

PERORATIO/EMOTIONAL SUMMING UP—6:12–17

EPISTOLARY CLOSING—6.18

The first thing one should always look for in analyzing a discourse is the thesis statement. That will provide the key to all that follows, and in this case the thesis statement can be found in Galatians 2:15–21. Here, we have a dramatic contrast between salvation being provided through the faithfulness of Jesus even unto death on the cross, contrasted with works of the Mosaic law, which can neither save a person nor complete one's working out of one's salvation. What is really at issue here is how Christians should live. According to the Mosaic law or according to the law of Christ? Paul argues, of course, for the latter and stresses that the Galatians must not follow the advice of the Judaizers and add Mosaic law observance to their already extant faith in Christ. The issue then is not primarily justification by grace through faith, though that is the starting point of salvation. The issue is whether keeping the Mosaic law will enhance one's Christian life and complete one's duty to God or not. Paul says this is entirely the wrong road to go down, and he says so because he believes that the Mosaic covenant was pro tempore, that is, given to God's people to keep them in line and alive until their Messiah should come. But, as Paul says, when the time had fully come, Christ, born of woman, born under law in order that he might redeem God's people out from under the law, was the change agent, the game changer. After all, the Galatians had received the Holy Spirit by hearing the gospel with faith and accepting it—not by doing works of the Mosaic law.

Notice that the thesis statement that tells us what the following arguments in the discourse are really about comes after a very lengthy "narration of necessary facts." Why does Paul go to such lengths to chronicle his various trips to Jerusalem and his confrontation of Peter in Antioch? Presumably he is setting the record straight, after the Judaizers had come to Galatia and muddied the waters by suggesting that (1) Paul had not given them the whole gospel; (2) Paul only had his authority from the Jerusalem church, and the Judaizers from Jerusalem knew better what the real gospel was; and (3) according to the Judaizers, even Gentile converts needed to become Jews in order to be full-fledged Christians like Jerusalem church Christians, and therefore, they needed to get themselves circumcised and keep the Mosaic covenant—not just the food laws or Sabbath laws but the whole covenant. Paul warns that if they do take on the sign of the Mosaic covenant, they will be obligated to keep all 613 or so commandments that are part of that covenant.

In one of Paul's most daring and creative arguments in Galatians 4:21–31 Paul tells a little allegory about Sarah and Hagar and the children of the free person and of the slave woman—and, of course, by implication of Paul's Gospel and the Judaizer's version of the gospel. Amazingly he puts Jerusalem, the Judaizers, slavery (and the slave woman Hagar), and the Mosaic law all into the same column and in the other column he places Sarah, her free children, and the Jerusalem that is from above and freedom. In essence he says that the Galatians must choose between the continuation of the Abrahamic covenant in the new covenant, and so freedom that the Spirit of God provides, and the keeping of the Mosaic covenant and the binding legal obligations it requires. There is no question which side of the argument he favors.

The final peroration is always meant to make an appeal to the audience's deeper emotions, thus sealing their consent to the arguments that preceded it. In Galatians 6:12–17 Paul talks about the real motives the Judaizers have for trying to compel the Gentiles to be circumcised—so that they can avoid persecution, presumably because Judaism was a sanctioned religion in the empire. Paul says, by contrast, that he himself has been not merely circumcised but crucified to the world and vice versa and that he bears on his body the marks of persecution, the so-called stigmata of Christ. This is said in order to produce pathos in the audience. One group is being characterized as cowards, seeking to avoid persecution, and the other as courageous, accepting suffering for the cause of Christ. Paul says that if one wants to boast about something, let it be Christ's cross, not one's own circumcision.

Figure 6.5 The aqueduct at Psidian Antioch, one of the cities to which the letter to the Galatians is addressed. (© Mark R. Fairchild, PhD)

One of the great virtues of rhetorical analysis of a letter like Galatians is that it shows us and helps us to understand the logic and flow of the arguments in a letter. Traditional interpretation of the text is seldom able to show the logic of why these arguments exist in the order they do and why there is a final emotional harangue. But orality and rhetoric are only two of the dimensions that distinguish ancient cultures from our own in various ways. We must consider several social dimensions of antiquity that make even clearer the differences between then and now, and there and here.

WHAT JUST HAPPENED?

In this chapter we learned just how different the biblical world was from ours when it comes to texts, education, and persuasion. Our world wants things in writing, whereas ancients were more likely to prefer and believe "the living voice." Our world believes education should be for everyone. In antiquity only a small percentage of people could read and write. Education was mostly for wealthy males only. Our world associates rhetoric with politics, hyperbole, and insincerity. In antiquity rhetoric was prized, and orators were some of the most highly paid persons in the ancient world. Indeed, speech making was a spectator sport all over the Roman Empire. We showed some of the different forms of rhetoric in the NT and how Paul's letters were basically speeches with letter features at the outset and conclusion because they were sent from a distance.

FOR FURTHER READING

Those wanting a brief overview of the rhetoric of the NT era and the rhetoric in the NT should consult my *New Testament Rhetoric: An Introductory Guide to the Art of Persuasion in and of the New Testament* (Eugene, OR: Wipf and Stock, 2009). For those wanting to understand orality and oral culture in general and the way ancient documents functioned in that setting, see Harry Y. Gamble, *Books and Readers in the Early Church: A History of Early Christian Texts* (New Haven, CT: Yale University Press, 1997).

7

SOCIAL REALITIES and CULTURAL SCRIPTS in BIBLE TIMES

The past is a foreign country. They do things differently there.
—L. P. HARTLEY *THE GO BETWEEN*

WHERE ARE WE GOING?

In this chapter we will examine ancient values and customs that shaped the cultures of the biblical world and in various ways distinguished that world from ours. Considering concepts or social realities like collectivist culture, patrons and clients, honor and shame, patriarchy, and limited good, we can paint a pretty clear picture of how different the ancient social world was in which the biblical figures lived.

The psychological dynamics of any given culture are not only unique and particular; they are often difficult to assess. For example, what is considered humorous in one culture may well seem offensive in another, and likewise what is considered persuasive in one culture may seem unconvincing in another. It's not just a matter of trotting out ironclad rules of universal logic. The issue is culture-specific. I say this now because a fair bit of the rhetoric of the NT will seem manipulative to us in our postmodern situation. It will look like emotive arm-twisting. Were we to examine in some detail Paul's tour de force argument in Philemon, we would see precisely this sort of thing, where Paul ends up saying "you owe me your very spiritual life" (Phil. 19) in order to get Philemon to set the slave Onesimus free and then warns he may be coming soon to Philemon's house, presumably to make sure the job got done right. To some degree this reveals something important about ancient cultures. They were very different from, and in various ways more emotive than, most modern cultures. Saying a few things about the social world of the NT will not go amiss here.

Ancient cultures were, to a far greater degree than most modern cultures, collectivist. By this I mean they did not promote individualism. Of course, there were individuals and, indeed, widely recognized high-status ones like an Alexander or a Julius Caesar; but identity in the ancient world was largely established by what group one was a part of and by factors like geography, gender, and generation. These were all patriarchal cultures where the question "Who was your father" was crucial. This is precisely why the gospel writers had to go to such lengths to explain Jesus's origins.

Have you noticed that people seem to have no last names in the Bible? The very marker that most distinguishes one person from another in our modern world hardly existed in biblical antiquity. Rather, people were identified by their geographical point of origin (Saul of Tarsus, Jesus of Nazareth, Mary of Migdal ["Magdalene"]), by who their father was (Simon bar Jonah, John son of Zebedee), or occasionally by their religious affiliation or role (Simon the Pharisee, Simon the Zealot).

Even in regard to the issue of salvation, which we tend to see as a very individual matter, it is interesting to listen to how Paul talks about it. He says, for example, in 1 Cor. 12 that it is a matter of the Holy Spirit baptizing a person "into the one body." You don't merely become a new person. You are joined spiritually to a new group. Or in Phil. 2:12–13 he literally says "work out ya'll's salvation with fear and trembling, for it is God who works in the midst of ya'll [you plural] to will and to do."

I remember vividly the day it was brought home to me that the "you" here was plural in the Greek. Salvation suddenly went from being an individual project to being a group exercise, and indeed, salvation was something that God was working in and into the group, its collective identity, especially as it met together as an assembly (*ekklēsia*). How does this affect the rhetoric of the NT? It was much easier to appeal to the notion of group loyalty, group identity, the need for concord and unity within the group because the cultural scripts had already undergirded such a value.

Another factor which certainly affected the rhetoric was the fact that ancient cultures had totally different economic systems from ours and, on top of that, were not democracies. There was no free market economy in antiquity. People "got ahead" in life on the basis of patronage and clientage. It was a reciprocity culture: you scratch my back, and I will scratch yours. This presented enormous problems for Paul in Corinth because when he decided to work with his hands, having refused patronage, this angered some of the more elite Christians in Corinth and led to trouble. Even more difficult was serving up the rhetoric of grace in a culture where it was believed that there was no "free lunch," that you did not get "something for nothing." Rather, it was all a matter of exchange. The idea that a human being, much less a deity, would do an act of undeserved favor or give an unmerited benefit to someone, without either demanding or asking anything in return, made little sense in a reciprocity culture. Yet this is how Paul depicted the nature of salvation and the God of grace. It surely must have been a hard sell in many quarters, requiring considerable rhetoric to persuade. All other deities were "payback" gods in antiquity. Why should the biblical God or Jesus be any different?

Finally, all ancient cultures were honor and shame cultures. At the top of the value hierarchy in an ancient culture was not the dyadic pair of truth and falsity or life and death (which certainly seems to be the top of the American value hierarchy, hence our cliché "it's not a matter of life and death") but rather honor and shame. The chief end in life was to obtain honor and avoid shame. If one needed to lie to achieve that end, so be it. If some needed to die to achieve that end, so be it. Establishing honor and avoiding shame was more important than truth, more important than life or death. How was one to change the cultural script so that truth was seen as the top value in the value hierarchy? This would take powerful rhetoric indeed. This did not mean that honor and shame or life and death did not continue to be very important to early Christians (cf., e.g., Paul's remarks in Phil. 1:20 about avoiding shame), but they were not as important as telling the truth about Jesus.

The rhetoric of the NT calls for a transvaluation of extant cultural values in various ways.[1] A good rhetorician knew that he had to start with a group (or a

---

1 For a brief helpful summary of the social world of the NT, see Bruce J. Malina, *The New Testament World: Insights from Cultural Anthropology*, 3rd ed. (Louisville, KY: Westminster/John Knox Press, 2001).

person) where they were culturally in order to lead them in a different direction. An appeal for group unity in Corinth was an easier sell in Paul's time than it is today, precisely because of the collectivist nature of ancient cultures. It also accented just how badly the Corinthians had been behaving, following the rivalry conventions of the day and applying them to church life. In short, rhetoric in the ancient cultures of the NT era worked differently compared to today, in various regards. The hermeneutical questions become difficult when one tries to transfer praxis from the early church to the church today, especially the church in the West, which unlike the Oriental church, does not have a collectivist and honor and shame foundation to build on.

Another of the major cultural building blocks of the ancient world was, of course, family. It was not just any sort of family but, rather, the patriarchal extended family that not only could include multiple generations, all under one roof, but also could involve slaves. Sometimes, interpreters of the Bible make the mistake of assuming that just because they find household codes in the NT, in Colossians 3–4 or Ephesians 5–6, there must have been a general endorsement of patriarchy and even slavery in the NT. Nothing could be further from the truth. De facto, this household structure already existed all over the ANE and the Greco–Roman world.

What we see in the Christian household codes is not an attempt to license or endorse something that had already existed for centuries but, rather, an attempt to limit the damage such a fallen system could do. What we see in these texts is the attempt to reform the household in light of Christian principles, injecting the gospel into preexisting fallen situations. When we hear Paul saying things like "the husband's body belongs only to his wife" (1 Cor. 7:4) or "submit to one another out of reverence for Christ" (Eph. 5:21), referring to mutual submission of all Christians to all other Christians including both men to women and vice versa, or we read the poignant discourse to Philemon, we know that Paul is not simply baptizing the existing social structures and calling them good—by no means.

Paul is trying to reform the existing conventions from within the context of the Christian household structure. This is all the more striking because almost all ancient marriages were arranged (there was no ancient equivalent to www.christianmingle .com) and involved property transactions. And yet still Paul is telling husbands to love their wives as Christ loves the church and gives himself up for it. What is most striking about the household codes is the number of exhortations given to the head of the household, who is at once husband, father, and master. Three sets of exhortations are given to him in a way that we never find in pagan household codes, limiting his power, directing his influence, insisting that he model his behavior on Christian principles, warning that he too has a master and he must treat those household servants as he would want them to treat him—as a person, as a person of sacred worth, as a person deserving respect and honor, and not merely as property. We do not find these sorts of exhortations to the head of the household in pagan household codes, for instance, in the advice Plutarch gives on the matter.

The final piece of the social puzzle worth mentioning is the concept of limited good. By this I mean that ancient persons had not bought the myth some moderns have that there is an infinity of resources in this world, plenty enough to go around and provide for everyone. In a world of limited good, if one person has a needed piece of valuable property, then the only way the other person can get it is by bargaining for it or stealing it or, if a relative, inheriting it (see the parable of the vineyard in Mark 12). There was only a limited amount of land in the Holy Land, only a limited amount of arable land that produced crops, and so only a limited amount of grain, a limited amount of bread, a limited amount of work for day laborers.

The ancient world was far more like, say, bread lines in Ethiopia during a drought, where the bread runs out too soon, than like an American grocery store, where you see signs saying "eat all you want, there is always more." There was not always more in the world of the Bible. This is one reason Jesus urged praying for "daily bread" and praying for it today. The implication was that his followers needed to keep looking for it, asking God for help to find it. Poverty and starvation were rampant in the ancient world, and obesity was only a problem of the extremely rich, who could afford food at any price, could afford to overeat.

WHAT JUST HAPPENED?

As you can see from this chapter, the cultures of the Bible were very different from ours in many ways, so we must take these contextual factors into account as we read the NT. A reading informed by knowing the basic narrative of the Bible, understanding its types of literature, and grasping the rhetorical and social nature of ancient societies gives us a foundation on which to stand and look deeply into the biblical text with insight. In this chapter we have focused on the social realities, remembering again that the words of the Bible only have meaning in particular contexts, so we must learn the contexts as well as the texts. Understanding comes when we learn both text and context and are able to see how meaning is formed in certain contexts.

I love taking my students to the lands of the Bible and watching them develop a slight case of cultural vertigo. It makes them realize how differently other people live and how their values do not always match up with our own. On one particular trip, we were in Luxor in Egypt at the temple of Thebes. To the left was a Japanese group taking lots of pictures. To the right was a German group listening intently to their guide. Up above, just outside the temple, the minaret started up the call to prayer in Arabic. My students had been eating Egyptian food, sweating in the Egyptian heat, absorbing Egyptian culture for days; and they were beginning to long for the things of home.

Our local guide could see that faraway look in their eyes and said, "Do not worry, my friends. Once we are done here I will take you to the American cultural embassy." Someone groaned and muttered "not another museum." With this the guide turned around facing out from the temple and pointed across the street—to a McDonald's restaurant. My students cheered. All of us are victims of a certain kind of parochialism, a narrow vision of life, a sort of cultural captivity. Cross-cultural experiences broaden our horizons. But studying the Bible is a cross-cultural experience you can do at home, if you will study both the text and its contexts diligently.

FOR FURTHER READING

Bruce J. Malina's *The New Testament World: Insights from Cultural Anthropology,* 3rd ed. (Louisville, KY: Westminster/John Knox Press, 2001), has become a standard textbook for explaining the social character of the world in which the earliest Christians lived. The truth is, however, that much of what he says in that book applies as well to OT culture. The OT cultures were even more collectivist, even more patriarchal, even more nondemocratic, and even more monolithic, with even more disparity between the tiny minority of the rich and everyone else, than in NT times. For a helpful study about ANE and OT culture, see John H. Walton, *Ancient Near Eastern Thought and the Old Testament: Introducing the Conceptual World of the Hebrew Bible* (Grand Rapids, MI: Baker Academic, 2006).

8

The THEOLOGICAL STRUCTURES of the GOSPELS

*Every painting must have a design structure, a foundation of
lines and shapes, on which to build the values, color, and detail.*
—CARLTON PLUMMER

WHERE ARE WE GOING?

*In this chapter we will examine the theological structuring of the gospel narratives.
While sharing a general chronological outline (events before, during, and after Jesus's
ministry), what really shapes the microarrangement of passages are theological and
ethical interests and concerns.*

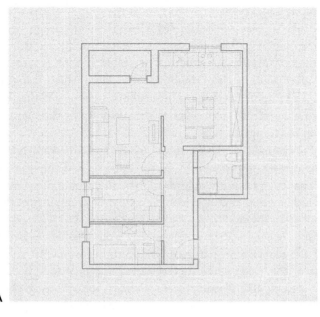

A

B

Figure 8.1 a&b If one can see the structure of something, its purpose and design become more evident. (Shutterstock/Redsapphire; Shutterstock/Viktoriya)

When you look at a blueprint what you see is the design of the skeletal structure for some building. You see the outline of where the walls are to be, the corridors, the doors, and so on. What you do not really see normally are the contents of the rooms themselves. Studying the structure of a biblical book is rather like studying a blueprint. It gives you a sense of the physical space in which things can be placed and arranged. The important thing to note about structure is that it is part of the context and, to a certain degree, dictates the meaning of the content by the very way the content is arranged.

Suppose, for example, we had a gospel which had an arrangement where John the Baptist was thrown into prison by Herod Antipas and the very next story said "and next John baptized Jesus in the Jordan." Not only would this sequence not make sense but it would be impossible and would destroy the credibility of the account as a whole, not to mention the credibility of the gospel writer. But if the sequence were the other way around, it would be both historically plausible and believable and would make sense of the sequence of passages. The meaning would be coherent, and the overall purpose of the writer would not be called into question. The point is simply this: structure affects, and in some cases dictates, the meaning of a sequence of episodes in a story. It thus will pay dividends to consider the issue of structures in the gospels, just as it does in the rhetorical letter discourses of Paul and others in the NT.

In my discussion of ancient biographies, I pointed out that while chronology in broad strokes was of some interest to biographers (and even more to ancient historians) once one drills down below the surface of the general structure of Jesus's life—baptism, ministry, Passion narrative about his last week, last supper, last breath, and then resurrection—what actually structures the telling of the ministry of Jesus are theological concerns more than chronological concerns.

MARK MY WORDS

This can be seen in two different ways in the earliest gospel, Mark. Firstly, there is the way the Christology of the book affects the structure. Here's the outline:

Mark 1:1–8:26 Questions raised about Jesus (who he was, why he behaved as he and his disciples did). Here are some of the questions:

Mark 1:27 "What is this?"—crowds

Mark 2:7 "Who can forgive sins but God?"—scribes

Mark 2:16 "Why does he eat with sinners?"—scribes

Mark 2:24 "Why are they doing what is not lawful?"—Pharisees

Mark 4:41 "Who then is this that even wind and water obey him?"—disciples

Mark 6:2 "Where did this man get this Wisdom?"—hometown folks

Mark 7:5 "Why do your disciples not live by tradition?"—Pharisees

Then we have a dramatic turning point in the narrative at Mark 8:27–30. We have Peter's confession that Jesus is the Christ (i.e., the Jewish Messiah), the Son of the living God. The "who" question about Jesus has been finally answered, and the answer matches up with what Mark told us at 1:1: "this is the beginning of the Good News about Jesus the Christ." It is only after the "who" question is answered that we begin almost immediately to hear Jesus discuss his coming suffering, demise, and resurrection. Four times in three straight chapters Jesus tells his disciples that he must suffer many things, be killed, and on the third day rise (Mark 8:31, 9:31, 10:32–34, and 10:45).

What this indicates, from Mark's vantage point, is that until you know who Jesus is, you cannot know why he had to die and be raised again. Once the "who" question is answered, the subject of his mission (the fact that Jesus was a man born to die) could be broached and an explanation of the significance of his death given, in Mark 10:45: "the Son of Man did not come to be served, but to serve and to give his life as a ransom for the many."

Finally, once the "who" question is answered and the mission is stated, we have the Passion and Easter narratives in the remainder of this gospel, in Mark 11–16. This leaves us with the following theological outline.

The questions—Who and why?—1–8:27

The "who" question answered—8:27–30, Peter's confession of faith in Jesus as the Christ

What is the mission—A mission of suffering—8:31, 9:31, 10:32

Mission accomplished—The Passion narrative—11–16

But there is another important way to look at the structure of Mark's Gospel, and that is by listing and comparing its revelatory peaks or disclosure moments. Mark presents the story of Jesus from an apocalyptic point of view. The Greek word *apocalypsis*, from which our English word *apocalyptic* comes, refers to the revelation of divine secrets. The idea is that unless God reveals the truth about this or that, often in a vision or a dream, no one would know it. Even Jesus is depicted at his baptism as needing a revelation from God to confirm his identity and begin his ministry.

Figure 8.2 The river Jordan near Yardenit. It was somewhere near here that Jesus was baptized. (Shutterstock/Roman Sigaev)

Mark is telling us that what happened in the case of Jesus and his ministry is that God began to part the clouds of unknowing and reveal his character and will and plan in the person of his Son, Jesus. Ched Myers should be credited for first fully seeing this as a key to understanding the Gospel of Mark.[1] He noticed that there are periodic apocalyptic or revelatory moments in the Gospel of Mark where Jesus's true or full identity is made known. Myers points to the following three:

BAPTISM	TRANSFIGURATION	CRUCIFIXION
Heavens torn	Garments turn to white	Sanctuary curtain torn
Dove descends	Cloud descends	Darkness descends
Voice from heaven	Voice from the cloud	Jesus's great voice
"You are my beloved Son"	"This is my Beloved Son"	"Truly this man was God's Son"
John the Baptist as Elijah	Jesus appears with Elijah	"Is he calling Elijah?"

1 Ched Myers, *Binding the Strong Man: A Political Reading of Mark's Story of Jesus* (Maryknoll, NY: Orbis, 1988), 390–392.

To this list of three we could add the story of the women at the tomb on Easter and their encounter with the angels, perhaps the Caesarea Philippi episode in Mark 8, as well where Peter confesses who Jesus is. The important point is that the whole story of Mark, from the beginning of the ministry to the end of Jesus's life, is punctuated by a few revelatory moments; and in between there is silence, silencing of the witnesses, and misunderstanding. Put another way, the commands to silence at particular junctures are balanced with commands to publication or proclamation after one gains understanding. The silence commands reveal that Jesus wants to let people know who he is on his own timetable and on his own terms. He does not wish to be pigeonholed into a bunch of preconceived messianic categories.

Even a few minutes' reflection on these sorts of structures and parallels shows that Mark, the earliest gospel writer, had some overriding and undergirding Christological and eschatological themes he wanted to stress; and he did so by the way he assembled the various stories of the ministry of Jesus and, to a lesser degree, the accounts of the last week of Jesus's life. Theology more than chronology is the engine driving the train.

A SCRIBE ASCRIBES WISDOM TO JESUS

Probably the second gospel to be written is Matthew. Matthew was a literate man, a tax collector; and whoever assembled the final form of the gospel with his name had scribal skills and an agenda to portray Jesus as Emmanuel, God's Wisdom come in the flesh. It thus becomes paramount to present as much of Jesus's verbal wisdom as he can, to show that he is one greater than Moses, Solomon, or, for that matter, any holy man or sage who came before him. To that end he presents us with five or six discourses by Jesus on key wisdom themes, interspersed with accounts of Jesus's deeds. Here is the basic theological structure of Matthew:

1. Narrative—Matthew 1:1–2:23 (Birth stories)

2. Narrative—Matthew 3:1–4:24 (Galilean ministry begins)

3. Teaching—Matthew 5:1–7:29 (Sermon on the Mount)

4. Narrative—Matthew 8:1–9:34 (On Christian discipleship)

5. Teaching—Matthew 9:35–10:42 (Teaching on discipleship)

Figure 8.3 Ancient Egyptian scribes copying documents on papyri. Notice that they are women. In early Christianity (second–fourth centuries) higher-status, literate women with a "fair hand" were sometimes used to copy the gospels, especially perhaps Matthew, which was the most popular gospel. (Werner Forman/Getty Images)

6. Narrative—Matthew 11:1–12:50 (On the Kingdom)

7. Teaching—Matthew 13:1–52 (Teaching on Kingdom parables)

8. Narrative—Matthew 13:53–17:27 (On community order, discipline, worship)

9. Teaching—Matthew 18:1–35 (Teaching on the same subjects)

10. Narrative—Matthew 19:1–22:46 (Controversies in Jerusalem)

11. Teaching—Matthew 23 (Judgment on Pharisees and scribes)

12. Teaching—Matthew 24–25 (Apocalyptic discourse)

13. Narrative—Matthew 26–28 (Passion and resurrection narratives)

It is safe to say that Jesus's daily life during the ministry didn't involve his being a talking head one week, a silent man of deeds the next, then a talking head for another week, then a man of deeds again, and so on. In other words, Matthew's structure reflects theological agendas more than chronological ones. This is not to say there isn't logic to the presentation. The logic, however, has to do with collecting sayings of Jesus on various different themes and key ideas (e.g., discipleship) and grouping them together topically. Obviously, Jesus did not tell all his parables or offer all his memorable discipleship aphorisms at one juncture in his ministry. The structure reflects the larger purposes of the Evangelist, which has to do with presenting Jesus as the sage and Wisdom Incarnate of God that eclipses all previous wisdom, even that found in the Torah. Interestingly, in Jesus's famous saying about "take my yoke upon you" (Matt. 11:29) this is precisely how early Jews talked about becoming serious in observing the Torah, the Mosaic law—only now it is Jesus as Wisdom come in the flesh and Jesus's teaching that is the yoke, not Torah.

THE GOSPEL OF THE WORD

Perhaps the most obviously theological of the gospels when it comes to both structure and content is the Fourth Gospel, which is our other biography of Jesus in the NT. Needless to say, the beloved disciple does his own thing when it comes to his gospel in so many ways. One way to portray the structure of this gospel is the following:

PROLOGUE—John 1:1–18

BOOK OF SIGNS—1:19–12:50

1. Water to wine at Cana—2:1–12

2. Curing the official's son at Cana—4:46–54

3. Curing the paralytic at Bethesda—5:1–15

4. Loaves and fish multiplied in Galilee—6:1–15

5. Walking upon the sea in Galilee—6:16–21

6. Curing the blind man in Jerusalem—9:1–41

7. Raising Lazarus from the dead—11:1–53

BOOK OF GLORY—13:1–20:31

EPILOGUE—John 21[2]

Notice that the Fourth Gospel really has no parables, nor does it have any exorcisms; and apart from points 4 and 5 in this list, it has no miracles in common with the Synoptic Gospels but rather tells its own unique miracle stories, mostly performed in Judea. In this gospel, miracles are called "signs." A sign, of course, is something that points to another reality outside of itself. In the Fourth Gospel the miracles are pointers to the coming of the King, the Word, Jesus. In fact in the Fourth Gospel we have a crescendo of the miraculous, a sort of "can you top this," with the raising of Lazarus being the last and climactic of the sequence, not least because it best foreshadows what would happen to Jesus at the end of the Passion.

Nothing happens in the Gospel of John by accident, and none of the arrangement of the material is careless. There are seven sign narratives, seven "I am" sayings, and seven discourses tagged to the "I am" sayings. If we remember that seven is the symbolic number in early Judaism for perfection, then this gospel is proclaiming over and over again that the Perfect One, the Savior of the World, has finally come, eclipsing all that has gone before. A further part of that motif is that in the early portions of this gospel we are told that Jesus sums up and fulfills all the earlier institutions of Judaism—he is the Passover lamb; he is the temple (the place where God dwells on earth); he is the manna which came down from heaven ("I am the bread of life"); he is the Day of Atonement, atoning for the sins of one and all; he is the one who replaces Jewish purification water with the new wine of the gospel; and so on. This in part explains why, in the Gospel of John, Jesus's cleansing of the Temple happens early in the story, rather than much later in the Passion narrative, which is where we find it in the other three

---

2 This outline I owe to Raymond Brown, *The Gospel According to John (i–xii)*, vol. 1 (New York: Doubleday, 1966), cxl–cxli.

gospels (cf. John 2:13–22 to Mark 11:15–19). All four gospels agree—Jesus cleansed the Temple in Jerusalem only once. But the placement of the story in John's Gospel is theological, not chronological. Another key structuring device is the "I Am" sayings, which are unique to this gospel. Let us first list the "I am" sayings:

1. "I am the bread of life" (6:35, cf. vv. 41, 48, 51)

2. "I am the light of the world" (8:12, cf. vv. 18, 23)

3. "I am the gate of the sheep" (10:7, 9)

4. "I am the good shepherd" (10:11, 14)

5. "I am the resurrection and the life" (11:25)

6. "I am the way, the truth, and the life" (14:6)

7. "I am the true vine" (15:1, 5)

These sayings, and the discourses that go with them, contribute to the uniqueness of this gospel. You will notice that we find the first five in the book of signs portion of this gospel and the last two in the book of glory portion. So they help link the two major parts of this gospel together. And none of them appears before the sixth chapter of this gospel.

The next thing to notice about this material is that almost every one of those predicates—light, life, bread, truth—had already been used of personified Wisdom in earlier Jewish Wisdom literature (in Prov. 3, 8, and 9; see especially Prov. 8:35–36, 9:5; Wisdom of Solomon 7:25–26, 8:8, 11:4; Sirach and *1 Enoch* 42). The point here is that Jesus in person is the embodiment of these things that previously were only a personification or, at best, were incarnated in Torah, the OT.

The fifth and sixth of these sayings are of the nature of summary statements. The essence is that Jesus is the true life and light revealed to humanity. He is both the revealer of everlasting life and the way to obtain it.

Besides these sorts of "I Am" sayings, there are other ones as well where the phrase "I Am" does not have a predicate. So, when Jesus walks on the water he tells the disciples that they shouldn't be afraid, "It is I" (6:20). More important is John 8:58, "before Abraham was, I am," a saying that confirms what John 1 told us—the Son was present in heaven before he took on flesh and dwelt among us. All of these "I Am" sayings are meant to associate the Son with the Father so that we are not surprised when we also hear "I and the Father are One" (John 10.30).

When we raise the question why none of this material is in the first three gospels, there is a reasonable answer we can now give. This is the sort of teaching Jesus did in Judea, but he took a different approach. By contrast, he offered many parables in Galilee. Indeed, as John 14–17 suggests, much of this Judean teaching was in-house teaching for the disciples as well. What is clear is that the beloved disciple has recast the teaching of Jesus in a Wisdom idiom to make clear various things about Jesus being God come in person to his people as light and life and healing.

If you are beginning to get the impression that the inspired gospel writers had freedom to arrange their material according to their special purposes, you would be correct. They were skillful theological arrangers of the sacred sayings and deeds of Jesus. What about Luke?

Luke, it will be remembered, is the historian among the four gospel writers, and he presents his gospel in a historian's way, not according to the conventions of ancient biographies. He is certainly more interested than the other Evangelists in chronology and in presenting a logical and chronological account of Jesus's ministry and then of the ministry of the earliest Christians—Peter, Paul, James, and others. Not surprisingly, in light of the fact that Luke says he used sources (Luke 1:1–4), Luke arranges his presentation by alternating between his three basic sources. Here is the way it looks in regard to his use of Mark and other sources:

SOURCE	LOCATION IN LUKE	MARKAN PORTION USED
Mark	Luke 4:31–6:11	(=Mark 1:21–3.6)
Non-Mark	Luke 6:12–8:3	(except 6:17–19=Mark 3:7–11a)
Mark	Luke 8:4–9:50	(=Mark 4:1–25, 3:31–35, 4:35–6:44, 8:27–9:40)
Non-Mark	Lukan travel narrative	(Luke 9:51–18:11)
Mark	Luke 18:15–43	(=Mark 10:13–52)
Non-Mark	Luke 19:1–28	
Mark	Luke 19:29–22:13	(=Mark 11:1–14:16)

Whereas Matthew uses some 95% of Mark's Gospel in his own, Luke uses about 55% and, thus, has room for a lot of unique material not found in the other gospels.

There is an overall structure to Luke–Acts, which may be stated as follows. Using a broadly chronological framework, Luke recounts the spread of the Good News up and down the social scale from the least to the greatest in Israelite society; and in the course of doing that, he maintains a "from Galilee through Samaria to Jerusalem" orientation in his gospel. Jesus must in the end go up to Jerusalem, and in the end the disciples must wait in Jerusalem until they receive power from on high. This stands in contrast to the "from Jerusalem to Rome" (and to other places in the Diaspora) orientation of the book of Acts.

Luke, in short, is interested in the universal spread of the Good News not only up and down the social scale but also geographically outward to the world. This theme of the universal scope of this gospel is announced in Luke 2:30–32: "for my eyes have seen your salvation, which you have prepared in the presence of all peoples, a light for revelation to the Gentiles and for glory to your people Israel." The spread of this Good News even to the least, last, and lost is made clear in the paradigmatic speech in Luke 4:18–21, where Jesus quotes Isaiah 61.

Luke's Gospel focuses more on the vertical (up and down the social scale) universalization of the gospel, while Acts focuses more on its horizontal (to all peoples throughout the empire) universalization. This means that one must take the material in Acts 2:1–21 as setting the agenda in Acts in the same way that Luke 4:18–21 does in the gospel. In Acts 2 various Jews from many nations hear the Good News in their own tongue, which suggests that this news is for peoples of all tongues and nations but for the Jews first. What lies behind this agenda is that Luke believes that Jesus is the *one* Savior for *all* peoples, and this is why he must be proclaimed to all peoples. There is stress upon both continuity of the Jesus movement with Israel and her Scriptures in some ways and discontinuity with Israel in others throughout the two volumes. It is hard to doubt that what determines the discontinuity is the universalistic agenda—those facets of Judaism that make difficult or impossible the welcoming of other ethnic groups into the people of God purely on the basis of faith, more particularly faith in the Jewish Messiah Jesus, must be critiqued or seen as obsolescent.

Even the geographical orientation of the Gospel of Luke is in part caused by the concern about salvation. Jesus must go up to Jerusalem, for it is the center from which Jews looked for salvation (Luke 9:51; 13:22, 33, 35; 17:11; 18:31; 19:11, 28). Jesus must accomplish or finish his earthly work there so that salvation and its message may go forth from Jerusalem to the world, as the Hebrew Scriptures had always suggested. The belief that salvation comes from the Jews engenders the "to Jerusalem" orientation of Luke's Gospel, which in turn explains why Luke relates the story of Jesus going up to the Temple as a boy (Luke 2:22ff.), why the prophecies of Simeon and Anna about Jesus as the world's Savior come from the Temple (2:25–38), why Luke wishes to show that Jesus is in the line of the OT prophets (13:33), and finally why Jesus's life and teaching are presented as a fulfillment of the prophecies of the OT (4:18–21; 16:31; 18:31; 24:27, 45). The disciples must remain in Jerusalem until they receive power from on high, for Jerusalem is not only the place from which salvation comes but also the place from which empowerment to preach it comes (Luke 24:47, 53; Acts 1:4). Thus, Luke 24:47, rounding out the gospel, foreshadows the fact that Acts will deal with the horizontal spread of the gospel "beginning from Jerusalem" to all the nations.

Several dimensions of Luke's theologizing call for comment. We especially see Luke's hand in the way he structures his so-called travel narrative. The middle of Luke's Gospel has been called the "Lukan travel narrative" (Jesus's journeying to Jerusalem between 9:51 and 18:14, in which there is next to no Markan material, only Q [the sayings source] and special L [unique to Luke] material alternating.[3] Luke 9:51 announces that Jesus has set his face like a flint to go up to Jerusalem, recognizing that the time was soon for him to go to heaven).

When we finally get to the triumphal entry in Luke 19, we feel like we have been on pilgrimage for a very long time. But then one also gets that feeling with Paul as he seeks to journey to Rome via Jerusalem, and this journey has some amazing twists and turns as well (see Acts 21–28). Many scholars have rightly noted that there is a method to Luke's way of presenting materials, and it involves both volumes, with the second volume extending some of the structural elements that were vertical in the gospels (up and down the social scale and in Judea, Galilee, Samaria) in a horizontal direction as the Word spreads from Jerusalem to Rome. This suggests that the book of Acts was not an afterthought but a continuation which Luke had in mind from the outset, hence all the parallel patterning. I would call this, to some extent, a theological and ethical structuring of materials. An example or two will have to suffice.

There are two paradigmatic sermons that set up the narratives that follow them, Jesus's sermon in Luke 4 and Peter's in Acts 2. Luke has carefully structured this material such that his narrative which follows this sermon will demonstrate how the Scripture he cites here (Isa. 61:1–2) is fulfilled. We can see this from the following:

---

3 Some of what follows here can be found in fuller form in my *The Indelible Image: The Theological and Ethical Thought World of the New Testament*, vol. 1, *The Individual Witnesses* (Downers Grove, IL: InterVarsity Press, 2008).

LUKE 4:18–19	LUKE 4:38–44	LUKE 8:1–3
v. 18 Preach Good News		v. 1 Preach and proclaim Good News
Recovery of sight to blind	v. 38 Jesus heals Simon's Mother-in-law and illnesses in women	v. 2 Healing evil spirits
	v. 40 Jesus heals sick	
Set at liberty the oppressed	demons cast out	examples of exorcism of Mary
v. 19 Proclaim acceptable year	v. 43 Preach Good News of the Lord to other cities	cf. 8:4–15

We can find something similar in Acts 2. Thus, we have an extended citation of the prophecy in Joel about the outpouring of the Spirit on a variety of persons, men and women, manservants and maidservants. It is no accident then that thereafter we have narratives that demonstrate the Spirit changing the lives of men and women and inspiring them to speak God's word in various ways and settings. For example, not only does Peter preach various sermons, as do Philip and Paul, but there is also the fact that we have various unexpected men and women telling the truth and telling the Good News, ranging from the Ethiopian eunuch (Acts 8) to Cornelius the centurion (Acts 10) to Rhoda, the maidservant in the house of John Mark's mother (Acts 12), to Priscilla, with her husband teaching the mighty evangelist Apollos (Acts 18), and we could go on.

What is especially important to note is not just that Luke believes that Scriptures are being fulfilled and coming to pass in the ministry of Jesus and his followers (which is true) but that he sees this as evidence of God's sovereign and saving activity in human history in an ongoing way. He does not wish to tell a narrative that has closure because salvation history is still going on in Luke's own era, from his point of view. The story continues. This is why even Acts 28, the last chapter of the two-volume work, does not tie up all loose ends with a neat bow. Luke is striving for something quite specific in his two-volume work. He wants not merely to chronicle the saving work of God through Christ in human history of his period but also to provide for the Christian movement a sense of direction, identity, and legitimation.

WHAT JUST HAPPENED?

The gospels and Acts appear on the surface to be beguilingly simple in construction, but as we have seen in this chapter, that is not quite true. They are rather complex and intricate in their structure, and the important part about that is that if you can see the method and emphases and the flow of the narrative, you can understand far better what the Evangelists are trying to tell their audiences about theology, ethics, and history. The rules about positive or negative repeated patterns of narrative or positive or negative characterization come into play and help us see what a gospel writer is really intending as we will soon see.

Thus far we have been focusing on form and skimming along the horizontal surface of biblical documents, talking about their genre, their structure, and the like. But now it is time to do some vertical digging, to take some core samples from the OT and the NT and see what we can discover. First, however, we will briefly review the rules for in-depth interpretation of the Bible.

FOR FURTHER READING

For those wanting to look more closely at the structure and structuring of the gospels, see my *Invitation to the New Testament: First Things* (New York: Oxford University Press, 2012) and Mark Allan Powell, *Introducing the New Testament: A Historical, Literary, and Theological Survey* (Grand Rapids, MI: Baker Academic, 2009).

The Biblical World in Pictures

Plate 1 An image of the earliest map of the Holy Land and its surroundings,
found in a fifth-century church in Medaba, Jordan.
© Mark R. Fairchild, PhD

Plate 2 The famous Cave 4 at Qumran, where the equally famous
full scroll of Isaiah was found.
© Mark R. Fairchild, PhD

Plate 3 The so-called tomb of Absalom is typical of such monumental tombs, and appears to have been the model for the tomb of Herod the Great.
© Mark R. Fairchild, PhD

Plate 4 A wealthy person's home in Ephesus, next to the famous Celsus library.
© Mark R. Fairchild, PhD

Plate 5 The Parthenon at night. Paul had his famous encounter with
the religious authorities nearby.
© Mark R. Fairchild, PhD

Plate 6 A rolling stone tomb in Jerusalem. Jesus was buried in such a tomb.
© Mark R. Fairchild, PhD

Plate 7 The earliest Christian missionaries such as Peter and Paul used the Roman roads to get more quickly from place to place spreading their message.
© Mark R. Fairchild, PhD

Plate 8 An inscription about the Ephesian silversmiths mentioned in Acts 20.
© Mark R. Fairchild, PhD

Plate 9 The so-called Temple Treasury at Petra. Probably the locale of
Paul's Arabian stay not long after his conversion.
© Mark R. Fairchild, PhD

Plate 10 The mosaic of Christ in glory in the Chora Church in Istanbul.
© Mark R. Fairchild, PhD

PART **II**

UNEARTHING the TREASURE

The BASIC RULES of the ROAD— HERMENEUTICS

Apply the whole of yourself to the text. Apply the whole of the text to yourself.
—JOHANNES BENGEL

If God has condescended to address men in the full particularity of their peculiar historical and cultured environments, then we have got to immerse ourselves fully and sympathetically in those environments, with their customs and values, ways of thinking and patterns of imagery, before we can understand either his demand or their response.
—D. E. NINEHAM[1]

[T]he main reason for studying texts, particularly old ones, is to expand the mind by introducing it to the immense possibilities in human actions and thoughts—to see and feel what other men have seen and felt, to know what they have known. Furthermore, none of these expansive benefits comes to the man who simply discovers his own meanings in someone else's text and who, instead of encountering another person, merely encounters himself.
—E. D. HIRSCH[2]

WHERE ARE WE GOING?

Before we turn to the detailed interpretation of biblical texts, it will be useful to review some of the basic rules for doing such in-depth study of the Bible. In this chapter we will review seven common hermeneutical principles often used to guide the interpretation of the Bible. We will also discuss how to move from determining the meaning of the text to applying the text and consider how one determines what is normative in a narrative text.

Hermeneutics is by definition the art of interpreting a text, in this case the text of the Bible. Historically, there have been a whole series of guidelines (rules of the road more than laws really) that have aided the interpreter of the Bible, and here is the right place and time to discuss them. So let's start by reminding ourselves of one rule that we have already had occasion to mention.

FIRST PRINCIPLE: CONTEXT, CONTEXT, CONTEXT

Any biblical book, passage, or verse needs to be interpreted in light of its various *original* contexts—narrative, literary, historical, rhetorical, social, and linguistic. In our discussion of translations in the epilogue, we will stress the linguistic context; and in the early chapters of this book, we dealt with the rest of this list of contexts in one way or another. Contextual interpretation is the foundation of all else and it is what prevents us from misusing the text or misunderstanding the text. Here it is perhaps useful to remind ourselves that even mere words do not have a meaning outside a particular context.

---

1 D. E. Nineham, *The Church's Use of the Bible Past and Present* (London: SPCK, 1963), 161.
2 E. D. Hirsch, Jr., *Validity in Interpretation* (New Haven, CT: Yale University Press, 1967), 25–26.

Take, for example, the English word *row*—this can refer to a line of seats, a verbal command to paddle water, an argument or a fight, a line of braided hair (e.g., a cornrow), and more. It can be a noun or a verb, but we will only recognize its meaning when we see it used in a sentence. It is not true that "in the beginning was the dictionary." Dictionaries do not define the meaning of words; they are the results of detailed study of word usage to determine the spectrum of meaning a word can have in various contexts.

SECOND PRINCIPLE: *SOLA SCRIPTURA*[3]

It was one of the battle cries of the Reformation to insist on *sola Scriptura*. By this Latin phrase was meant that the final authority over the church was "the Bible alone." What was not said in this slogan, but was meant, was the Bible alone, rightly interpreted. Protestants have continued to affirm this principle in one form or another ever since the Reformation. One of the things this principle implied, of course, was that no nonbiblical tradition itself was immune to revision or critique on the basis of the Bible, no matter how long-standing the tradition.

With the Bible seen as the court of last resort and the litmus test of truth about matters that the Word of God spoke to, this in itself set up a kind of suspicion about pneumatic claims. What I mean by this is that if someone said, "The Spirit told me . . ." and what was said was clearly at variance with what the Bible said on the selfsame subject, then this fresh "revelation" must be critiqued by the canonical one. Sometimes this approach went so far as to suggest that the Holy Spirit wasn't speaking independently of God's Word anymore but was simply leading believers into the truth that was in that Word. Sometimes as well this was taken to mean that while the Spirit could lead persons to say things that went beyond the clear teachings of the Bible, the Spirit that inspired the Scripture itself would never lead a person to claim something that contradicted or went against the text of the Bible. This principle was especially to be put to the test whenever a more pneumatic, charismatic, or experientially oriented revival movement arose within post-Reformation church history.

This kind of tension between the Word and what is thought to be the voice of the Spirit still arises today when some churches or their representatives claim, for example, that God's Spirit has shown that same-sex sexual relationships are not, or

---

3 Some of what follows here can be found in another, more detailed form in my *The Living Word of God: Rethinking the Theology of the Bible* (Waco, TX: Baylor University Press, 2007), 152–170.

are no longer, sinful. Sometimes this hermeneutical move involves arguing that the Bible doesn't say what it appears to have said, but more often, since this move cannot explain away all the biblical data on this or that matter, the claim is made that new revelation has superseded the old, just as the NT eclipsed various things in the OT.

The living voice of prophecy is appealed to, to justify breaking with traditional exegesis of various biblical passages and ultimately with some parts of the Bible itself. Not surprisingly, Evangelicals who have been well schooled in rule two, *sola Scriptura*, have largely taken a negative or dim view of these sorts of pneumatic claims as they seem to compromise the authority of the Bible as God's definitive revelation of his will and truth. If rule two really is *sola Scriptura*, then Evangelicals are right to take a dim view of pneumatic claims that go against the explicit teaching of the Bible.

THIRD PRINCIPLE: SCRIPTURE IS ITS OWN BEST INTERPRETER

In this day and age, one hears a great deal about canonical criticism and canonical theology that is indeed a manifestation of the old principle that the first and best interpreter of the Bible is the Bible itself. One was to compare and contrast various texts within the Bible to gain an understanding of its meaning. What was assumed was that the text was clear, and the reader was especially encouraged to interpret the more difficult or puzzling passages on the basis of the clearer ones. The assumption behind all of this is that there was ultimately the single coherent mind of God behind all the Bible and, therefore, that there is a consistent and coherent revelation within the Bible.

Part of the problem with this principle is that it sometimes leads to a rather flat view of the whole Bible such that Levitical laws, for example, were thought to be able to fully inform the proper interpretation of NT institutions, which led to such problematic notions as Sunday being the Sabbath, the Lord's supper being seen as like the Levitical sacrifices, church buildings being seen as temples, and a clerical class of Christians being seen as priests. The problem is that while one can find all of these institutions in the OT, one is hard-pressed to find any of them imposed on Christians in the NT. Sometimes this way of interpreting the NT so heavily in light of the OT has led to the elimination of the whole notion that much new is even going on in the NT. The NT is seen rather as just the fulfillment or completion or even the renewal and perfect expression of the old. This way of looking at things has especially characterized certain forms of Reformed covenantal theology and still does today.

At risk in this sort of approach to the Bible was losing any sense not only of the newness of the new covenant but of progressive revelation in the Bible. Statements, for example, by Jesus in Mark 10 about Mosaic legislation being given originally because of the hardness of human hearts (but that now that the Dominion is breaking in, new rules apply and the original creation intent of God before Moses is being reinstated) are either ignored or misinterpreted in the service of preserving one's covenantal theological approach.

This is chiefly a front-to-back approach, by which I mean you start from the front of the Bible and read to the back, and this in turn means that your hermeneutic is so heavily OT that by the time you get to the NT it can hardly be more than just a fulfillment or renewal of the OT. The problem with this approach is that it is not the approach of various NT authors, who begin with the Christ event and reread the OT in light of the Christ event.

A flat approach to the Bible sometimes involves the "one covenant but just in various administrations" view, and this was seen by some Protestants as putting the emphasis entirely too strongly on the OT being allowed to determine how the NT can and ought to be understood. Yet there was general agreement that texts like Hebrews, especially Hebrews 1:1–4, established with clarity that Christ and the revelation of God in Christ was to be seen as the *climax* of the revelation of God's truth and Word. And if one is thinking narratologically, then of course a story must be read in light of its climax; and this changes not only what comes thereafter but also how one views what came before the climax.

There is enormous debate about how much of the OT is still binding on Christians. One hermeneutical move suggested that all of the OT was still directly binding on Christians except for the portions that were said in the NT to be fulfilled or abrogated or superseded. The other major hermeneutical move, which caused far fewer difficulties in terms of Christian practice, was the suggestion that only those portions of the OT Law which are reaffirmed in the NT explicitly are binding on Christians. This meant, for example, that since nowhere in the NT are Christians said to be required to observe the Sabbath, indeed there are texts that warn against being trapped into such practices (see Col. 2:16), that this is no longer an obligation for Christians. For the most part, some form of this second hermeneutical suggestion about the relationship of Christians to obeying OT principles has been accepted and practiced.

FOURTH PRINCIPLE: THE ANALOGY OF FAITH

One of the more dominant principles of interpretation in Protestantism, even until today, is the idea that there is a central theme of Scripture, the great theme of God's divine saving activity or, even more specifically, justification by grace through faith. This theme is then viewed as a norm that is so powerful that it led to the suggestion that if there was a passage of Scripture that seemed at odds with it, then someone was obviously misunderstanding the import and message of that problematic passage. Martin Luther famously questioned whether James should be in the canon at all because in his mind it questioned the doctrine of justification by grace through faith. He even called that letter "a right strawy epistle."

The phrase *analogia fidei*, or "analogy of faith," comes from the rendering of Romans 12:3 into Latin; but this probably involves a rather clear misinterpretation of the meaning of that verse, which should be compared to Romans 12:6. The proper translation should likely be "according to the measure of faith." Prophets should prophesy, teachers should teach, leaders should lead according to the measure of their current faith and not beyond it.[4]

In other words, this passage has to do with a limitation, but it is not an attempt to provide a hermeneutical rule by which one can measure the interpretation of difficult passages or provide a central theme and norm to guide one in the interpretation of such difficult texts. To the contrary, it is about limiting other ministerial activities (scriptural interpretation is never mentioned here) according to the measure or quantity of one's faith, whether great or small. The Reformers naturally had a problem with this Pauline idea of degrees of faith since they saw all saved persons as having the same saving faith, but in fact both Jesus and Paul regularly talk about little or large, small or great faith; thus, it is no surprise that Paul would see this as something which should limit or guide the degree to which one exercises one's gift—one should do it in proportion to one's faith. Notice he does not say in proportion to one's abilities.

FIFTH PRINCIPLE: *SENSUS LITERALIS* VERSUS *SENSUS PLENIOR*

This Latin distinction has to do with the difference between a "literal sense" of the text and its "fuller sense" (which is what these two Latin phrases mean, respectively). By "fuller sense" is meant its deeper or even hidden meaning. This mode of

---

4 See Ben Witherington III and Darlene Hyatt, *Paul's Letter to the Romans: A Socio-Rhetorical Commentary* (Grand Rapids, MI: Eerdmans, 2004).

interpreting the text became common in the Middle Ages and led to the allegorizing of the text, especially, for example, the parables. Augustine's interpretation of the Good Samaritan parable is notorious. In it he claimed that the Good Samaritan was Jesus, that he was administering the sacraments to the man lying on the side of the road who was dead in sin, and that the church was the inn, with the innkeeper being the minister, the coins paid being penance money, and so on. All of this was justified on the basis of the principle of the "deeper sense" of the text, but of course, the problem with this was it was not a deeper meaning that either Jesus could have encoded into this parable or his original audience could have understood him to be discussing. There was no church with sacraments in that sense when Jesus taught this parable.

If we ask whether an author can say more than he or she realizes, the answer must be *of course*! In dealing with an inspired text one can argue that God was speaking at a deeper level than the human author fully realized at the time (e.g., in a prophetic text like Is. 53). Did the human author of Isaiah 53 realize he was talking about Jesus or even an individual messianic figure? Perhaps not. Elsewhere in Isaiah 40–55 "my servant" is said to be Israel. Some prophetic and poetic texts may then have a fuller sense. If some texts, perhaps particularly prophetic texts and the Psalms, were thought by the earliest Christians to have a fuller meaning, only to be discovered later, do we then look for fulfillment of the literal sense of those same texts, only for their deeper sense, or both? Or should we stick with the notion that a text may have a fuller significance later, not a fuller meaning? Much depends on one's view of the roles of the human and divine authors.

Sensus plenior, or "fuller sense," thinking argues that when the text was originally written God encoded a deeper sense to it, which is very different from giving the reader permission to "find" a meaning in the text. With fuller sense readings, unlike "meaning is in the eye of the beholder" readings, one can assume that there is a deeper meaning in the text, so one does not need to creatively read one into the text.[5]

This whole sort of approach to interpretation has quite naturally made Protestant interpreters nervous because there seem to be no limits to what one can claim is a

---

5 Reader-response criticism is a form of creative reading of the biblical text based on a theory of meaning which does indeed suggest that since all readers are active readers, we are bound to, and indeed need to, read things into the text. In short, meaning is largely in the eye of the beholder. Whatever else one says about this highly subjective theory of meaning, it does not accord with what the biblical authors thought about meaning. On these sorts of epistemological questions, see Kevin J. Vanhoozer, *Is There a Meaning in This Text?* (Grand Rapids, MI: Zondervan, 1998). As the blurb for the book on Amazon says, "Vanhoozer defends the concept of the author and the possibility of literary knowledge. . . . He argues that there is a meaning in the text, that it can be known with relative adequacy, and that readers have a responsibility to do so by cultivating 'interpretive virtues.'"

"hidden" or "deeper" meaning in the text. There seem to be no controls. And when an example like Augustine's allegorizing of the text is pointed out, this makes such exegetes all the more skeptical about the idea. It's better to stick to the notion that an author can say more than he realizes under inspiration, but it still had to be consistent with the surface meaning of the text and intelligible to its original audiences.

SIXTH PRINCIPLE: PREDICTION VERSUS FULFILLMENT

Prediction is when a biblical author prophesies (or promises) certain coming events. This may be distinguished from the concept of fulfillment. Christ is said in the NT to be the fulfillment of all sorts of ideas and institutions in the OT that were not predictive prophecy (e.g., the Temple or the sacrificial system). Fulfillment then is a much larger category than prediction. Note the use of the Psalms in the NT, which are songs, not prophecies, to speak of Christological matters (cf., e.g., Mark 1:11).

Isaiah 40–66, which is poetic prophecy, and the Psalms, which are not prophecies, are the two most used portions of Scripture in the NT. Only a few of the Psalms could be said to be royal or messianic in their original settings, looking forward to an ideal king, Psalm 2 being one of them. Nevertheless, many more of them are used in the NT to describe personal experiences (e.g., Jesus on the cross quoting the beginning of Ps. 22). Here, we are actually dealing with the principle of analogy, namely, that believers' experiences are parallel in various of the eras of salvation history. Thus, while the Psalmist's words were about himself, they certainly accurately described the experience of Jesus as well.

There is a kind of principle of analogy that is found in the Bible itself, the principle of **typology**. *Typology* involves the notion that there is an historical type and an ante-type, for example, Jesus and Melchizedek in Hebrews, and the ante-type foreshadows the type and indeed sets up an anticipation that there will be a greater and more fulfilling example of this sort of person later. The idea in this case has to do with God operating in a similar fashion in various eras of salvation history, preparing for the climax of revelation in its earlier stages by prefigurements. This whole notion presupposes the idea of progressive revelation and, as such, is an idea that not only the author of Hebrews but also Paul seems to operate with (cf. 1 Cor. 10, where the Exodus events are seen as analogous to some aspects of Corinthian experience). More could be said along these lines, but we need now to move on.

The typological use of the OT in Hebrews and elsewhere reminds us once more that the earliest Christians all thought that the OT speaks to Christians even in their new situation after the Christ-event. But how? I would suggest that we first must recognize that (1) Christians are not under the old covenant anymore in any of its administrations but that (2) a good bit of the old covenant is renewed in the new, and (3) even in texts which are not ethically binding on Christians, if we will but ask the right questions of the text, we can certainly find a Word of God to preach or teach from that text to a Christian audience.

Here are some of the questions I would suggest we ask of OT texts that are not binding on Christians: (1) What does the text tell us about God? (2) What does the text tell us about God's people? (3) What does the text tell us about the inter-action between God and his people? These questions can be asked of any text, and much can be garnered and learned from the answers we discover. But there is one more way, an experiential way, that a text of Scripture will come to life, namely, when *God uses it* to speak to us more directly in a crisis situation. Let me give a personal example.

My wife was in the hospital in Durham, England, in 1979, and we were expecting our first child. We were thousands of miles from home in the United States and from any close friends or family. Unfortunately, my wife's blood pressure had gotten out of control, and the doctors had placed her in the hospital some three weeks before our child was due. The blood pressure kept rising, and finally the doctor said that Ann would need to be induced. This upset her to no end as we had gone through all the Lamaze classes, and my wife is a biologist anyway. She did not want the baby drugged as it was coming into the world. I remember very well being at the hospital with her, and we had been reading through some of the doom and gloom chapters of Ezekiel, particularly Ezekiel 36. Suddenly in the midst of a passage of dire warnings there were these words of reassurance: "And I will multiply your kindred, and I will keep you safe, and I will bring you home."

Well, of course, those reassurances were meant for the exilic Jews in Babylon long before the twentieth century. But God used those words to reassure my wife and me as well, and I said to her, "Honey, I think the baby is on the way. We've gotten a word from on high." I went home that night and did not change out of my clothes but rather paced the floor. My neighbor, who had a car, knocked on my door at 4 something in the morning to collect me and was shocked to find me ready. He asked me how in the world I knew he was coming at that hour. I told him we had had a divine reminder to be ready. Sure enough, Christy Ann was on the way without Ann being induced and was born in the late morning of August 14, 1979.

Turns out, God knows how to use his ancient Word to speak to us in our very different situations, and he applies the text more effectively and directly than we could possibly manage to do. We, on the other hand, need some guidelines and rules for using the text.

SEVENTH PRINCIPLE: A QUADRILATERAL OF AUTHORITIES?

One of the pressing questions for Christians that arises from the rules already cited and from our personal experiences concerns the relationship of Scripture, reason, tradition, and experience. I would suggest that if we are talking about a subject on which the Bible directly teaches us something (matters theological, ethical, historical, or involving Christian praxis), then there is a principle that must be stated about the interrelationship of these four things. We can say that reason, tradition, and experience can all be seen as windows into the Scripture or avenues out of the Scripture by which we may express the truth of Scripture; but in no case and on no occasion should reason, tradition, or experience be seen as a higher authority than Scripture by which Scripture could be trumped on some issue that it directly addresses and about which it makes claims on God's people.

This further principle is really the only one involving these four things that does justice to the foundational principle of *sola Scriptura*. Suggesting that reason, tradition, or experience has equal authority with the Bible in one biblical matter or another, or even higher authority, is a recipe for trouble and for compromising some of the essential verities of the Word. This is not in any way to deny that reason is a good thing or experience is a good thing or tradition is a good thing, but they all must be "normed" by the Scriptures. One example must suffice.

A person can have a genuine experience, a genuine religious experience, without it being a good one. That something is genuine and real does not in itself tell us the ethical or spiritual quality of the experience or whether in the end it is good or bad for the person. Without the final objective norm of Scripture, it becomes difficult, if not impossible, to tell the difference between a heartwarming experience brought about by the work of the Spirit and some sort of emotive "spiritual" experience that is neither edifying for the person in question nor glorifying to God.

For example, not far from where I live is Shaker Village in Pleasant Hill, Kentucky. One of the founders of the sect, Mother Ann Lee, had experiences that led her to claim (and her disciples to claim about her) that she had all the perfections of God in her, in female form. This went far beyond what the Wesleys said about being perfected in love by God's holy presence such that God's love could cast out all fear in the believer, cleanse fully from inward sin, and leave just the living sense of God's loving presence. And it certainly went beyond what Paul claimed in Philippians about not having yet obtained a beatific state. Mother Ann Lee may have had real spiritual experiences, but when compared to what the Scriptures say about such experiences, she was probably rightly judged by most to have had experiences engendered by some spirit other than the Holy Spirit or at least she badly misinterpreted the meaning and significance of her experiences.

It is similar with traditions. There are many traditions in many churches, and many of them are good. But if they fail the litmus test of being consistent and coherent with, and a legitimate extension of, Scripture, then they should not be made requirements. For example, some low-church Protestant groups have long had a tradition of no sacraments at all, including no Christian baptism. But this is surely a direct violation of the command to baptize persons in the great commission in Matthew 28.

And, of course, with "reason" we also have to be careful. A person can be perfectly reasonable and logical but be thinking in too narrow and small a compass or circle of thought. For example, it was reasonable on the surface of things to suggest that Hebrews 6 had something to say about the issue of postbaptismal sins, a major issue in the early centuries of church history, until more careful and detailed exegesis of this text showed that the subject of conversation was not sins after baptism but rather apostasy after conversion, a far bigger and graver matter.

ON MOVING FROM INTERPRETATION TO APPLICATION

Different kinds of literature function differently as they try to convey their message to an audience. Narratives accomplish this basically by *showing* what they want the audience to know about belief and behavior, whereas letters, laws, sermons, and prophecies (except for visionary prophecy) accomplish their tasks more by *telling* what they want or expect. Of course, we have all these sorts of literature in the Bible and, generally speaking, fewer mistakes in application seem to be made with material that is obviously didactic and direct than with narrative. There are many considerations to reflect on.

Sometimes when application is the topic, the material of the Bible is broken down into two categories—principles and practices. This sort of process of discernment or ferreting out of materials from the text is undertaken in recognition that the text was written at another time, in another language, and to other contexts than our own; that there are sufficient differences between then and now and that culture and ours; and that in many cases it is not possible to directly apply the text without such a process. But prying abstract principles out of biblical texts is not that easy and, in some cases, not possible at all, especially when one is dealing with narrative. There is a further problem when you begin talking about "theological principles" derived from the text when in fact what has been derived are ethical principles, for example, the principle to encourage one another in love.

One of the questions that has to be raised from the outset is whether there is any such thing as a biblical culture or whether we should urge that the biblical patterns of belief and behavior be indigenized into any culture. Of course, some Jewish and Christian groups have thought there was such a thing as a biblical culture. A good example of this is the Amish, who have chosen seventeenth- to eighteenth-century German agrarian culture as somehow the epitome of what biblical culture amounts to and should look like. The problem with this, of course, is that when one freezes the cultural expression like that, not only does the world pass the group in the fast lane as it continues to change but the Amish become glorious anachronisms, echoes of a bygone era which make the Bible look antique and of no real relevance to where the world is today.

Not surprisingly, most modern discussions on this issue have opted for the view that there is no particular biblical culture either to be found on the earth today or required or enunciated by the Bible itself. Of course, it is true that when one requires certain kinds of patterns of belief and behavior across generations and centuries there are things that are identical between believers then and now, and many other things that are similar. All Christians have always believed that Jesus Christ is the crucified and risen Lord, and all Christians have always known that there was a high standard of ethical behavior and praxis required of them, which included things like truth-telling and loving one's neighbor, on the one hand, and worshipping God and sharing fellowship, on the other.

What is noticeable in discussions in the NT, in places like Acts 10 and 1 Corinthians 9, is that the audiences are being told that there should be fewer barriers between ethnic groups of people. They are being told that God is impartial and the God of all nations. They are being told in effect that all are one in Christ even though Jews don't cease to be Jewish and Gentiles don't cease to be Gentiles. But the implication is that there is a far wider realm of "things indifferent," which scholars call **adiaphora**, than there had been before the Christ-event.

By this I mean, for example, in regard to dress, Christians are not told how to dress in the NT except they are told to dress decently or modestly, in a fashion that will not distract people as they are worshipping God (see 1 Tim. 2). Or in regard to food, in various places (cf. Mark 7:15–19, Acts 10) Christians are told that no food is unclean anymore, though some eating venues, such as pagan temples, should be avoided. Or in regard to housing or modes of transportation and other such practical aspects of life, the NT does not mandate things. In fact, it does not mandate much about day-to-day life except that one's entire lifestyle honor God and be a blessing and a help to others and self, on the one hand, and that one avoid sin, which destroys relationships with God and human beings and damages one's self, on the other hand.

There is, however, an enormous freedom of choice about mundane things in the NT. The absence of ritual purity rules and other sorts of OT practices that could be said to be ethnocentric and nurture ethnocentricity stands out in the NT compared to the OT. All of this is probably the natural outworking of a religion that was ardently evangelistic and universalistic in outlook and wanted to convert other ethnic groups to Christ, not to a particular form of cultural expression.

Because there are many commonalities between the experiences of God's people in many different eras, we find that by analogy there is a relevance and a pointedness to many ancient texts when it comes to our lives. The principle of analogy, of course, especially comes into play as we read these texts and understandably so. From a Christian point of view, God is the same God, human nature is the same, and God's solution to the human dilemma is the same today as it was in the time of the NT. Sometimes this principle of analogy is stated in the form of preserving the principle of the original in some equivalent practice when one is dealing with an issue of praxis or polity.

As one moves from interpretation to application there are a series of careful steps one can take to ensure one is making an application that is consonant with the original text. (1) Understand as much as possible about the original historical setting and context of the text, remembering that the true meaning of the text must be something the human author and/or God would have wanted to say or allude to, to that audience (e.g., 1 Cor. 13 "when the perfect comes" does not refer to the canon but rather to the second coming of Christ). Failure to attend to this rule leads to numerous errors and especially to anachronistic misreadings of the NT. (2) Hear the Word as it is addressed to that original situation (the context of the original audience is crucial here). (3) Hear the Word as it addresses our situation (here again careful attention to context and the way the Bible can speak is crucial). (4) Apply the original meaning to new situations that are analogous and appropriate.[6]

Of course, it is never as easy as that little outline suggests. The principle of analogy recognizes that no two cultural situations are ever exactly alike, but one looks for enough continuity between the two so that the original sense of the text can meaningfully be applied today. For example, the household codes reveal houses with slaves; but we do not have such households today, so some of this material is not applicable or analogous.

The basic rule of thumb is that while principles (whether theological or ethical) remain the same, practices often and should change with the differing cultural situations (e.g., appropriate clothing in church will differ culture to culture). But there are clearly various mandated practices in the NT, such as baptism and the Lord's supper; and this in turn means that the NT cannot be reduced to just a bunch of principles. Indeed, narratives especially resist such reductionism. The OT as well mandates both principles and various practices. There can be said to be more emphasis both in the OT and in early Judaism on orthopraxy than on orthodoxy, but the emphasis in the NT and early Christianity is more on theological and ethical principles rather than on rituals or specific practices.

Especially important to consider is how narratives function normatively and with authority. Of course, stories are not told in the Bible merely or mainly for entertainment. They are told to inform, inspire, and motivate; and they have a pedagogical dimension in these ways and in others. Sometimes the implicit message is "go and do likewise," for example, when we hear about the evangelistic efforts of Peter or Paul, the faith of Abraham, or the faithfulness of Hezekiah. Sometimes the implicit message is "go and do otherwise," for example, when we read the story of Judas betraying Jesus, the story of Ananias and Sapphira in Acts 5, or some of the stories about Samson.

The question then becomes how to tell the former sort of stories from the latter. My suggestion would be that one looks for *positive repeated patterns* in the text. For example, the summaries in Acts 2:42–47 and 4:32–35 of how the early church worshipped and fellowshipped reveal a positive repeated pattern. Or if there is only one pattern (e.g., that Christian baptism was required for all disciples—see Matt. 28), then we can be reasonably sure that the author wants to inculcate similar beliefs and practices in the audience. Or there are many examples where we see devout prayer being answered by God in the OT. Repetition is the key clue.

---

6 I learned these principles under G. D. Fee. See his helpful summary of his teaching on these things in *New Testament Exegesis*, 3rd ed. (Louisville, KY: Westminster/John Knox Press, 2002).

But what if we find varied patterns? For example, in some places in Acts we find people being baptized with water before they receive the Holy Spirit (see Acts 8, the story of Samaria). In some places we see them receiving the Spirit before they are baptized (Acts 10, Cornelius and family). In some places the two seem to be part of one event (Acts 8, the Ethiopian eunuch). In some OT narratives we hear about patriarchs treating their wives as if they were their sisters. In other narratives, this practice seems to be condemned as deceptive. What should we conclude from this? In my view we should conclude that there is no normative ordering principle being taught in these stories.

Narrative parables function similarly to other sorts of narratives in this regard, and there can be little doubt that certain principles of belief and behavior are being inculcated by the parables (see, e.g., Luke's interpretation in 18:1, "then Jesus told his disciples a parable to show them that they should always pray and not give up"). These parables are not just nice little sermon illustrations but Jesus's public teaching, meant to instruct the audiences on important Kingdom matters, not only in regard to what God is up to but also in regard to what they ought to be doing. Of course, parables often have unsavory characters in them, for example, the thieves in the Good Samaritan parable. Thus, caution must be exercised before one jumps to the conclusion that Jesus wants us to go and be like this or that character in the story. Sometimes he wants just the opposite.

In his recent discussion of how narrative or story functions with authority or has authority, N. T. Wright says the following:

> There are various ways in which stories might be thought to possess authority. Sometimes a story is told so that the actions of its characters may be imitated. It was because they had that impression that some early Fathers, embarrassed by the possibilities inherent in reading the Old Testament that way, insisted upon allegorical exegesis. More subtly, a story can be told with a view to creating a generalized ethos which may then be perpetuated this way or that. The problem with such models, popular in fact though they are within Christian reading of Scripture, is that they are far too vague: they constitute a hermeneutical grab-bag or lucky dip. Rather, I suggest that stories in general, and certainly the biblical story, have a shape and a goal that must be observed and to which appropriate response must be made.
>
> But what might this appropriate response look like? Let me offer you a possible model, which is not in fact simply an illustration but actually corresponds, as I shall argue, to some important features of the biblical story, which (as I have been suggesting) is that which God has given to his people as

the means of his exercising his authority. Suppose there exists a Shakespeare play whose fifth act had been lost. The first four acts provide, let us suppose, such a wealth of characterization, such a crescendo of excitement within the plot, that it is generally agreed that the play ought to be staged. Nevertheless, it is felt inappropriate actually to write a fifth act once and for all: it would freeze the play into one form, and commit Shakespeare as it were to being prospectively responsible for work not in fact his own. Better, it might be felt, to give the key parts to highly trained, sensitive and experienced Shakespearian actors, who would immerse themselves in the first four acts, and in the language and culture of Shakespeare and his time, and who would then be told to work out a fifth act for themselves.

Consider the result. The first four acts, existing as they did, would be the undoubted "authority" for the task in hand. That is, anyone could properly object to the new improvisation on the grounds that this or that character was now behaving inconsistently, or that this or that sub-plot or theme, adumbrated earlier, had not reached its proper resolution. This "authority" of the first four acts would not consist in an implicit command that the actors should repeat the earlier parts of the play over and over again. It would consist in the fact of an as yet unfinished drama, which contained its own impetus, its own forward movement, which demanded to be concluded in the proper manner but which required of the actors a responsible entering into the story as it stood, in order first to understand how the threads could appropriately be drawn together, and then to put that understanding into effect by speaking and acting with both innovation and consistency.

This model could and perhaps should be adapted further; it offers in fact quite a range of possibilities. Among the detailed moves available within this model, which I shall explore and pursue elsewhere, is the possibility of seeing the five acts as follows: (1) Creation; (2) Fall; (3) Israel; (4) Jesus. The New Testament would then form the first scene in the fifth act, giving hints as well (Rom 8; 1 Cor 15; parts of the Apocalypse) of how the play is supposed to end. The church would then live under the "authority" of the extant story, being required to offer something between an improvisation and an actual performance of the final act. Appeal could always be made to the inconsistency of what was being offered with a major theme or characterization in the earlier material. Such an appeal—and such an offering!—would of course require sensitivity of a high order to the whole nature of the story and to the ways in which it would be (of course) inappropriate simply to repeat verbatim passages from earlier sections. Such sensitivity (cashing out the model in terms of church life) is precisely what one would have expected to be required; did we ever imagine that the application of biblical authority ought to be something that could be done by a well-programmed computer?[7]

This is a very intriguing suggestion, and there is much to commend in it. However, this sort of approach helps to answer the question of how we should live or behave, but it doesn't do much for the question of what is true and how timely truths are incarnated in differing cultural settings. What is especially unclear from this proposal is what role direct imperatives that exist in the NT are to play while we are busy improvising on the basis of the earlier story. Wright is trying to avoid the "timeless truth" model that involves the strip mining of stories and other sorts of texts in such a reductionistic way that all that is left is a pile of principles and practices. I am sympathetic with his concern about reductionism, but I do not think we can avoid the truth claims issues or even the issue of timeless truths or principles.

There can also be the objection to the suggestions of Wright that I have already stressed—sometimes the function of a narrative is to tell us that we should "go and do otherwise" and sometimes it is to tell us that we should "go and do likewise," and even mostly positive characters in a narrative sometimes have feet of clay. Any history that involves human behavior is bound to be messy and ambiguous, and thus, while I would argue that the storied world does provide us examples to emulate and avoid and at least with Acts gives us a sense of the ethos of the early church, the stories are told to inculcate certain beliefs and behaviors, beliefs and behaviors that are often more directly and clearly spoken of in the letters and sermons of the NT or the laws in the OT, beliefs and behaviors that involve truth claims.

The authority of all of these stories has to do with their being grounded in both God and God's revelatory truth for the world that in the NT focuses on God's Son, Jesus. There are *timed* truths (truths for only a specific time period, such as the Levitical sacrificial system) and *timeless* truths (both theological and ethical, as found in various places in the NT), and all of the NT can be said in one sense or another to involve *timely* truths—Words of God on target for the situations to which they are addressed. The issue after all is a truth one, for even in regard to stories one must ask whether and in what sense the stories being told are "true."

There is no shortcut or substitute for doing the hard work of interpretation before one gets to the point of application. But the interpretive task is no harder

---

7 This is from his essay "How Can the Bible be Authoritative," which is posted on his website, www.NTWrightpage.com.

than the application of the text; indeed, in many cases it may be easier for the good reason that figuring out how to live out of the text faithfully today, especially in an increasingly less Christian culture, is often more difficult than understanding the text.

Just prior to his expulsion from Germany in 1935, Karl Barth had a chance to offer a formal farewell to his students as the Nazis moved to strengthen their grasp on the intellectual life of the country. He ended with these words: "so listen to my piece of advice: exegesis, exegesis, and yet more exegesis! Keep to the Word, to the Scripture that has been given us."[8] This is still the right advice and perhaps the single most important key to making sure we do not misapply the text today.

Application without exegesis is bound to lead to misapplied, however well-intentioned, Bible teaching. But exegesis without application falls short of the call to holiness of life and behavior, which must accompany the need for right thinking and true believing. Biblical thinking and believing must be fleshed out in biblical living, or we are like barren trees with no fruit; and it is well to remember that what attracts a hungry world to a tree is its fruit, not its bark or leaves.

WHAT JUST HAPPENED?

It stands to reason that before one begins to do any serious amount of driving, one needs to learn what the basic rules of the road are, for instance, which side of the road to drive on. In this chapter, we reviewed various of the hermeneutical rules of the road usually used to guide the interpretation of the Bible, in preparation for doing in-depth explorations of particular texts. What you notice about these rules in general is that they deal with ways one can use this or that individual passage responsibly today. Even more to the point, those rules that deal especially with the NT are rules of the road for how Christians can and should use the Bible. The unspoken assumption of this chapter as well as other chapters in this study is that the biblical writers themselves knew better than we do what they were trying to say and convey, and therefore, the more we dig deeper and bring to the surface internal clues to their intentions and meanings, the better. We are now prepared to go further than we have in previous chapters and explore in depth what the Bible has to offer us.

---

8 Quoted in Fee, *New Testament Exegesis*.

FOR FURTHER READING

Three books that will provide further insights about the material in this chapter are my *The Living Word of God: Rethinking the Theology of the Bible* (Waco, TX: Baylor University Press, 2008), Kevin J. Vanhoozer, *Is There a Meaning in this Text?* (Grand Rapids, MI: Zondervan, 1998), and Anthony C. Thiselton's classic study *The Two Horizons: New Testament Hermeneutics and Philosophical Description* (Grand Rapids, MI: Eerdmans, 1980).

10

DIGGING DEEPER— HISTORICAL NARRATIVES

In history, a great volume is unrolled for our instruction, drawing the materials of future wisdom from the past errors and infirmities of mankind.
—EDMUND BURKE

A small body of determined spirits fired by an unquenchable faith in their mission can alter the course of history.
—GANDHI

WHERE ARE WE GOING?

In this chapter we will explore the use of historical narrative in the OT and the NT, considering a sample from the stories about Moses and another from the book of Acts. We will examine how narrative is used to reveal the character of God, of his people, and of their relationship and along the way to provide some ethical guidance for God's people. We will point out that one of the most striking things about biblical narrative is its honesty about the flaws and virtues of even its central figures. In this respect, Jesus stands out from all the other characters in the Bible as without flaw or sin.

WHAT IS HISTORY?

Human history, by its very nature, is messy. It is almost always complex, and its patterns and trajectories usually only emerge after the fact. In any case, history is one thing; history writing is another. At best, history writing records a subset of what actually happened and what its significance was and is. And honest history writing will quite naturally reflect the sometimes ambiguous, sometimes unclear nature of historical reality. The good guys sometimes do bad things. The bad guys sometimes do good things. Sometimes you can't tell who's who without some guidance or editorial commentary from the writer. Narrative, as opposed to law or poetry or letters, is sometimes the most difficult kind of literature to decipher. What are the reasons a particular story is told? Who, if anyone, are we supposed to identify with or like in the story? And from a scriptural point of view, what truth is God trying to reveal to us? Is it a truth about God, about us, or about both?

History writing is never just a presentation of the facts. It is always a matter of facts plus interpretation. Always. For example, the history writer must decide which are the important facts, the facts of "historic" importance, because especially in antiquity, before the rise of rapid writing and endless computer documents, a writer had to be quite selective in what he or she would record and relate. Critical judgment had to be applied to the storytelling. This was all the more the case when it came to recording what we have come to call *salvation history*, the story of God's intervention in human history to rescue, save, redeem, and create a people for himself. Furthermore, if the Bible really is a revelation from God, then what we are being told in the Bible is not merely the perspective of one human being or another who only has limited knowledge or insight. We are being told in some way God's perspective on the human dilemma, the human story, particularly the story of God's people. In this chapter we will concentrate on sampling two stories, one from the OT and one from the NT, which help us see how narrative works in the Bible and what its aims and purposes seem to be. Before we do so, it might be helpful to consider briefly a "problem" narrative that various commentators, both Jewish and Christian, have had trouble interpreting.

Without question, there are numerous OT passages that have and should raise serious ethical questions for Jews and Christians. One such passage is 2 Kings 2:23–25, which reads as follows:

> From there Elisha went up to Bethel. As he was walking along the road, some boys came out of the town and jeered at him. "Get out of here, baldy!" they said. "Get out of here, baldy!" He turned around, looked at them and called down a curse on them in the name of the LORD. Then two bears came out of the woods and mauled forty-two of the boys. And he went on to Mount Carmel and from there returned to Samaria.

The story is problematic not only because it appears that a vain Elisha is responding to taunting by children in a horrible manner, a manner not consistent with being a true prophet of God, but also because it suggests that God zapped the boys, for Elisha calls down a curse on the boys.

On the one hand, of course, Christians need to learn not to expect Christian behavior of pre-Christian biblical figures; but even by OT standards, this behavior by Elisha is objectionable. Suppose, however, the point of including this narrative in a sacred book is that we are to learn something about how even godly men can misbehave at times, even badly misbehave? Even godly men can abuse the power God has given them. It is well to remember that Elisha had asked for "a double portion of the spirit of Elijah," and he received it. What we learn from the story of Elijah's ascension and Elisha's commissioning earlier in 2 Kings 2 is that when God empowers a person, it is possible for that person to use properly, or abuse, the power and authority given to him.[1] Here, we see the abuse of power by an all too human prophet. God is off the hook for this disaster. The prophet is not. This is a cautionary tale for spiritual leaders and the message is "go thou and do otherwise."

---

1 Consider the earlier incident of Moses striking the rock with his staff, which produces water, but he goes beyond God's commission to only *speak* to the rock on this occasion. This going beyond the command produces censure, even though the striking miraculously produces water (Num. 20:8–12).

Don't let personal pique or vanity or anger dictate your behavior, perhaps especially when you are reacting to children misbehaving.

HEROES WITH FEET OF CLAY

The Call and Commission of Moses—Exodus 3:1–4:17

It is widely known that there are numerous call narratives in the OT, perhaps the most familiar of which are the prophetic ones in Isaiah 6 (see Chapter Eleven) and Ezekiel 1. It is the nature of this call narrative in Exodus 3–4 that sets Moses off from the patriarchs mentioned in Genesis and sets him in the line of the prophets. Moses, unlike the patriarchs, is not merely called to go and to do, to bless and be a blessing, to receive and believe in the promise and its fulfillment. He is also called upon to proclaim God's word even to an inhospitable audience, to perform miraculous deeds and wonders, and to lead his people home, to set them free. As a prophet, Moses is much like his descendants, Isaiah, Jeremiah, and Ezekiel; but he is also unlike them in that he is a liberator, not just a proclaimer or just a claimer of God's promises.

This particular narrative begins with Moses out on the Sinai peninsula tending sheep, and he appears to be looking for better pasture when he comes to Mt. Horeb. Horeb appears to be just another name for Sinai, and already it is called the mountain of God. If this is Jebel Musa, it is an impressive 7,500 feet high. It is surely no accident that the very mountain where God will reveal his will and presence to his people later is where he first reveals his will and presence to Moses. Moses is simply minding his father-in-law's business, not seeking any close encounters of the first kind with the deity.

The text says Moses went to the back of the desert (to the west). Semitic peoples reckoned directions by facing east, not north, and so west was behind or at the back of the way one was normally facing (toward the rising sun). The *malak YHWH*, or messenger of God, appears to Moses, the one we have come to call "the angel of the Lord." Several commentators suggest that this messenger of God is actually God himself; that is, it is not merely God's angelic representative. The angel/messenger of Yahweh, however, appears in the older parts of the historical books of the OT directly (Judg. 2:1, 4; 5:23; 6:11ff), and it is probably him here as well.

The peculiarity of seeing a bush burn without being consumed intrigues Moses, so he draws closer. God's presence as a flame would seem to imply his holiness (cf. Exod. 3:5) and purifying force but perhaps also his miraculous power.

Any being who can set a bush on fire and not destroy it is a unique being. This suggests harnessed energy and power inexplicable in merely human terms. This event does not seem to be presented as a supernatural vision (unlike Ezek. 1) but, rather, as a miraculous natural occurrence happening outside of Moses's psyche.

God calls Moses by name two times, indicating a certain urgency; and Moses responds immediately, "Here I am." Throughout this discussion, while Moses complains about his inability to be a public speaker, he shows himself more than capable of carrying on a dialogue with God at length! Verse 5 should be translated "stop coming near (as you are doing)." One could say God does not want Moses to experience a premature ministerial burnout! The point is that Moses is not ready yet to come into God's presence; he must be prepared and know not merely what he is dealing with (a burning bush) but with whom he is dealing. This he finds out in verse 6. The place is called a holy place because God is there, not because it is inherently sacred or hallowed ground. This *holiness* characterizes the story of God and his people in Exodus in a way that is not true in Genesis. God is holy, and he requires a holiness and strictness of his people's behavior in a way that is at least not made explicit before the Mosaic era. The taking off of sandals may be because they were dirty, or it may simply be Middle Eastern practice in God's presence to be without various articles of clothing.

Beginning with 3:7, God explains that he has not ignored the cries of his people. Rather, he has both heard them and come down to do something about their suffering. He cares so much that he has come from heaven to intervene on their behalf. The story makes clear that it is God, not Moses, who is the prime rescuer of his own people: "I have come down to rescue them . . . and bring them up out of that land" (3:8). He also plans to provide a homeland for them, a land presently inhabited by various peoples and groups. Further, it is not just any land but a good and broad land, "oozing with milk and honey," to give a literal translation of the Hebrew here.

Moses's initial response is understandable; he is overwhelmed. It is too great a task for one who is only a simple shepherd, and in any case he is unworthy of such a job. He implores, "Who am I that I should go to Pharaoh?" Moses is not yet making excuses but simply sees himself as inadequate to the task. In one sense this could be seen as disingenuous unless Moses has totally forgotten his roots, forgotten that he was raised in the Egyptian palace and had an important status there at one point earlier in his life.

But it is not the adequacy of Moses or his worthiness that is at issue since God, who is fully adequate and worthy, will be with him. Moses's own shortcomings will not prevent God from using him. The first part of God's answer, "I will be with you," is perhaps a play on God's name, Yahweh (vv. 14–15).

The second part of God's twofold answer to Moses in verses 13–15 is one of the greatest storm centers of controversy in all of OT studies. What is God's name? What does it mean? What sort of question is Moses asking? The matter is extremely complex, but the evidence leads us to the following conclusions.

First, in verse 12 God had said to Moses, "I will be with you" (the verbal form *ehyeh*).

Second, in verse 14 we have the same form of the verb *ehyeh* from the root *hayah*. The use of this verb in verse 14 suggests that we are being told something about God's activity or his self-revelation in his activity, not something about his being or essence. It is probably incorrect then to translate the Hebrew here as "I am that I am" and interpret it to mean God is a self-existent, self-contained being.

Third, normally when God was going to act or had just revealed himself, he was given a new title or name (see Gen. 16:13). Notice that Moses does not say "Who are you" or "Who shall I say you are," but rather he expects to be asked not whether this God exists but "What is his name," by which is likely meant "What new revelation have you received from God?" or "Under what new title has he appeared to you?"

Fourth, Moses's question is not posed as a merely hypothetical one but as the natural and expected reaction of the oppressed Israelites. The authenticity of Moses's mission is linked to a revelation of the divine name, confirming that God is going to do something. Verses 14b and 15 do not suggest that the key Hebrew phrase *ehyeh asher ehyeh* is taken to be a refusal of God to reveal himself. It cannot be a totally enigmatic response. Further, verses 14b and 15 should be seen as parallel explanations or responses, and verse 15 is clear enough. It is the God of their fathers who is speaking to them and promising this.

Fifth, it is probable that the Tetragrammaton, or four consonants in God's Hebrew name (*YHWH*), is a shortening of the whole phrase *ehyeh asher ehyeh* into a personal name.

As Exodus 4 progresses, it becomes clear how much Moses is looking for a way out of this, until finally he exclaims, "Send someone else to do it!" (v. 13). Though the question in 4:1 is "What if they [the Israelites] do not believe me [Moses]?" it is clear the real issue is not whether Moses will be believed by others but whether he is willing to believe and trust Yahweh. It is Moses, not Israel, who needs convincing here. God more than adequately provides a way for Moses to answer the Israelites' disbelief with three miraculous signs. God's power is obvious.

The only thing left for Moses to do is begin making excuses (v. 10, "I am not eloquent, I am heavy of mouth"). Moses is presumably not lying but showing lack of faith in God. There may be an implied rebuke, however, when Moses adds that his condition has not changed since this revelation began (v. 10b). God's answer is proper and final: "Who has set a mouth in humankind?" God is obviously angry with Moses's excuse-making and says, "Now go and I will teach you and help you speak." So finally Moses must decide what to do; he can evade the matter no longer with questions. Even given Moses's plea and God's anger, God in his mercy takes part of the burden off Moses by providing his brother Aaron to help him and to be his mouthpiece. Moses will speak for God, and Aaron will speak for Moses. Moses provides Aaron with the revelatory message, and thus, it is "as if you were God to him"; that is, Aaron does not get the revelation directly but through Moses. God will use Moses whether he likes it or not.

This narrative is at one level powerful and at another level painfully honest. Moses is surely not presented as a clear role model of what to do when God calls you to serve in some way. And yet, of course, in the end Moses obeys, however much he tried to evade the commission at the outset. Is he like the son in Jesus's parable who refuses to go when his father tells him to but then turns around and does (Matt. 21:28–32)? The narrative shows the ethical *ambiguity* of the whole situation and of such narratives—should we see this story as teaching us "go and do likewise when God calls" (and, if so, in what respect), or is this a tale about "how not to respond to God when he tries to light a fire under you" (or, in this case, in front of you)?

As we stressed in Chapter Nine when we discussed hermeneutical rules for narratives, what we should look for is positive repeated patterns if we are trying to discern what sort of behavior the author is commending or negative repeated patterns if we are trying to figure out what sort of behavior he is condemning.

At the level of theology, of course, this story teaches us about a God who keeps coming to his people, keeps commissioning his people, however reluctant they may be, however flawed they may be. And we probably learn something important about the biblical God—God's name, God's character being revealed in what he will do, in this case in Egypt under the auspices of Moses's mission.

The Wake-Up Call of Peter and the Conversion of Cornelius—Acts 10

It is probably true to say that for Luke the Cornelius story is the turning point which makes the mission of the church a deliberate mission to Gentiles as well as to Diaspora Jews and God-fearers. It was not many years after this incident that

Gentiles began to predominate in early Christianity. The importance of this event is shown by the fact that it is recounted three times and is the crucial matter at the Jerusalem Council in Acts 15 (cf. Acts 10, 11, 15). Positive repetition in a historical narrative where the author has a limited amount of space is a key indicator of what an author deems important.

If Luke was trying to answer the question of how Christianity developed from being a Jewish sect to a world religion, the two crucial episodes are the Cornelius story and the story of Paul's conversion, both of which are referred to three times in Acts.[2] Thus, Acts 9 and 10 are the key events that explain the course the early church took.

Historical narratives should be judged not in isolation but rather in relationship to the larger story of which they are a part. You would not know just how crucial the Cornelius story is for Luke if you did not read on beyond Acts 10 and discover the story is retold twice more and is in fact interwoven with the story in Acts 9 of the conversion of the apostle to the Gentiles. Acts 9 introduces Paul, and he is commissioned to go to the nations. Acts 10 introduces the first major Gentile convert. You can see that Luke is quite concerned to explain how a Jewish movement became a predominantly Gentile one by his own day, if not before then.

Acts itself could be seen as the human response to God's initiative with Paul and Cornelius, which allowed Gentiles into Christianity without requiring them to submit to the Mosaic law. At verse 2 we are told that Cornelius is devout, a God-fearer, and a charitable man. In other words, he is already a synagogue adherent and is not a total stranger to biblical religion. Cornelius is told at verse 4 by an angel that God had taken note of his prayers and charitable gifts. He is given orders to send messengers to fetch Simon Peter in Joppa, who was staying at Simon the tanner's house. At verse 9 we are told that Peter goes up to the roof to pray at noon, which is not one of the usual hours of prayer for a Jew and, thus, points to the devoutness of Peter. Peter is also hungry but at the wrong time of day. Jews normally had a mid-morning brunch and a large meal in the late afternoon, The Greeks and Romans, however, did eat at noon. While Cornelius had a vision, God puts Peter into a trance while he is hungry and thinking about food. Not surprisingly, what Peter sees is potential food! Notice how God uses the natural to reveal the supernatural or provide an occasion for such a revelation. In both cases, God speaks to the one who comes to him in prayer (cf. 13:2). Shockingly, God tells Peter to "rise, kill and eat." At least some of the creatures in the vision were clearly not kosher.

---

2 The three tellings of the conversion of Paul are found at Acts 9, 22, and 26.

According to verse 14, Peter is repulsed by the order. "Surely not, sir," he says, which implies that he is not clear who is speaking to him. It may be significant that the voice says to Peter, "What God has cleansed, do not call common [unclean]." Notice the text does not say "what *animals* God has declared clean." This is important because later Peter interprets the vision to mean not merely the abolition of food laws but a declaration that *there are no unclean persons*. At verse 16 we are told the command is reiterated three times, perhaps because of Peter's disbelief. Verse 17 indicates that Peter was left bewildered by all this, but the Spirit (v. 19, not part of the vision) prompts him to go downstairs to meet his visitors, Cornelius's messengers.

At verse 22 we get new information. Peter was to come and speak to Cornelius. An important factor in this story is the matter of table fellowship. For a Jew to maintain a kosher table, he could let Gentiles share in his food, but he could not eat in a Gentile's home, where there would be unclean food. Thus, verse 23 is not out of the ordinary or in response to the vision.

The next day, Peter goes with the messengers some thirty miles from Joppa to Caesarea. Cornelius was anticipating a meeting with an important person and had called in all his relatives and close friends. At verse 25 when Peter arrives, Cornelius shows him the extreme form of respect, bowing down, or doing obeisance, which Peter refuses, saying that such an act should be reserved for God (cf. 14:14f; Rev. 19:20; 22:9).

Verse 28 reveals that Peter had meditated on the meaning of the vision and had understood it to mean that no person was unclean, so he could visit and enjoy fellowship with Gentiles. Peter apparently does not yet realize this means that Gentiles can have a full place in the Christian community.

Verse 34 makes clear that God shows no partiality. As James 2:1 and 9 make clear, Christians must have the same attitude. This also means that evildoers cannot expect God will show partiality on their behalf at judgment day either (cf. Rom. 2:11; Eph. 6:9; Col. 3:25; 1 Pet. 1:17; Deut. 10:17). Peter stresses that God accepts people from all nations on the same basis, that is, if they fear God and do what is right (Micah 6:8). Verse 37ff provides a summary of the kind of evangelistic preaching done in the early church. Peter's sermon is interrupted, however, by the incursion of the Spirit. The Spirit falls on all who hear the message (v. 44). The result of this was both speaking in tongues and the praising of God (which may be two ways of saying the same thing).

Much has been made here of the parallel to Acts 2, and some have called this text the "Gentile Pentecost." However, the parallels are not exact. There is no mention of other languages here or of hearing in foreign languages. Peter does not deduce that Cornelius and his kin had exactly the same experience as he previously had but that they had received the same Holy Spirit he and others received on Pentecost. Notice he does not say they spoke in tongues the same way he did. Here, in Acts 10, surely what is meant is *glossolalia*, speaking in an angelic language praising God. In Acts 2 the story is about a miraculous ability to speak on a particular occasion in a foreign language (a miracle my students studying Greek and Hebrew regularly pray will happen for them). Peter stresses that it makes no sense to withhold water baptism when these people have already received the Spirit. Water baptism is, after all, but a symbol of the reality that the Spirit produces in the individual. If one has the substance of that reality, how can its sign be withheld? It must be stressed that here Gentiles are incorporated into the church by a miraculous work of God, not because of any planned Gentile mission. The church in Jerusalem is amazed and accepts Peter's report as genuine, but it does not immediately set up an ongoing Gentile mission. This issue would not be fully resolved until the big council in Acts 15. What is clear is that the Cornelius episode began a trend that precipitated a crisis that had to be resolved. God's action creates a crisis that the church must respond to by changing its view and practice of missions.

The ongoing nature of a continuous narrative like this affects the way we assess its meaning. For example, had we read Acts 9 before reading Acts 10 we would have noticed the positive repeated pattern of how God communicated in visions to both Saul and Ananias to produce the conversion and acceptance of Saul into the Christian fold (as indicated by his baptism), and likewise in Acts 10 two visions of a sort are required, one to Cornelius and one to Peter, for the acceptance of Cornelius's conversion and admission into the Christian community, signaled by his baptism.

We are apparently meant to think it takes an extraordinary work of God to move the earliest Jewish Christians in the direction of an intentional gospel mission to the Gentiles. Furthermore, the vision and experience of Peter become crucial in the all-important Acts 15 council, as he gives the key testimony that it should not be necessary for Gentiles to get circumcised and keep the Mosaic covenant to become followers of Jesus. Put another way, Gentiles did not need to first become Jews in order to be followers of Jesus. Thus, it is right to say that the crucial turning point in Luke's narrative that explains the primary trajectory of evangelism and mission the church would pursue from about AD 50 onward are these stories in Acts 9 and 10.

As with the story of reluctant Moses, we find in the story of Peter a person who is reluctant but for a different reason, reluctant to associate with Gentiles or go into their houses, until God explains to Peter that the Gentiles are no longer unclean.[3]

---

3 The text says, "What God has cleansed . . ." and it is appropriate to ask when that happened. Apparently, this is an indirect allusion to the effect of the death of Jesus for all persons.

In both the story in Exodus and the story in Acts, God has to overcome obstacles to persuade his messengers to do his will. But here a cautionary word is in order.

A Christian reading the Bible needs to have some sense of what can be called progressive revelation. While it is possible to compare and contrast the Moses and Peter stories as we have done here, at the end of the day there are fundamental differences. The story of Moses is a story of a call and a commission but not of a conversion. Furthermore, Moses is not a Christian, and it is a mistake to read all sorts of Christian ideas back into the story of Moses. For example, "the angel of the Lord" is just that, an angel or messenger of God. It is not Christ in some sort of preincarnate state. According to the New Testament, there was no incarnation of the Son of God before it happened in the womb of Mary, Jesus's mother. And as we shall see in our discussion of Philippians in Chapter Fourteen, early Christians believed the Son of God was much more than an angel. We should not view Moses and various other positive figures in the OT as Christians before there ever were Christians. There is a development of God's people over time, and there is also a development of understanding of God over the course of the Bible. The true God is viewed in the NT as more than just the person called Yahweh. This is not the case in the OT.

Furthermore, there is a change of covenants involved between the time of Moses and the time of Jesus. In the Mosaic covenant, the laws of clean and unclean are established according to Leviticus. In the new covenant the laws of clean and unclean are said to be abolished, abolished by the teaching or the death of Jesus or both, apparently (see Mark 7:15–19). In the Mosaic era if one wanted to be a full member of God's people, one had to get circumcised and become a Jew. Once Jesus inaugurated the new covenant, this was no longer necessary, as Acts 10–15 makes abundantly clear. Gentiles could be part of God's people without keeping the Mosaic covenant. There had been a change in covenants and covenant requirements, a change accordingly in views about the nature of the people of God, a change in views about the nature of salvation (one had to believe in Jesus in order to be saved), and even to some extent a change in the way God was viewed as a multipersonal being (see 1 Cor. 8:6).

Luke's narrative reflects all these changes, and he tries to faithfully show that some of these changes were seen as shocking, unexpected, resisted even by some Jewish followers of Jesus. Indeed, even the leaders of the early Jesus movement— Peter, James, and Paul—had to have a conversion involving even a conversion of their Jewish imaginations in order to be convinced that God was doing something new and unprecedented as a result of the coming of Jesus and his death and resurrection.

As with all such historical movements, some people understood the significance and implications of what had happened sooner than others. And some never accepted the implications. The challenge then for Luke, as for the persons who wrote down the stories of Moses, was not only to accurately relate individual episodes but to accurately interpret their relationship to events before and after them and to accurately interpret the significance of the events for the ongoing life of God's people. This was no small or easy task, not least because there was both continuity and discontinuity between the OT stories and the story from the time of Jesus and after. God's faithfulness to Israel had been seen as a kind of partiality to a particular people. But now, Peter is told, God is no respecter of persons; God is impartial to both Gentile and Jew and wants them both to be a vital part of the people of God and on new terms. Gentiles do not have to become Jews to do so.

The challenges for the reader of such biblical historical narratives are as follows. (1) One needs to bear in mind where one is in the story. In reading the OT one should not expect characters to behave like Christians, talk like Christians, or share the full range of Christian values. Yes, there is some continuity between OT and NT characters, but there is also some discontinuity when it comes to theology, ethics, and practices. One should not expect the new covenant to simply be a renewal of one of the old covenants (e.g., the Abrahamic or Mosaic covenant). (2) One needs to bear in mind "who is speaking" in the narrative. Is it God (who knows all things)? Is it a human being merely giving his or her own views? Or is it a human being with a revelation from God like in the story in Acts 2? (3) One needs to learn to ask the right questions of narrative texts like the following: What does it tell me about God? What does it tell me about human beings and more specifically God's people? What does it tell me about the way God relates to his people? (4) Since it is a characteristic of biblical narrative to "tell it like it is" and portray even the positive biblical characters as flawed persons (with the exception of Jesus), it follows from this that we should not seek to glorify them or hide their shortcomings in our teaching or preaching about them.

WHAT JUST HAPPENED?

In this chapter we focused on two important historical narratives, one from the OT and one from the NT. We noticed similarities and differences in the accounts and stressed that the stories need to be interpreted in their individual historical contexts and in light of where they come in their respective narratives. We stressed the honesty of the biblical accounts in reporting even the weaknesses and flaws of the central characters, and we stressed that in order to properly use these stories for teaching or other purposes one needs to understand the author's point of view and the nature of his presentation. One needs as well to ask the right questions, especially when dealing with a narrative text. Not everything in the narrative is being commended or condemned, so one has to develop an understanding of the positive and negative elements and patterns in the accounts to draw any ethical conclusions about the stories. One can also ask theological questions of the text. Finally, we stressed that the reader needs to have a sense of the progressive nature of the biblical story—indeed, the progressive revelation of the character of God, of salvation, of the people of God, of the covenants—in order to rightly interpret the whole narrative of the Bible.

FOR FURTHER READING

For an insightful treatment of the narrative portions of the Bible, see Robert Alter, *The Art of Biblical Narrative* (New York: Basic Books, 2011). An interesting treatment of the Bible compared to ANE literature is John N. Oswalt's *The Bible Among the Myths: Unique Revelation or Just Ancient Literature?* (Grand Rapids, MI: Zondervan, 2009). On the history of the NT period, see my *New Testament History: A Narrative Account* (Grand Rapids, MI: Baker Academic, 2003). On history in the OT, see V. Philips Long, *The Art of Biblical History* (Grand Rapids, MI: Zondervan, 1994).

11

DIGGING DEEPER—The PSALMS

[T]he Psalter is the very paragon of books. . . . Moreover, it is not the poor every-day words of the saints that the Psalter expresses, but their very best words, spoken by them, in deepest earnestness, to God Himself, in matters of utmost moment. Thus it lays open to us not only what they say about their works, but their very heart and the inmost treasure of their souls; so that we can spy the bottom and spring of their words and works—that is to say, their heart—in what manner of thoughts they had, how their heart did bear itself, in every sort of business, peril, and extremity. . . .

And (as I said) the best of all is, that these words of theirs are spoken before God and unto God, which puts double earnestness and life into the words. For words that are spoken only before men in such matters do not come so mightily from the heart, are not such burning, living, piercing words. Hence also it comes to pass that the Psalter is the Book of all the Saints; and every one, whatsoever his case may be, find therein Psalms and words which suit his case so perfectly, that they might seem to have been set down solely for his sake, in such sort that anything better he can neither make for himself, nor discover, nor desire. One good effect of which, moreover, is that if a man takes pleasure in the words here set forth and finds they suit his case, he is assured he is in the communion of the saints, and that all the saints fared just as he fares, for they and he sing all one song together, particularly if he can utter them before God even as they did, which must be done in faith, for an ungodly man relishes them not.

—Martin Luther, Preface
to the Revised Edition
of the German Psalter (1531)

WHERE ARE WE GOING?

In this chapter we will explore in some depth the Bible's prayer and song book, the Psalms, by digging into particular select texts and seeing what they mean and how that meaning is conveyed in this kind of poetic and figurative language. This is an appropriate spot to dig deeper into the Bible as the Psalms are central to the OT and, apart from Isaiah, the most quoted portions of the OT in the NT. We will begin with a general discussion of the types and forms of psalms, followed by a more in-depth discussion of particular passages.

If the proof of the pudding is in the eating, the proof of the principles of interpretation is actually doing the job of **exegeting**, or unpacking and interpreting some texts. What we intend to continue doing in the next several chapters is provide some more core samplings of what it looks like to take into account the things we have discussed in Chapters 1 through 10 and then apply both that knowledge and the principles of interpretation to specific texts. In view of the fact that the Psalms is one of two books in the OT which is most used in the NT (the other being the later portions of Isaiah, found in Isaiah 40–66), we will start by examining the Psalms.[1]

---

1 For a review of the traditional principles of interpretation see Chapter Nine.

INTRODUCTION

Perhaps no portion of the OT is more familiar to the Christian than the Psalms. Here, we hear the sound of a heart that beats like our own; here, we are not lost in the complexities of historical narrative; here, we have prayers and songs that can and do speak for us. Yet, Christians, precisely because they have made these wonderful songs their own, have often overlooked or obscured their original meaning. We cannot say what this or that text might mean to us today if we have not first tried to hear what it originally meant when the inspired author wrote it. This is so because the meaning of the text has not changed through the ages. What it meant is still what it means today. The significance of the text for us or its application may change but not the meaning. And that meaning is best discerned when one has good knowledge of the context in which the text was first given.

The word *psalm* comes to us from the Greek word *psalmos*, which is in turn a translation of the Hebrew *mizmor*, which means either instrumental music or song. Thus, to a large extent when we talk about psalms, we are talking about songs. In fact, the analogy between the psalter and a modern hymnal is quite apt. This book was Israel's ancient hymnbook, used in worship in the temple and in the synagogues in a later era. Though the traditional Hebrew title for this book (*sefer těhillim*, "book of praises") might suggest otherwise, even a cursory reading of the Psalms will show that we have not only praise songs but also individual and corporate laments, wisdom poems, salvation historical songs, etc. The following will show that the most frequent kind of psalm is some form of a lament:

INDIVIDUAL LAMENTS—Pss. 12, 44, 58, 60, 74, 79, 80, 83, 85, 90, 94, 123, 126, 129, 137 (cf. Lam. 5).

CORPORATE LAMENTS—Pss. 3, 4, 5, 7, 9, 10, 13, 14/53, 17, 22, 25, 26, 27:7–14, 28, 31, 35, 39, 40:12–17, 41, 42, 43, 52, 54, 55, 56, 57, 59, 61, 64, 69, 70, 71, 77, 86, 88, 89, 109, 120, 139, 140, 141, 142 (cf. Lam. 3).

HYMNS/SONGS OF PRAISE—Pss. 8, 19:1–6, 29, 33, 46, 48, 66:1–12, 76, 84, 87, 93, 96–100, 104, 105, 113, 117, 122, 135, 136, 145–150. One subset of this category is songs of Zion—Pss. 46, 48, 76, 84, 87, 122.

THANKSGIVING SONGS—Pss. 67, 75, 107, and 124 are community thanksgiving songs, while Pss. 18, 30, 32, 34, 40, 66, 92, 116, 118, and 138 are individual thanksgiving songs.

MESSIANIC/ROYAL PSALMS—Pss. 18, 20, 21, 45, 72, 101, 110, 144:1–11. Strictly speaking, most of these are Thanksgiving songs. Some of these are about the king—some by the king, some for the king. One could add Ps. 2 with its coronation liturgy here or the second half of Psalm 24:3–6 with its entrance liturgy (cf. Ps. 15). One could also add Ps. 22 in light of its later messianic use.

TORAH OR WISDOM PSALMS—Pss. 1 and 119 are Torah/Law songs. Closely related to this sort of psalm are the wisdom psalms—Pss. 32, 34, 37, 49, 111, 112.

PILGRIMAGE PSALMS—Pss. 120–134. These are songs sung on the journey up to the festivals on Mt. Zion in Jerusalem.

Over one-third of the psalms are some form of a *lament*, a cry or complaint to God, whether by an individual or by the community as a group. By and large these laments manifest a common form involving (1) an address to God, (2) the complaint, (3) a confession of trust, (4) a petition, (5) words of assurance, and (6) vows of praise. These laments were probably originally composed for worship, which means that we do not have here just the spontaneous outcry of the human heart but a carefully constructed poetic response meant to help the worshipper have words to speak of his or her own or the nation's distress. The very generic character of the laments enhances their universal use, for most people have been able to identify with one or more of these laments at one time or another.[2]

Another major category of psalm is the *hymn*, or song of praise. Examples of this type of psalm may be found in Psalms 8, 19:1–6, 29, 33, 46–48, 66:1–12, 76, 84, 87, 93, 96–100, 104, 105, 113, 117, 122, 135, 136, and 145–150. Some of these are more specific than others and have been called "songs of Zion" because they are about Zion or Jerusalem (cf. Pss. 46, 48, 76, 84, 87, 122). The hymns in the Psalter are hymns of thanksgiving, with a definite structure involving an introduction, a body, and a conclusion. The introduction usually includes an address to self or others. This is followed by the reasons for this praise (e.g., "praise the Lord, for his name is great"). There are usually one or two standard reasons that he is praised in

---

2 One of the major differences between the OT psalms or songs, which often double as prayers, and NT hymns and prayers is that we basically do not have laments in the NT. We have prayers of praise and thanksgiving and sometimes cries for help, and we have hymns that glorify Christ and his saving work; but we do not have laments, unless one counts "How long oh Lord," the cry of the saints in heaven in Revelation 6:10—but they are simply quoting the psalms. By contrast, the lament is the largest single type of psalm in the OT.

INTRODUCTION

these hymns—for his works/creation (Ps. 8) or for his saving acts in Israel's history (Ps. 78). This latter feature distinguishes Israelite hymns from other hymns of other ethnic groups and religions in the ANE.

Another important category of psalm includes thanksgiving songs, which do not have the specific structure of the hymns. Psalms 67, 75, 107, and 124 are community thanksgiving songs, while Psalms 18, 30, 32, 34, 40, 66, 92, 116, 118, and 138 are individual thanksgiving songs. Some are called "royal psalms," the psalms of a king. Sometimes the royal psalms are about the king or some aspect of his life, and some of these have been called "messianic psalms" (Pss. 18, 20, 21, 45, 72, 101, 110, 144:1–11) because they are about the ideal or final great king. The origin or root of the messianic psalms is to be found in 2 Samuel 7, the oracle of Nathan where there is a promise that kings will follow in the Davidic line in perpetuity so long as God's people, and particularly their king, are faithful to God.

Another sort of psalm is the law or Torah psalm, such as Psalm 1 or 119. Closely related to this sort of psalm are the wisdom psalms—Psalms 32, 34, 37, 49, 111, and 112. There are also psalms of ascent or, as I like to call them, "pilgrimage songs," which were sung when people were going up to Jerusalem. Some focus on the opening up of the city gates ("lift up your heads, O ye gates"); others, like various of the ones grouped together in Pss. 120–134, are more general. Psalms 15 and 24:3–6 are *entrance liturgies*, words said or sung as a king enters the city in ceremonial procession.

One of the major keys to understanding the psalms is to realize that these are the songs, prayers, and words of real human beings to God. They are primarily a revelation not of God's character but rather of human character.[3] They function as the Word of God to us rather differently from a prophetic oracle which says "Thus saith the Lord" and indeed reveal God's perfect will, character, and plan.

To use the words of the great poet George Herbert, what we have in the psalms is "the heart in pilgrimage, the soul in paraphrase." The psalms, then, are often a true revelation of (and brutally honest about) the human heart, and sometimes the emotions or thoughts expressed in these psalms are truly human but truly less than divine. What we learn from some of these psalms is how to go and do otherwise, not how to go and do likewise.

Take, for instance, a cursing or imprecatory psalm like 137:9, where God is implored to dash the heads of infants against rocks because of what their parents did to Jerusalem. Such a cry is understandable, but it hardly comports with the

---

3 Luther understood this. See the quote at the beginning of this chapter.

sentiments of Jesus, who, when he underwent unjust treatment, said "Father, forgive them, for they know not what they do" (Luke 23.34). If we can treat the psalms as a true revelation of the human heart expressed in prayer and song, we are well on the way to understanding this part of Scripture. Our human hearts may well often identify with the heart cries heard in the psalms, but we should only emulate them when they reflect what we have learned elsewhere about proper human desires and actions.

Let us now consider how the book of Psalms was put together. Here, we have a collection of collections. This is especially evident at the end of Psalm 72, where we are told, "This concludes the prayers of David . . ."; but we go on to have another collection of Davidic psalms beginning with Psalm 101. This makes clear that there was a shorter collection of Davidic psalms which originally ended with Psalm 72 but that that collection has been added to the larger whole which we now have. Some of the smaller collections include (1) the psalms of Asaph (78–83), a Levite musician who played a leading role in worship during David's era (1 Chron. 15:17–19; 16:4–5), and (2) the psalms of the sons of Korah (42, 44–49, 84, 85, 87, 88), who were also levitical musicians involved in Temple worship (1 Chron. 6:22).

When we ask about authorship, it becomes clear that we have psalms from a wide variety of periods in Israelite history, from as early as the time of David to as late as the postexilic and Second Temple age. This necessarily means that there must have been a variety of authors for these psalms, although 34 of the psalms are anonymous. That still leaves us with some 116 psalms that have titles, though not all the titles include names.

Traditionally, and I think correctly, the origin of the Psalter has been traced back to David. He was the one who set the process in motion; many later figures followed his lead and composed psalms. We have corroboration that some of David's psalms made it into the psalter, for in the case of Psalm 18, we find a variant form in 2 Samuel 22 attributed to David. In the book of Psalms this song has been retooled for worship and now addresses a wider audience—all Israel.

This example, however, provides us with a significant clue: it suggests that various of the psalms may have begun as wisdom poems or as prayers and been reshaped so they might be sung or otherwise used in worship. A further clue that all the psalms in their present form were meant for some form of worship is the little word *selah* that occurs regularly (e.g., 3:2, 8; 9:16, 20). This word probably indicates a break in the public recitation in worship (meaning something like "pause"). There are also musical notations, names of tunes, and directions to the choirmaster in various psalms. All of these factors make clear that this material in its present form has been adopted and adapted for worship.

Something further should be said about the royal or messianic psalms at this juncture. Various psalms, especially Psalm 110, were used by the early church and, if Mark 12 is a clue, by Jesus himself to exegete and interpret the meaning and experience of the Christ. This is part of the canonical interpreting of the material for us, giving a clue of how it may be used. Yet we must also raise the larger question of whether David and other OT psalm writers had Jesus *specifically* in mind when they said things like we find in Psalm 2:7, "You are my son, today I have become your Father."

It is probably true that the original or at least primary referent of these royal psalms was the Davidic king and his descendants. But Christians can say, based on how the writers of the NT used such a psalm, that God planned for Jesus to be the ultimate son of Jesse, being born into that line of monarchs, so that later Christological interpretation of these psalms was not only natural but a legitimate extension of their original meaning to the final Davidic king. It is not a matter of arbitrarily reading Christ into a psalm that has no relevance to his life or work. In short, the human author sometimes said more than he realized. Jesus *fulfilled* in his life and death various of these psalms, even if they originally were directed to earlier Davidic monarchs.

AN ODE TO CREATION (PSALM 8)

One of the major motifs in the psalms is praising God for his work as creator. Psalm 8 is the perfect example of this sort of psalm, manifesting the normal structure of invocation (v. 1 expanded by a "who" clause in v. lc), motive for praise (v. 3ff), and refrain (v. 9). There is little doubt this psalm was sung in Israelite worship services. Two of the great imponderables are addressed in this sublime hymn: (1) who God is and (2) what our human role on earth is in light of who God is. As often noted, this hymn has echoes of Genesis 1, including the discussion of creation, the mention of humankind in the image of God, and the task of dominion given to humans by God. We have been uniquely made for personal relationship with God, and as persons like unto God, we are able to share some of his majesty, both by being an image-bearer and by fulfilling the task of having dominion over the earth.

The tone of this psalm is set from the opening invocation: it expresses awe, wonder, and joy. The central theme of the psalm could be said to be the majesty and magnificence of God as it is revealed in nature and human nature or human roles. At verse 4 (in English translations it is v. 3), the psalmist begins to reflect on creation, which because of its vastness and beauty causes a sense in us of human insignificance. What kind of God could it be that could make all of this? In view of the size and scope of the universe, what are puny human beings that God should pay any attention to them? And yet God is mindful of his human creatures, not only caring for them but in fact exalting them to a place of honor. We are told that we are made but a little less (or lower) than *elohim*. Now this might mean "angels" (this is how both the Greek OT and Heb. 2:6–8 take it), or it might mean "God."

Next, we are told that humankind is bequeathed both glory and the functions (though on a lesser scale) of God—to rule over all of creation. Notice that it is God who is the actor in all these actions ("you made . . . you put"). We are talking about not human accomplishments or what we deserve but rather the plan and gift of God. We were meant and made to be ruler over all the works of God's hands.

As Bernard Anderson reminded us some time ago, this stress on human dominion over creation was a revolutionary doctrine. Other ANE cultures saw the gods as part of nature, and all humans as under the sway of the stars (hence the need for astrology). But it is not by recognizing nature as our mother but rather God as our Father that we come to understand why we are here. Only by God's special revelation do we learn of our true place and task in life. We are to be God's governor or representative on earth.[4]

This hymn does not remind us that we have taken the great power and privilege granted us by God and often used it to exalt ourselves and serve our own ends. The NT develops the theme of this psalm a bit further than the original author by applying this task of having dominion especially to Christ, the one unfallen human who will not abuse creation and who can rule it justly (cf. 1 Cor. 15:27; Eph. 1:22; Heb. 2:6–8). Ultimately, when Christ returns, he will reveal the sort of dominion we were meant to have over creation, for he will order all things under himself (1 Cor. 15). He is indeed the last Adam, the one who fulfills properly and finally the task given to the first Adam. When he accomplishes this, humanity will have dominion and there will be a new heaven and a new earth. Then again will the closing words of this hymn ring out, "Oh Lord, our ruler, how magnificent is your name in all the earth."

---

4 Bernard W. Anderson, with Steven Bishop, *Out of the Depths: The Psalms Speak for Us Today* (Louisville, KY: Westminster/John Knox Press, 2000).

THE LAMENT OF THE LORD (PSALM 22)

Of all the royal and possibly messianic psalms in the Psalter, Psalms 22 along with 110 are the most cited or alluded to in the NT. In fact, the Matthean crucifixion narrative seems to be deliberately cast in light of Psalm 22, showing how the end of Jesus's life fulfilled this psalm. It is possible that the stimulus for seeing the psalm in this way was actually Jesus's cry from the cross, which is an **Aramaic** quote of the first line of this psalm. In any event, we must first ask what this psalm meant to its original audience. The psalm begins with the psalmist, perhaps David, in deep distress. The cry "*My* God, *my* God" (author's italics) indicates that the psalmist has not forsaken Yahweh, but it appears to him that he has been forsaken by Yahweh, hence the urgency of the cry. What is especially striking about this is that the psalmist asks not why these things are happening to him but why God has seemingly abandoned him in his hour of need. His complaint is not so much "why have you allowed this to happen?" but rather "where are you when I need you so badly?" The biblical God is deeply concerned and compassionate and will come to the rescue. Probably, we should not see these words as an attempt to berate God for not doing his job but as a cry of desperation. Nonetheless, the psalmist is clearly terrified by his God-forsakenness, especially because he is beset by a fierce and powerful foe.

Verse 1b reads literally "far from help [or helping me] are the words of my roaring." Even his most vehement shouting seems useless, stressing how far away God seems, not even hearing the psalmist's strongest cries. Even though the psalmist had been taught to trust God (the verb for *trust* occurs three times in vv. 4 and 5) and was crying to him both day and night, his experience seems to give the lie to his theology. How very often does our experience cause us to doubt, reject, or reshape our theological assumptions? Then at verse 3, the psalmist begins to think of the character of God: he is holy and enthroned on the praises of Israel. Maybe it is because God is so holy that he seems so distant. He is literally set apart from the human scene, as the Hebrew word *qadosh* ("holy") suggests. The psalmist seems to be remembering the worship service when Israel would sing praises. They would lift God up and exalt him in song. Perhaps he is envisioning the ark on which God was enthroned above the cherubim (the creatures who were thought to lift him up). Some have seen here the smoke of the burning incense, a symbol of prayer and praise, rising up to God during worship.

At verse 4 the psalmist looks back over the history of God's people. He remembers that there was precedent for God rescuing his people when they were in dire straits. But then the psalmist seems to think, "they were worthy of such help, and

I am not; I am but a worm." The psalmist is probably envisioning the Exodus here, for he uses the verb that means "to slip through" (cf. Judg. 3:26). God helped them to "slip through" the hands of Pharaoh and escape Egypt. They were not put to shame or disappointed. Yet the psalmist is overcome by his sense of unworthiness. A worm is something trampled under human feet, not treated decently as a person should be. Sometimes when people are abused in this fashion they begin to wonder whether they deserve such treatment. After all, wonders the psalmist, why does everyone despise me? It is bad enough to be suffering, but to suffer while being taunted by one's own people and seemingly abandoned by one's God is intolerable.

Verse 7 speaks of derision, 7b reading literally "they separate with the lip"; that is, they sneer at him and shake their heads (cf. Matt. 27:39; Mark 15:29). What is especially galling is that the crowd taunts him in regard to his faith: "He rolled his burden to the Lord, so let the Lord deliver him." The psalmist had petitioned God openly and now awaited the response, for it is clear the crowd would not help him. Verse 8 must be seen as the words of the enemy, but at verse 9 we return to the psalmist's reflections. He asks himself, "would God stop caring now?" After all, God drew him forth from the womb and placed him at his mother's breast. Indeed, God had cared not only for the forefathers but also for the psalmist himself, so there was good reason to expect it to happen again. Yet God seems so distant that the psalmist implores, "Do not be distant!"

Beginning in verse 12 the adversaries are described as bulls of Bashan (cf. Amos 4:1, "cows of Bashan"). The fertile pastureland east of the Jordan called Bashan was well known for its strong breeds of cattle. At verse 13 we have a different metaphor: the foes are like hungry lions ready to rend one in pieces and roar, or possibly we should read "ready to rage and roar." These images were often used of savage leaders in antiquity, for instance, the Assyrian conquerors. At verse 17 we hear of dogs surrounding the psalmist, standing around waiting for a carcass to dismember.

The self-description in verse 14 is very moving. The word translated "potsherd" often denotes pieces of broken earthenware, but here the subject seems to be the palate. The author feels totally washed out, a bag of disjointed bones. Indeed, his foes are already casting lots for his clothes, as though he were already dead. The psalmist is emaciated, and his tongue clings to the roof of his mouth. Verse 15b indicates that God ultimately put the psalmist in the dust of death. The most difficult verse in the entire psalm is 16c. How are we to render the Hebrew here? The obvious sense of the phrase is "like a lion," but how does that relate to hands and feet? John Calvin points out that if we do render it literally, then we must supply the verb from the previous clause, "encompassed" or "beset." The Greek OT at this point has "they pierced my hands and feet." It is important to note that the NT cites this verse but mentions the nailing of Jesus's hands and feet only after the resurrection (cf. John 20:25–28). If the original text had read "they pierced my hands and feet," then it is surprising that no Evangelist cites this verse. Thus, I suggest that we take it in its most natural sense and translate, "like a lion they beset me, hands and feet," that is, all around or completely. The image could be of hands and feet being gnawed. Since the lion metaphor had already been used, it is natural to see a development of it here.

Beginning at verse 23 there is an address to the whole congregation, and verse 25 in all likelihood means that the psalmist would not have sung this part had he not had a change of fortune. Thus, this whole psalm cannot be applied to Jesus as it is, for Jesus died but the psalmist did not. Verse 28 is interesting. Here, the psalmist gives a more universal perspective on things. The Lord is seen as one who rules over all nations and to whom one day all the ends of the earth and all nations will run and bow down. The nations are seen as converted by the all-encompassing rule of God. Then at verse 29 we hear, "Lo, those who sleep in the earth must worship him, before him all must bow who went down into the dust." Here, clearly, we have the consummation of human history, and this seems to allude to life beyond death, if not resurrection of the body per se. It appears to refer to conscious life beyond the grave, though in what form is unclear. The point is that no one gets beyond God's rule, not even the dead. We can see a clear progression here: (1) in verse 28 all present nations must worship, (2) in verse 29 all past human beings will do so, and (3) in verse 30 all future persons will do so. When one dies, one's descendants will serve God and tell their descendants to do so, so the reign of God will be passed down from generation to generation. Thus, this magnificent psalm is full of rich ideas including the afterlife, the problem of evil, and rescue by God in times of trouble.

There was, of course, one God-forsaken person to whom this psalm was appropriately applied in the NT—Jesus. Though probably David or the psalmist did not know he was speaking of Jesus when he wrote, the divine author could well have led the human author to say more than he fully understood. Not all of the psalm fits Jesus, who was not rescued *from* but rather *beyond* death; but a great deal of it does apply very well, which is probably why Jesus chose it to frame his own last words. Notice how this psalm ends, as Philippians 2:5–11 does, with every knee bowing and every tongue confessing the true God. The Evangelists are telling us that Christ endured our God-forsakenness, taking it upon himself, so that we would not have to bear it any longer.

THE SHEPHERD'S SONG (PSALM 23)

As Henri Nouwen reminds us, when one is most personal one is most universal.[5] This certainly applies to Psalm 23. There is general agreement among scholars that this should be seen as a song of trust. We have, however, the difficulty of deciphering what the Hebrew phrase **lĕ David** means here. Does it mean by, for, or about David or for use by a Davidic king? The character of the psalm makes it believable that it could go back to David himself, who was indeed a shepherd.

Verses 1–4 focus on the Lord as shepherd and verses 5 and 6, on the Lord as host. Some question may be raised as to whether we should see these as two distinct images or whether verses 5–6 are speaking about a shepherd hosting someone in his tent, in which case there is a natural development of a single metaphor here. This song does not appear to have any royal focus, and it seems likely that it was originally a personal song of trust and confidence in Yahweh, not a song for worship. The two major themes are that Yahweh protects and provides.

The psalm begins with a clear statement of faith, "Yahweh is my shepherd." The psalmist is on very personal terms with Yahweh, for he uses not only God's personal name but also the possessive "*my* shepherd" (emphasis added). This implies both a special sense of belonging and a unique relationship. It was not unique in the ANE to call a god a shepherd,[6] but here what stands out is that the psalmist is making a claim not for corporate Israel (cf. Ps. 80.2.77.21.95.7) but for himself. The psalm starts on a serene note, "Because Yahweh is my shepherd I suffer no lack or want." The psalmist is not saying that God protected him from ever having any hard times. Rather, the point is if you have the Lord as your shepherd, you have all you need to endure and prevail, whether in good times or bad.

We, who live in a materialistic world, have a hard time relating to the claim that God is all one needs. It is, however, true that God is the only absolute necessity in life, for with God come all other blessings according to God's plan and provision. As John Calvin reminds us, it is the sign of a true believer that he or she recognizes and glorifies God whether in good times or bad. One should not forget God in the good times or call upon God only in the bad times. In short, the true believer's faith is not dependent on his or her circumstances. Calvin speaks of the believer using God's benefits as ladders to climb up closer to God, not as a means to lead one to think one can do without God and be self-sufficient. Our psalmist

5 Henri J. M. Nouwen, *In Memoriam* (Notre Dame, IN: Ave Maria Press, 2005).
6 James Pritchard, ed., *Ancient Near Eastern Texts* (Princeton, NJ: Princeton University Press, 1969), 387.

is supremely confident not in himself but in God. He is also not naive, for he has walked through the valley of deep darkness; he has had his brush with death or great evil.

In verse 2 God is the subject of the action, as is true throughout the psalm, except for the last verse, where "I" reappears. What we are talking about here are the consequences of God's gracious action. The believer not only trusts in God and God's providence but also sees clearly that he or she could not make it without God. The believer sees him- or herself as a sheep that needs to be told when to rest and when to run, that needs to be led and fed, that needs to be guided and guarded, and that needs on occasion to be rescued and disciplined.

Even a person with only a minimum of knowledge about farm life knows that sheep are not terribly bright. They need constant supervision or unbreakable fences. This must be kept in mind as the psalm progresses. This shepherd cares enough to make the sheep lie down in green pastures where it will have plenty to eat. He also places the sheep beside placid waters. This might mean gently flowing waters, for if a sheep gets too near swift waters it may lose its footing and quickly drown. In short, the image is of both provision and protection.

What could be in view is the nomadic shepherd who has led his flock to an oasis and naturally camps there so that both he and his flock can rest and refresh themselves. Out of the resting and refreshment place one becomes restored; one's life energy comes back. Hence, verse 3 means "he restores my life" (*nefesh* means "life," not "soul"). In the desert there are many paths, and it is easy to get lost; but God leads his sheep not only in the right paths but also in the paths of righteousness. Notice, though, God does not do it simply for our good but also for his own sake. What is at stake here is not just human dreams and wishes, but God's character and will for his human creatures. His glory will either be poorly or well reflected on earth, depending on the paths we follow here. Because God wishes for us to reflect and reveal his will for humanity so that all nations may give him the credit the true God is due, he wants to make sure we do not make him look bad. We are his witnesses. Here there may be an allusion to God's deliverance of Israel in the Exodus events for his own name's sake.

Verse 4 should be translated "even though I walk through the valley of deep darkness." The word *tsalmavet* can mean "very deep shadow" or possibly even "total darkness." The use of this same word should be compared in Amos 5:8, Isaiah 9:2, and Psalm 44:19, which suggest that the translation "valley of the shadow of death" is going a bit far. Danger, however, does seem to be connoted here. One commentator suggests seeing the deep valleys of Israel where one's enemy could stand on the rim of a hill and fire arrows at those below. Job 10:21–22 suggests that the threat of death is involved here, though the words simply mean "deep darkness." Notice that the psalmist fears no evil, not because there are no dangerous people out there but because the Lord is with him, giving him confidence. He believes that greater is God who is with him than any other force that exists in the world. Verse 4b speaks of the comfort of rod and staff. The shepherd carried a crook and club (or rod), the former to pull sheep out of holes and to guide and control them and the latter to ward off attacking wild beasts. Here, the image seems to be of fending off the enemy in the darkness of the valley and the rescuing of the sheep should it fall into a hole. In this sense, these tools of the shepherd are a real comfort to the sheep.

In verses 5 and 6 the imagery changes dramatically. Now the creature whom the psalmist envisions is not a sheep but a human being for whom God has prepared a feast in his tent but in the presence of his enemies. Understanding of Bedouin customs helps us here. Once a person came into a Bedouin's tent, that person was safe, guaranteed immunity from harm while under the protection of the host. One may think of the story of Lot in Sodom in Genesis 19. It is not completely clear whether we are meant to think of the psalmist's enemies surrounding the tent where he eats or whether God has actually planned for him to eat with the enemy, in which case the Shepherd is trying to bring peace and reconciliation between the parties.

Much depends on whether one sees verses 5 and 6 as being set in a tent as I have suggested or in the temple, the house of the Lord. We must not overlook the fact that the Hebrew word for temple is not used here, only the word for "dwelling/house," which could equally well refer to the tent of the nomad or possibly the tabernacle of God in the period of Israel's history before the Temple. If one sees the temple in view here, then the psalmist would be talking about a postsacrificial sacred meal meant for reconciliation and fellowship between those who had been enemies. But if this is an early psalm that goes back to David, then one must remember there was no Temple in David's day.

It was customary to anoint the head of a guest with oil, when he or she came in off the road, having experienced the hot baking sun that dried out one's scalp. This was a basic act of hospitality referred to on various occasions in the gospels (see Luke 7:46). Also, the filling of the cup to overflowing was seen as a part of good hospitality in one's tent and makes sense here at a festive meal. The Greek OT has "and your cup cheers me like the best wine." The psalmist has seen Yahweh bring about reconciliation even between old foes; thus, he is able to exclaim with confidence, "surely goodness and *hesed*" (possibly meaning "covenant loyalty and love") "will follow me all the days of my life."

In short, the psalmist is looking toward a future based on his experience of what God has done for him in the past and present. The very last clause of the psalm indicates the psalmist's personal response to all God's effort on his behalf. He will repeatedly return to the tent of Yahweh and become a sojourner there in order to show his faithfulness and loyalty in response to God's unmerited favor. The psalmist will give God his due, for the God he worships is due repeated and heartfelt responses of loyalty and love, so gracious has Yahweh been through all life's vicissitudes. Thus, the psalmist concludes by saying that as long as he lives he will keep going to the tent to meet and enjoy fellowship with his Shepherd.

It is no accident that Jesus calls himself the Good Shepherd in John 10:11. It implies his oneness with Yahweh, who is always Israel's shepherd, and possibly it implies his royalty since Israel's leaders were also called shepherds. This psalm makes clear that though the words are about an ancient culture, we all may have the same experience as the psalmist since God and human need have not changed over the centuries.

PSALM 139—THE OMNI GOD

Psalm 139 is certainly one of the richest and theologically most profound of all the psalms, yet surprisingly it is never quoted or alluded to in the NT. In many regards, it creates the same sort of problems for the Christian reader as does Psalm 133, for in the midst of some of the most sublime poetry in the OT we also hear at verse 19 "I wish you would kill the wicked, God" and then at verse 21 "do not I hate those who hate you." It is no wonder that some scholars say that for many the magnificent Psalm 139 is ruined by verses 19–22. It may help some to point out that the psalmist's hatred and death wish are not for personal enemies but for the enemies of God, but frankly we cannot go along with Augustine when he suggests that this psalmist really means he hated in them their iniquities (i.e., he hated what was wicked in them). Of such nice theological subtleties as hating the sin but loving the sinner the psalmist knows nothing. He simply says he hates *them*, indeed, hates them utterly and wishes them dead.

It may be worth noting also the various names used for God in this psalm. God is called "Yahweh" in verses 1, 4, and 21; "El" in verses 17 and 23; and "Eloh" in verse 19. As far as the structure of the psalm, it may be divided up into three or four **strophes**, four seeming the most natural: verses 1–6 are about God's omniscience; verses 7–12 are about his omnipresence; verses 13–18 are on his omnipotence and inscrutability; and verses 19–24 are personal petitions, which fall into two subsections: petitions about God's foes, followed by petitions about self. It has been noted that actually verse 1 reads "Thou hast searched me and known" (there is no personal pronominal suffix after *yada*; hence, I have not added "me" after "known"). The point would be that God knows all, having examined the psalmist. It is also interesting that the Hebrew word translated "search" or "examine" has as its basic meaning "to dig," and at Job 28:3 refers to digging for precious metals. It suggests a thorough examination, a getting to the root or heart of the matter.

Verses 2–6 will expand upon what the psalmist means when he says God knows and examines him. God knows when the psalmist sits down, when he rises, when he walks (travels), and when he lies down to rest. In short, Yahweh knows all of his activities; his "ways" (*děrakhim*) or behavior are thoroughly known to God. Then we will hear that God knows all his thoughts before even he speaks them. The verb used at the beginning of verse 3 actually means "to sift" or "to winnow." The point here is that one's activities have been thoroughly sifted and weighed, analyzed, and judged. Verse 4 could mean either that God knows what the psalmist will say before he does or that the psalmist doesn't need to say anything for God to know what he is thinking. Either way, God knows one internally and externally: there are no secrets from God, nor, as we shall hear, is there any place to hide.

Verse 5 speaks of God besetting the psalmist. Indeed, the verb can mean "besiege" in a hostile sense, but it also can mean "protect" in a positive context. Likewise the noun used of God can be used to speak of God's hand, or literally palm, of protection or punishment. Is the point here that the psalmist cannot escape God? That is what the following verses seem to suggest, in which case we should interpret verse 5 to mean that God encompasses and surrounds the psalmist; he is being pursued by "the hound of heaven." God gives him no quarter or perhaps restricts his freedom. The point seems to be that even if the psalmist wished to escape God, he could not. Everywhere he turned he found God, and everything he thought, said, or did was known by God. Such complete knowledge by God is incomprehensible to the psalmist; it is awesome and too amazing to take in (v. 6).

Verse 7 begins the second strophe with a question: where could the psalmist go to get away from God's spirit? This is a rhetorical question, to which the implied answer is "nowhere." The reference to God's spirit here is not to the Holy Spirit but to God's presence in general. Both his spirit and his face express the immanence and presence of God. There may be some sense, though, in distinguishing between constant encounter and automatic immanence (part of the process). Some have seen here merely the assertion that God is ever present with the believer, as Psalm 23:6 asserts. This may be so. Verses 8 and 9 are going to tell us that no height and no depth, no distance in the far east or west, is beyond the parameters of God's presence (this suggests a broader concept of omnipresence than just explained). **Sheol**, here as elsewhere in the OT, refers to the grave or the land of the dead, not hell. It may be significant that the psalmist tells us God is in both places, for in pagan mythology it was asserted that one might escape one deity who was of the sea by going to the mountains or another deity who was a sky god by hiding in the earth. But the God the psalmist worships is the only one, and he is everywhere.

Verse 9 seems to refer to the idea of traveling as fast as (or by) the wings of the dawn. One possible way to render it would be "If I should lift up wings such as the morning dawn," alluding to the swiftness with which light travels across the whole sky once the sun has risen. The psalmist envisions going to live at the other end of the Mediterranean. But even there God's hand would be present to guide him, indeed grab him if necessary. Verse 11 expresses the pointlessness of asking night to come and cover one, for to God light and dark are all one. God can still see and know, no matter what the conditions.

Verse 13 is especially interesting. God created the psalmist. The text literally says God made his kidneys (thought to be the center of conscience). He wove together or knit together his sinews and bones. God is directly involved in the creative process in the womb. Verse 14 is a reverie on human creation: it actually reads, "I am awesomely wonderful." This is not an ode to egotism, for the psalmist goes on to add that this is so because "wonderful are the things you have made. You know me through and through."

The psalmist returns to his anatomy lesson in verse 15 and says that even though he was formed in a hidden or secret place, the womb, his bone structure was not concealed from God's all-seeing eye. Then he speaks of being made deep down in the earth. This seems to be an allusion to the original creation story of Adam formed from the dust of the earth (cf. Job 10:9). Notice Job 1:21, where womb and earth are equated. It is not clear whether we are to see earth here in this psalm as simply a metaphor for womb or whether what is meant is that each individual was individually formed by God, like Adam from the dust of the earth. Verse 13 would favor such an interpretation.

Verse 16 speaks of God seeing the psalmist's *golem* (from *galem*, which means "wind up" and is used in the Talmud of every kind of unshapen stuff or raw material, such as the wood or metal which would be used to form a vessel). Here, what is meant is embryo, it seems, since the psalmist clearly sees a continuity between his present self and this *golem*; but it is as yet unshaped, unsculptured, until God takes his hands and does his work. This metaphor may indicate some medical knowledge of how the fetus gradually forms. Verse 16b indicates that in the book of life all the days of one's life are written down, planned in advance, before any of them come to pass. This does not say that the plan does not take into consideration what God knows we will or would do in various circumstances, but it is definitely talking about a sort of predestination. Notice verse 4 in this psalm indicates that the psalmist's personal choice to speak or not is not annulled by this fact. God's sovereignty and human freedom are both affirmed in the Bible. What is clearly in view here is the determination of length of life (cf. Exod. 32:32–33). Literally, it speaks of days being fashioned for us. The book of life (cf. Ps. 56:8; 69:28) is here a book about earthly life and its extent, *not*, as in the NT, about who makes it into "the Lamb's book of life" and so into everlasting life.

It is not surprising, in view of verse 17, that the psalmist says he finds God's thoughts difficult and yet wonderful. Unlike the days of a human life, God's thoughts are so vast and so many that they are literally as innumerable as grains of sand on a beach. Verse 18b literally says "if I awoke I would be with you still." Some have seen here an allusion to resurrection, but more likely what is meant is that even if the psalmist falls asleep counting God's thoughts, when he awakes, he would still be with God and still involved in counting.

Then suddenly at verse 19 the tone shifts dramatically. It is not too difficult to imagine the semantic shift here. The psalmist has been thinking about an omni-everything sovereign God. If there is such a God who is good, then why is there evil and wickedness in this world? The psalmist cannot answer that question, but he does think that if God is that sovereign, he could at least eliminate the wicked, wherever they may have come from. He asks God to kill the wicked, to make the "men of blood" (probably meaning bloodthirsty men) leave him alone. These men mention God (pronounce his name is what the phrase seems to mean here) maliciously, perhaps in a curse. They speak falsely; they even oppose or possibly attack God. The psalmist is trying to show his utmost loyalty to God here. He hates those who hate him. God's enemies are his. But in view of verse 19 one wonders if he is not in fact saying "let my enemies be yours, God." Yet though he classifies his enemies as wicked, he does not see himself as beyond scrutiny. Verses 23 and 24 should be seen as a protest of innocence at least in this matter. "Examine me God, probe me, and see my anxiety. See if I walk in the way of pain." What he is talking about is the way of sin which leads to internal and external punishment or torment. Rather, he wishes to be guided in the *derek olam*, the everlasting way (i.e., possibly the way that leads to everlasting life).

One of the characteristic ways of speaking of opposite ethical choices in the OT is to refer to the two ways, one that leads to death and destruction and the other, to life and light. We see this language in Deuteronomy 30–32 and in the covenant where Israel is presented with a choice between the two ways and asked to pledge allegiance to the right way, the way of the covenant. The point is that the psalmist indicates his loyalty to the covenant: he has not been going down a road that leads to pain and torment. Thus, the psalmist asks to be vindicated not as a perfect person but as one in right relationship with his sovereign God. Notice that he leaves his enemies to God's disposal. He does not take matters into his own hands.

Thus concludes a psalm with many lessons for us and a thousand good sermons. Leslie Allen concludes about the themes of this psalm that it affirms "not omniscience but constant exposure to divine scrutiny . . . not so much omnipresence as confrontation with an unseen person at every turn, not omnipotence but divine control of a creature's life. These are the heart-searching themes of the psalm."[7] God is very real to this psalmist, indeed inescapable, and yet ironically here he is called upon to be the psalmist's means of escape from the wicked. Such are the imponderables when one truly believes in the God of the Bible. An omnipresent God can give one a feeling of complete security if one is in positive relationship with him or of complete helplessness if one is trying to run and hide.

WHAT JUST HAPPENED?

In reviewing the content of this chapter, what you have seen is what detailed exegesis, or interpretation, of biblical texts looks like. And you have learned a few things indirectly about what it takes to do such interpretation. In the first place, it requires a knowledge of the biblical languages. Thus, you saw sprinkled throughout this chapter comments on the possible meanings of various Hebrew words and how they are translated sometimes poorly and sometimes well.

Let's suppose, however, that you have not learned the languages of the Bible and cannot read the original-language text that is the basis of all translations. Has your understanding of the Bible met an insuperable roadblock? Not necessarily, if you are prepared to read good commentaries on the original language text and learn from them. Later we will refer to David Bauer's guide to good commentaries as a key reference tool in helping you to build your library. For now, however, what you should have learned is that without a knowledge of the kinds of things we discussed in the first ten chapters, which do not necessarily require a knowledge of Hebrew or Greek, and without the help of biblical scholars, understanding the real meaning of a whole host of biblical texts is quite difficult and, in some cases, impossible.

---

7 Leslie C. Allen, *Psalms 101–150*. World Biblical Commentary, vol. 21 (Nashville, TN: Thomas Nelson, 1983), 263.

This is not because the Bible is unclear; it is because the modern reader is unfamiliar with the contexts and the original meanings of the texts in question. While it flies in the face of the assumptions of some Bible readers, the truth is that simply using your brain, and the aid of God's Spirit, is often not enough to grasp the meaning of the Bible. We all need further help to do so, not least because our own cultural context and language are vastly different from biblical cultures in antiquity. In short, we need to give our brains and the Spirit more to work with in order to more fully grasp the meaning and understand the message of the Bible.

FOR FURTHER READING

There are numerous helpful guides and introductions to the Psalms, and I have already listed one by Bernard Anderson in the notes. In addition to that, try N. T. Wright's *The Case for the Psalms: Why They Are Essential* (New York: Harper One, 2013). Another stimulating book is Robert Alter's *The Book of Psalms* (New York: Norton, 2009).

12

DIGGING DEEPER—ISAIAH

The people who were honored in the Bible were the false prophets. It was the ones we call the prophets who were jailed and driven into the desert, and so on.
—Noam Chomsky *Tablet: A New Read on Jewish Life*, November 12, 2010

THE ORACLE

Call them forth,
Call them forth,
From the passive past.
The soothsayers and truth sayers
The yea sayers and nay sayers
The foretellers and forthtellers,
Scanning the skies,
Hoping for the horizon,
Acting out the plan
Signing forth the ban

Boon or bane
Commendation or condemnation
Blessing or curse,
Let them wrap their mantles
'Round their hoary heads
And cry: "Thus sayeth the Lord"
Once more.—BW3

WHERE ARE WE GOING?

After an introduction to the setting and context of the book of Isaiah, we explore certain key texts that are of importance for understanding both OT prophecy and the NT. We examine the call of Isaiah and the early prophecies of the coming great King and then focus on some of the Suffering Servant songs of Isaiah 40–55.

The OT prophetic book which is most quoted, alluded to, or echoed in the NT is without question Isaiah. Indeed, so important is Isaiah to the theologizing of the writers of the NT that this book has sometimes been called the Fifth Gospel. Jesus cites it, Paul cites it, Peter cites it, John of Patmos cites it, and we could go on. There are literally hundreds of references of one sort or another to Isaiah in the NT. It follows from this that it is very important to understand Isaiah if one wants to understand the Bible as a whole or either testament individually. We will look at some of the texts we find in both the OT and at least partially cited in the NT.

BACKGROUND ISSUES

Without question, Isaiah is one of the most interesting and complex books in the whole Bible. It is the longest of the classical prophetical books, with 66 chapters, and the most quoted in the NT, some 411 times. This fact alone should make it of supreme interest to us. Unfortunately, Isaiah has been a battleground for various crucial issues of OT studies.

Who is this Isaiah? He may well have been a court prophet. This would explain not only his knowledge of political affairs but also his free access to the king. We are told he was married, though it is not completely clear whether the Hebrew refers to his wife as a prophetess or means she was the wife of a prophet—probably the former. Isaiah engages not only in oracles and visions but also in prophetical sign acts like his predecessors, so he is not a one-dimensional prophet. Perhaps the largest of the scholarly debates is whether the Isaiah referred to in Isaiah 6 wrote this whole huge corpus of literature or perhaps was responsible for only the first 39 chapters, before the style of the document changes rather remarkably in Isaiah 40–66.

The problem is not just one of style, however, because a good deal of the material in Isaiah 40–66 seems to have been written while the writer was in exile and some of it perhaps even later than that. It is not likely that Isaiah actually lived the extremely long life he would have had to live to do so. For example, the Judean exile lasted about seventy years, and Isaiah was a prophet before then. More certainly, the Isaiah referred to in the early chapters of the book was a prophet during the reign of King Uzziah and at least one subsequent king, which places him sometime in the eighth century BC, not in the seventh century or the sixth century when Judah was taken into exile. We will be able to say a bit more about this in due course as we discuss three key texts from Isaiah.

ISAIAH 6:1–10—THE CALL

Without question, this chapter is one of the most quoted texts of the OT. Yet it is also seldom understood in context. If we see chapters 1–5 as introducing and summarizing the overall message of Isaiah, then chapter 6 climaxes that complex of material. Yet it can also be argued that chapter 6 introduces what follows when the prophet gives more specific pronouncements about the coming judgments. In fact, this revelation of God's holiness and human sinfulness explains precisely why the following chapters go on to record judgment and woe. For instance, Isaiah 6 explains well why Isaiah likes to call God the Holy One—he has had an experience of his holiness and glory of overwhelming proportions.

Much of the controversy about this passage concerns whether it may be seen as a call narrative or not. Is this the event that engenders Isaiah's prophetic ministry or something else? Much hinges on how we interpret the key verse 5. Probably it should read "Woe is me that I was silent [or because I was silent], because I was a man of unclean lips." It is possible to read this as suggesting that Isaiah had previously been a prophet but had refrained from publishing or making known all God had told him. In fact, Jerome tells of a legend that Isaiah had lost his inspiration and now was being cleansed and recommissioned. Jewish exegesis has related this passage to 2 Chronicles 26:16–22 and Uzziah's wrongs about which Isaiah was silent. Perhaps Isaiah had been silent about Jerusalem's and Judah's and Uzziah's sins, critiquing the northern tribes alone. But now he is being commissioned to proclaim the whole counsel of God, even against his beloved city and region and king. It may well be quite significant that this vision comes in the year when King Uzziah died.

It is not clear whether we are to think of Isaiah being in the Temple in Jerusalem or having a vision of the heavenly temple. The Hebrew word here in itself simply means "the hall," or possibly "the palace," and does not indicate whether it is an earthly or heavenly one; but perhaps this is a false dilemma. The opening vision is of God himself on a throne that is high and lifted up. So immense is God that even the hem of his garment, or the lower extremities covered by the skirt of the garment, fills the temple. Notice that the prophet does not describe God himself. Above and around the deity fly seraphim. This last word, which is a transliteration of the actual Hebrew word, may in fact come from the word for fire and, thus, means the "fiery ones" or "brilliant ones." If so, it is only appropriate that one of them carries the hot or fiery stone that purifies Isaiah's lips. The seraphim address each other, not the prophet, and it is as though the prophet overhears the conversation in the heavenly palace. This comports with other texts which suggest that prophets were listening in on the heavenly counsel and so on God's plan for human history. They proclaim God's very nature—holy. One commentator has said that *holy* is what God is in himself, while *glory* is the appearance or impression he makes on those who encounter him. The word *qadosh* suggests God's holy otherness, his distinctness.

At verse 5 Isaiah indicates his unworthiness to be having such an experience, and he becomes profoundly uncomfortable in God's presence, for an unclean person in the presence of a holy God is in danger of judgment and destruction. This text, however, says nothing about an unclean heart in Isaiah. It says that he is a man of unclean lips, which strongly suggests that his proclamation had not previously been all it ought to be and in fact comported all too well with the character of God's people, which was likewise unclean. The one who had pronounced prophetic woes on others must now pronounce woe on himself. Isaiah was not able to remedy his unclean lips, so a seraph touches his lips with a hot, smooth stone or a coal taken from the altar. With this act, Isaiah is told his guilt has departed and his sin atoned for by God's very agent. Isaiah is being given a second chance here, and immediately he is given an opportunity to serve. Note that he is not drafted but given an opportunity to volunteer.

The Lord asked, "Whom shall I send, whom will go for us?" (6:8, "us" being God and his heavenly agents). Isaiah's response is "Behold me," which may suggest an invitation to scrutiny. Isaiah has now been cleaned up in the organ that is his instrument of service. He is prepared to go out and speak the pure word of God. But what he is to proclaim will be a very distressing message. We must always bear in mind the power of God's word as spoken by the prophet. It does not merely announce coming things but in a real sense brings them about or sets them in motion.

This in part explains the difficult saying in verses 9 and 10. Isaiah is called to go and say "Hear and hear, but do not understand; see and see but do not perceive or know." The word of the prophet will in fact have the effect of hardening the people in their rebellion, not enlightening them. It is a message that will blind and deafen. Now, this effect is clearly not permanent, in view of what follows in this book; but it will last until judgment falls even on Jerusalem and Judah. It will last until after the period of desolation described in what follows, a desolation which seems total but, as we shall see, will involve a remnant.

Even though the tree of Judah is chopped down, a small shoot will sprout from the stump—but not until the ax has done its work. Verse 13 indicates that there is still hope. But the nation must first be cleansed or purged of its sin just as Isaiah has been. That Isaiah is cleaned without being totally destroyed is a hopeful sign for the unclean people he addresses and represents.

ISAIAH 7—THE COMING KING

Dealing with this text is like walking through a minefield: it is very difficult to get through the text and all the thorny issues it raises. The matter is complicated by the fact that Isaiah 7:14 is quoted in Matthew's Gospel in the LXX or Greek OT version, and it refers to Jesus. As any careful reader will see by examining Isaiah 7:16, Isaiah indicates that the child he is talking about will be born and grow up *before* the lands of Israel and Syria will be laid waste (i.e., by the period 733–722 BC at the latest).

This text should be read in light of the first half of Isaiah 7. Isaiah in both cases is addressing the situation that existed shortly after Ahaz had ascended to Judah's throne and after the Syro–Ephramite alliance was threatening Ahaz for not joining up with them in resistance against Syria. Ahaz was quite young and inexperienced at this time and no doubt needed advice and reassurance. The former oracle affirms the destruction of the alliance by Assyria; this oracle stresses the continuing of the royal family line.

The oracle begins by Isaiah telling Ahaz to request a sign. This is not without precedent, and signs did not have to be negative; in this case, the sign could very well be seen as positive and confirmatory (cf. 7:9—confirmed). Ahaz is instructed to ask for any sign he might choose. We might say "the sky is the limit." This could imply a willingness to perform a miraculous sign, but it could also imply simple providence without any especially miraculous element. Ahaz refuses to ask, feigning modesty and not wishing to test Yahweh. This reaction may reflect two things: (1) Ahaz, being young, may have been frightened of Yahweh and afraid to ask; (2) he may have already made up his mind what his policy would be and did not want to be redirected into some faith venture, away from what he saw as a pragmatic course of action. Clearly, however, Isaiah sees Ahaz's refusal not as modesty but as revealing a lack of faith in Yahweh.

When the actual oracle about the sign begins at verse 13b, the addressee is not Ahaz in particular but the house of David, and the plural is used in this context. This suggests strongly that this oracle is addressed to and is about the royal line. It is not simply for Ahaz, although he is the first intended recipient. He is only one of those who wearies Yahweh (the "you" in "you weary" is again plural, referring to more than Ahaz). The idea here is that God's infinite patience is being tried severely. Verse 14 indicates that God will give a sign to "you" (plural), to the Davidic line, including Ahaz.

The sign is as follows: "the *almah* shall conceive and bear a son, and she shall call his name Immanuel." This child shall eat the food of royal infants (curds and honey represent the food of royalty in some Mesopotamian texts) until he comes to the age of moral discernment. Indeed, before he comes to that age the two kings Rezin and Pekah (the ones Ahaz now dreads) will have withdrawn from Judah's soil. It is quite clear from the definite article before *almah* in the Hebrew that the prophecy has a specific woman in mind. Perhaps the most reasonable conjecture is that Isaiah has in mind a young maiden, perhaps a princess in the royal household. One conjecture is that Abia is the princess in view, for she was the daughter of Zechariah, a friend of Isaiah's (cf. 1 Kgs. 18:2). The child then would be Hezekiah. Since we know that Hezekiah likely assumed power in 715 BC, it is possible that he had not yet been born to Ahaz in 734 or slightly earlier when this oracle was given. The record will also show that Hezekiah was in many ways a godsend. Furthermore, the very survival of the Davidic monarchy when Tiglathpileser invaded Palestine in 733 BC, killed Pekah, and took over everything in sight (except Jerusalem and parts of Judah) was nothing short of a real miracle. This was indeed also a propitious sign for the Davidic line during Ahaz's early days. Isaiah had counseled no alliance with Rezin and Pekah, but he had also advised not to call for outside help from Assyria or others. Rather, the king should simply rely on Yahweh, who continued and preserved the royal line, as this oracle indicates.

In regard to the crucial word *almah*, in a positive context, as this is, it simply means a sexually mature young woman and, thus, a suitable candidate for marriage. The word is not a technical term for virgin, though virginity would certainly be implied in a positive context such as this one. Thus, when the LXX translates *almah* by *parthenos* ("virgin") it is not incorrect; the Greek is just more technical and specific than the Hebrew term. Thus, this text can be perfectly well interpreted in its original historical context without reference to Jesus.

But this leads us to look at the other two uses of the name "Immanuel" in this book. First, we note that Immanuel is an incomplete phrase meaning simply "God with us," and the verb that one inserts in the phrase depends on the context. Here, probably what is meant is "God is with us," but at Isaiah 8:8 it appears to mean "God will be with us" and at 8:10, "God is with us" again. In neither of those two texts does it seem to refer to a human person, only to the idea of God being with his people. I do not think we should translate these verses with the proper name Immanuel.

The conjecture that Isaiah's own son is this Immanuel figure is not impossible in light of the early part of Isaiah 8. Against this must be the fact that if we take Immanuel as a proper name at 8:8, in what sense can Judah really possessively be called "the land of Isaiah's son"? Such a claim would much better suit Hezekiah. But, as I have said, I think neither is in view in Isaiah 8. One other point needs to be kept in mind. The name "Immanuel," if we are talking about a royal Davidic heir, need not be seen as the child's personal name but as a throne name, for instance, like the names in Isaiah 9:6. A throne name is more like a royal title than a proper name. Notice that in Matthew 1:23 Jesus is not *named* Immanuel but rather given his personal name, Jesus. Immanuel is simply something that the child would be called, descriptive of what he meant to his people and family.

What then are we to make of Matthew's use of this text to refer to Jesus? I would suggest that we note that Matthew doesn't say that Jesus was *predicted* in Isaiah 7:14 but rather that Jesus was the fulfillment of what was spoken of in the text. This is not quite the same thing. It is perfectly possible for God to fulfill his word more than once, without Isaiah having foreseen some savior figure 700 plus years in advance that was no immediate help to Ahaz (though such foresight cannot be completely ruled out). Thus, I think we should say that Jesus was the more perfect fulfillment of Isaiah's word about Immanuel. In a much truer sense than any mere human Davidic child, Jesus could really be God with us since he had a divine nature. Surely, Isaiah did not have full understanding of how these prophecies would later, and legitimately, be used by Christians.

ISAIAH 52:13–53:12—THE SUFFERING SERVANT

We have now entered the realm of pure poetic verse that characterizes Isaiah 40–55. There is little question but that this passage is the most important to Christians of the whole prophetic corpus, and thus, we must look at it in detail and with some care. This Fourth Servant song is in two parts: what certain people say about the *eved* (i.e., the servant, 53:1–11a) and what God says (52:13ff; 53:11b–12). Both segments tell of the Servant's humiliation and his exaltation. These are set in contrast to one another, as is what people expected of this *eved* and how they reacted to him and, by further contrast, what was actually the case and how God reacted to him. This material can be said to show the whole career of the *eved* from womb to tomb and beyond, and as such, it bears the same sort of elements we find in the Christian creed: born, lived, died, buried, exalted beyond death.

The song begins on a high note: God's *eved* will prosper and be exalted. There will be a total reversal of evaluation of this man; those who were aghast will be astonished. Here, we see a total reversal of fortunes. We are to envision here a person who has no form or physical beauty. This seems to have two reasons: (1) he has been disfigured, indeed badly disfigured, by persecution and (2) he has been stricken. Isaiah 53:4 uses a verb that can refer to being stricken with a dread disease like leprosy (cf. 2 Kgs. 15:5). There is no doubt that this word indicates one afflicted by a dread disease, one that probably causes disfigurement and repulsive appearance; and leprosy best fits this sort of description.

People were horrified, for this person was marred beyond human semblance. One must envision the usual human reaction here to seeing one who is badly disfigured. Who could believe that this sort of person could be exalted by God? The author is trying to make clear that we are dealing with a totally unique set of circumstances; indeed, it appears he means to indicate that this is an unrepeatable set of circumstances.

To understand this passage one must bear in mind the common theology of the day: (1) that outward beauty is an indication of being blessed by God, and thus the opposite is a sign of being smitten by God, and (2) that a person who suffers is assumed to be smitten by God. This passage blows those theologies right out of the water. Not only are we taught here not to judge by appearances, but we also learn that suffering does not necessarily mean that someone is a sinner or that God is displeased with that person.

Isaiah 53:2 is meant to indicate that the *eved* came forth from unpromising or at least ordinary circumstances. There was hardly anything auspicious about his origins. At Isaiah 53:3 we hear that the servant is "a man of blows, humiliated by or familiar with sickness" (or possibly pain). Various scholars have noted the very close parallels throughout this song to the psalms of lament, where being despised and rejected is always associated with personal suffering and humiliation. Psalm 22 should especially be compared to our *text*. This *eved* was one shunned by humankind, one from whom people hid their faces. He was not highly esteemed—quite the opposite.

Then at 53:4 comes the beginning of the surprise: the reason for this sad state of affairs for the *eved* was that he was bearing *our* sickness and pain. He was crushed because of *our* iniquities (the verb here means crushed, shattered, broken in pieces). Verse 5a suggests a wound incurred by violence done against one's person. The author then makes clear why this was happening—"the punishment lies on him, in order that we might have peace [*shalom*]." There is very little doubt that here we are talking about vicarious or substitutionary suffering. What is quite amazing is that it is not a person the people might have evaluated as suitable or exceptional who is called upon to perform this substitutionary suffering for us but one who to all outward appearances seemed ordinary, if not repulsive—the least likely candidate, humanly speaking. When we are told that Yahweh laid on him the iniquity of us all, we must take this to mean he endured the punishment and accepted the guilt for it since sin is not a substance to be borne. We might say he took the blame on his shoulder. Yet the *eved* did not complain; he simply and quietly bore the punishment.

Verse 8 seems to be talking about one who has been incarcerated and is taken before a court, condemned, and executed. None were concerned about the effect on his family or his hope of having progeny and preserving the family line. He was simply cut off from the land of the living. He was ranked with those who were criminals, but surprisingly he was buried with the rich, presumably as a sort of consolation prize or, as the songwriter says, "because he had done no wrong to deserve all this grief."

At verse 10 we have an adversative conjunction, indicating a clear turning point in the song; I translate it "and yet." Yet God reversed these misfortunes. The one who had been made by God to be an offering for sin, in fact shall see his days prolonged and have seed. Because he has born the sins of and justified many (notice it does not say all), the *eved* is given a portion with the great. It seems clear that life beyond death is in view here, although resurrection is not mentioned specifically, and exaltation to heaven may be in mind. This reward is granted because the *eved* poured out his *nefesh* to death (i.e., his life, or possibly here lifeblood). He was a guilt offering (v. 10). He has made *paga* for transgressors. This means "to make entreaty for" or "intervention for," but in this case we are not to think of his mediator role of offering prayers for us in heaven. Rather, his death is an intervention on behalf of sinners, a stepping in the path of punishment and so deflecting it from sinners.

What should be seen from this passage is that the Servant definitely performs here not merely a prophetic role but a priestly one. Yet this was contrary to all expectations since a diseased and ordinary person could not be a priest. Indeed, it is even possible to take 52:15 to mean "he will sprinkle many nations"; that is, he performs a purifying rite (cf. Lev. 14:7a). This is following the Hebrew text rather than the LXX. Who then is this Suffering Servant? None fit the description in our Isaiah's day, and indeed none in any day fits the description so well as Jesus himself. One must, however, bear in mind that this is poetry and not every detail should be pressed—for instance, the matter of being stricken with a dreaded disease. Had that been the case, Jesus would have never drawn a crowd or have been allowed in a temple. The point is that the Servant took upon himself all the effects of sin and punishment of sin for our sake.

WHAT JUST HAPPENED?

In this chapter we took a look at the prophecy that shows up in the book called Isaiah. Notice that it involved more than one kind of literature. There was more classical prophecy in Isaiah 1–39 and more song/poetic prophecy in Isaiah 52–53. We also examined the call narrative of Isaiah in Isaiah 6. In all this there was a relevance of the material to the immediate situation. This was especially clear in Isaiah 6–7, but that does not mean there could not be a fuller or final fulfillment of prophecy later, by someone who better sat for the portrait of Immanuel or the Suffering Servant. With this chapter we began to see how our studies in the genre of narrative, prophecy, and poetry have prepared us to read a complex book like Isaiah in a way that comports with its narrative, literary, and prophetic character. We have also begun to see why detailed exegesis or close careful reading of a biblical text is so important and always more illuminating with some knowledge of the original languages, not to mention the historical and religious contexts.

FOR FURTHER READING

As with the Psalms, there are numerous useful introductions to Isaiah, but J. Alec Motyer's *The Prophecy of Isaiah: An Introduction and Commentary* (Downers Grove, IL: InterVarsity Press, 1993) is one of the more accessible ones. Perhaps even better is Brian E. Beyer's *Encountering the Book of Isaiah: A Historical and Theological Survey* (Grand Rapids, MI: Baker Academic, 2007). I would especially commend John F. A. Sawyer's *The Fifth Gospel: Isaiah in the History of Christianity* (Cambridge: Cambridge University Press, 1996).

13

DIGGING DEEPER— The PROPHESIES and PARABLES of JESUS

To say he had a face is to say that like the rest of us he had many faces . . . the face of a man is not a front for him to live his life behind, but a frontier, the outermost ever changing edge of his life itself in all its richness and multiplicity, and hence they spoke not of the face of a man or of God, but of his faces. The faces of Jesus then—all the ways he had of being and of being seen.

—F. Buechner[1]

---

1 *The Faces of Jesus: A Life Story* (Brewster, MA: Paraclete Press, 2005), vii–viii.

Figure 13.1 One of the most well assured results of history is that Jesus was crucified under Pontius Pilate in about AD 30. (Shutterstock/jorisvo)

WHERE ARE WE GOING?

In this chapter we will examine the ways in which Jesus could be called both a prophet and a sage or wise man. We will sample his prophetic discourse in Mark 13 and then consider various of his parables of the Kingdom. We will point out that Jesus was a complex person who doesn't easily fit into one or another pigeonhole, whether it be prophet, priest, king, or sage. Indeed, one could say that all these terms describe him to some degree but each one in isolation is an inadequate description.

Most of the teachings of Jesus are in wisdom form—parables, aphorisms, riddles, proverbs. But occasionally Jesus spoke as a prophet. What is interesting about this is that unlike the classical prophets, Jesus never quoted God—he just spoke in his own voice, in the first person. What I mean by this is that he never used the formula "thus says Yahweh" (or, as he would have put it, "thus says Abba, the Father")—not once. Jesus does prophetic sign acts like OT prophets (cursing a fig tree, cleansing a temple—cf. the prophetic sign acts of Ezekiel, e.g., Ezek. 12, where he depicts the exile). But he speaks on his own authority, again and again; and from the first, people noticed this about Jesus and questioned him about it (Mark 1). Nobody spoke on his or her own authority in that Jewish context, not even prophets. Rabbis would cite the wisdom of previous rabbis, sages would quote wise literature from the past, prophets would offer a verbatim quote from God, priests would quote the liturgy in Torah, religious officials would gather in Sanhedrin and act on legal precedent, even rulers cited the law of the land as their authority to act; but in a culture of derived authority Jesus spoke on his own authority. But what did he say? Before we answer that question it is important to realize that Jesus, like the apocalyptic prophets of old (Daniel, Ezekiel, Zechariah), had visions.

JESUS THE PROPHET

At his baptism Jesus sees the Spirit descending from heaven and hears the voice of God confirm he is God's beloved Son. If we compare Mark 1 to Revelation 1, we see that the language used to describe the event in Mark 1 is nearly identical to the language used to describe John's first visionary experience—the heavens open, God's Spirit envelops the man, and suddenly he hears the voice of God. In both cases, the visionary remains on earth, but his mind is elsewhere. Similarly, in the wilderness Jesus "sees" the Devil, the temple, the whole world, and yet he is still in the Judean wilderness forty days later. Jesus says things like "I saw Satan fall like lightning from the sky," and of course he himself appears with images of Moses and Elijah on the Mt. of Transfiguration. Yes, Jesus was a seer, a visionary. But there is more to Jesus's prophetic character than this.

In Mark 13 we have a large block of Jesus's prophetic teaching, often called the Olivet discourse. We need to spend a little time probing deeper into the character of Jesus's prophecy. First of all, here is the text in question:

> As Jesus was leaving the temple, one of his disciples said to him, "Look, Teacher! What massive stones! What magnificent buildings!" "Do you see

all these great buildings?" replied Jesus. "Not one stone here will be left on another; every one will be thrown down." As Jesus was sitting on the Mount of Olives opposite the temple, Peter, James, John and Andrew asked him privately, "Tell us, when will these things happen? And what will be the sign that they are all about to be fulfilled?"

A

Jesus said to them: "Watch out that no one deceives you. Many will come in my name, claiming, 'I am he,' and will deceive many. When you hear of wars and rumors of wars, do not be alarmed. Such things must happen, but the end is still to come. Nation will rise against nation, and kingdom against kingdom. There will be earthquakes in various places, and famines. These are the beginning of birth pains. "You must be on your guard. You will be handed over to the local councils and flogged in the synagogues. On account of me you will stand before governors and kings as witnesses to them. And the gospel must first be preached to all nations. Whenever you are arrested and brought to trial, do not worry beforehand about what to say. Just say whatever is given you at the time, for it is not you speaking, but the Holy Spirit. "Brother will betray brother to death, and a father his child. Children will rebel against their parents and have them put to death. Everyone will hate you because of me, but the one who stands firm to the end will be saved. "When you see 'the abomination that causes desolation' standing where it does not belong (let the reader understand) then let those who are in Judea flee to the mountains. Let no one on the housetop go down or enter the house to take anything out. Let no one in the field go back to get their cloak. How dreadful it will be in those days for pregnant women and nursing mothers! Pray that this will not take place in winter, because those will be days of distress unequaled from the beginning, when God created the world, until now—and never to be equaled again. "If the Lord had not cut short those days, no one would survive. But for the sake of the elect, whom he has chosen, he has shortened them. At that time if anyone says to you, 'Look, here is the Messiah!' or, 'Look, there he is!' do not believe it. For false messiahs and false prophets will appear and perform signs and wonders to deceive, if possible, even the elect. So be on your guard; I have told you everything ahead of time.

B

"But in those days, following that distress, the sun will be darkened, and the moon will not give its light; the stars will fall from the sky, and the heavenly bodies will be shaken. At that time people will see the Son of Man coming in clouds with great power and glory. And he will send his angels and gather his elect from the four winds, from the ends of the earth to the ends of the heavens.

A′

"Now learn this lesson from the fig tree: As soon as its twigs get tender and its leaves come out, you know that summer is near. Even so, when you see these things happening, you know that it is near, right at the door. Truly I tell you, this generation will certainly not pass away until all these things have happened. Heaven and earth will pass away, but my words will never pass away.

B′

"But about that day or hour no one knows, not even the angels in heaven, nor the Son, but only the Father. Be on guard! Be alert! You do not know when that time will come. It's like a man going away: He leaves his house and puts his servants in charge, each with their assigned task, and tells the one at the door to keep watch. "Therefore keep watch because you do not know when the owner of the house will come back—whether in the evening, or at midnight, or when the rooster crows, or at dawn. If he comes suddenly, do not let him find you sleeping. What I say to you, I say to everyone: 'Watch!'"

A few preliminary remarks are necessary. Scholars talk about the way that prophets sometimes spoke with a "foreshortened perspective." What is meant by this is that while they certainly tended to concentrate on present events or events in the near future, sometimes they would talk about more distant events in the same breath with events that were already transpiring or would happen soon. The image that is helpful is as follows: picture someone looking at a mountain range. Because there are so many peaks in this range they appear from the distance to be juxtaposed very closely, almost on top of one another. In actuality, there are deep valleys and considerable distances between them. So it is with prophets: sometimes they talk about near and far events in the same breath, especially if the far events are germane to the discussion of the near ones. Thus, in Mark 13 we have this kind of prophetic speech. This is not surprising since Jesus believed that the final eschatological Kingdom was already coming, so it seemed natural to talk about the nearer and more distant eschatological events together.

Jesus in Mark 13 clearly talks about things that will transpire within a biblical generation, which is to say within about forty years. In fact, Jesus probably spoke this discourse in AD 30, and the Temple in Jerusalem was toppled by Titus's army in August AD 70—almost exactly forty years later. Jesus here talks about not one stone upon another, and Josephus, the Jewish historian, gives an eyewitness account of the destruction of the Temple and the toppling of the huge Herodian stones in his account in *The Jewish War*, book 6. I would encourage you to read the account online or even buy the audio recording and listen to the dramatic account. Jesus was right—Herod's Temple was the temple of doom, going down for the count, and Jesus sees this as a judgment of God. Like Ezekiel, he foresees God's spirit abandoning the Temple and going elsewhere.

We have seen in the last few chapters how truly important it is to catch the structural signals of a book, a discourse, or passage, if we are to interpret them properly; and Mark 13 is not different. There is an A, B, A', B' structure to this discourse, which if ignored, leads to all sorts of wrong conclusions. I have marked the divisions of the discourse in the translation above with the appropriate letters. A and A' refer to events on the *near* horizon, events that will transpire within a biblical generation; and in fact, they did so. These prophecies were fulfilled, especially during the period of the Jewish wars of the AD 60s and leading up to the destruction of the Temple in AD 70. We should not look for them to be fulfilled again since Jesus said they would all transpire basically within the lifetime of his young disciples (who were likely all in their twenties or thirties at most).

There are little linguistic markers used to help the hearer identify that period—Jesus talks about "these things" and what will happen in "those days," and he is prepared to say "these things" will transpire within a generation. Notice something else about "these things": they involve events on the earth—wars, persecution of disciples who are hauled before authorities, earthquakes, and a series of tribulations leading up to the "abomination that makes desolate." That phrase is a direct quote from Daniel 9:27. It refers to the defiling of the holy of holies in the Jewish Temple when unclean pagans enter and do unclean things there, not least of which is stealing things from the holy of holies. All this did in fact transpire in the events leading up to and culminating in AD 70.

But there is another category of events, B and B'. Notice about these events that the timetable for when they will transpire is not given. The text of verse 24 simply says "but in those days following that distress." It does not say how long after the tribulation and fall of the Temple; it simply says "later." In regard to those later events, Jesus talks about cosmic signs in the heavens and the return of the Son of Man (i.e., himself) on the clouds to judge the world. He speaks of this a second time in Mark 13:32–37, the B' and final section of the discourse; and here he makes specific that no one, not even the Son or the angels in heaven, knows when this second coming of the Son of Man will transpire. It will happen at a surprising and unknown time in the future. Therefore, since it could happen soon after the fall of the Temple or much later, one must always be alert and prepared. It's coming like a thief in the night or like when a person comes back from a long journey abroad at an unexpected time. This contrasts completely with what Jesus has said about the events leading up to the destruction of the Temple that will happen before "this generation" will pass away.

So once again preliminary eschatological events lead up to the destruction of the Temple. These events all transpire on the earth. Final eschatological events are accompanied by cosmic signs in the heavens—Jesus returns with his angels for final judgment, something Jesus later warned the Jewish leaders of the Sanhedrin about when ironically they were trying to judge him (Mark 14:62). Jesus says in effect, "you think you're judging me, well, I'll be back from heaven to judge you later!"

There is indeed a clear connection between the preliminary eschatological events and the final ones. The destruction of Jerusalem and the Temple was in many ways the end of early Judaism as it had previously existed. And, of course, to this day there is no Temple in Jerusalem, only the Temple Mount, or platform on which it stood (the so-called Western or Wailing Wall is what we see in Fig. 13.2). Judaism had focused on three *T*s prior to AD 70—Temple, Territory, and Torah. Thereafter, and especially after the failed second Jewish rebellion led by Bar Kokhba in the second century AD, Judaism became Torah-centric, focusing only on the Law.

For a first-century Jew like Jesus, it was natural to connect the fall of the Temple and Temple-centered religion that brought the end of the then known Jewish world with the actual end of human history when Jesus returns to Jerusalem to judge the world. Jesus believed there was a connection between both the preliminary judgment on Jerusalem and the final judgment, namely, himself. In Jesus's view, the judgment on him in Jerusalem and on Golgotha precipitated the judgments on Jerusalem and its Temple and, indeed, the final cosmic events and judgments that have yet to transpire.

Figure 13.2 The Wailing Wall is the western wall of the platform on which originally stood the Temple of Herod in Jerusalem. (© Mark R. Fairchild, PhD)

Notice as well that Mark himself has probably inserted a couple of parenthetical clues for his readers into the discourse: (1) before Jesus returns, the gospel must be preached to all nations (13:10) and (2) he inserts the reminder to the official reader of the document "let the reader understand" (13:14) to be sure to explain to the audience what that elliptical phrase "the abomination that makes desolate" means, as they may not know Daniel (which may mean the audience is mainly Gentile). This latter parenthetical remark may also be a clue to us that Mark was writing near the time the Temple would fall, and most scholars do put the writing of this earliest gospel somewhere around AD 68–70.[2]

What is the cost for not recognizing the A, B, A′, B′ structural signs of this discourse? It has led many readers, including scholars such as Albert Schweitzer, to conclude that poor Jesus had predicted his second coming before a generation passed away and that, unfortunately, he was wrong. Sadly, you still find this

---

2 For all these sorts of background issues about authorship, audience, date, etc., see my *Invitation to the New Testament* (New York: Oxford University Press, 2012).

mistake in many scholarly works as well as in the speculations of laypeople. If, however, one knows how to read the structure of the Olivet discourse in Mark 13, one will not make this major mistake in interpretation.

JESUS THE SAGE

Of the forty some parables of Jesus, we want to take a little time to look in depth at a couple of the most famous of the longer or narrative parables—in Mark 4 the parable of the sower and in Luke 10 the famous parable of the Good Samaritan.

By way of reminder, the Greek word *parabolē*, from which we get the word *parable*, has a broader range of meaning than our English word. For example, in Luke 4:23 the metaphorical saying "Physician heal yourself" is called a *parabolē*. So, what does this word mean in the Greek? Basically it refers to metaphorical speech that involves an analogy ("the kingdom of God is like a sower who . . ."). The analogy can be short or long. It can involve a simple sentence, a proverb, or a riddle; or it can be as complex as a short story—like the parable of the Good Samaritan. Note that metaphors or extended metaphors compare two things that are basically unlike each other, except in some particular respect where they are similar. So when the psalmist says that when God came down to judge the earth and "the hills skipped like rams," there is only one way in which hills and rams are alike—they bounce or bound from time to time when danger or disaster is afoot. C. H. Dodd added that parables are meant to "tease the mind into active thought." They are not intended to be simple, obvious stories; they are meant to prompt deep reflection and musing.

Here is the text of the famous parable of the sower in Mark 4:2–9:

He began to teach them many things in parables, and in his teaching he said to them: "Listen! A sower went out to sow. And as he sowed, some seed fell on the path, and the birds came and ate it up. Other seed fell on rocky ground, where it did not have much soil, and it sprang up quickly, since it had no depth of soil. And when the sun rose, it was scorched; and since it had no root, it withered away. Other seed fell among thorns, and the thorns grew up and choked it, and it yielded no grain. Other seed fell into good soil and brought forth grain, growing up and increasing and yielding thirty and sixty and a hundredfold." And he said, "Let anyone with ears to hear listen!

The first thing to bear in mind is that this is not a full-fledged allegory. Not every detail in the parable has some symbolic reference to something outside the parable. For example the sun in the parable is not some sort of allegorical reference to the Son. But there are definitely allegorical elements in early Jewish parables. After all, they are a form of metaphorical analogy, and the subject is God's divine saving activity. It is also good to remember that these parables are not necessarily true to early Jewish life; they are true to the Kingdom. It is doubtful early Jewish farmers with only a little arable land would simply scatter seeds in a rocky field. They would first clear out the rocks the best they could, often making a retaining wall around the field with them. Or again, a hundredfold yield on an ancient grain crop would be miraculous, not merely "a really good year." But then the Kingdom, the divine saving work of God, is about miraculous events involving humans. Is it about ancient agriculture? Not so much. Finally, ancient farmers were unlikely to throw precious seed on a road. They were far more likely to prepare the soil, till it up, and then sow the seed. The sower in this parable does otherwise.

On careful reflection we have here a picture of Jesus the sower, presumably setting an example for his disciples of sharing the Good News (presumably the seed) with all sorts of people. One of the more interesting features about the parable is that what makes the decisive difference in the story is not the sower or the seed but, rather, the quality of the soil. The sower is the same and the seed is the same in each case, but the reception of the seed depends on the condition of the soil. In other words, this parable makes clear that the sower does not predetermine who will accept the seed and be fruitful and produce a crop. It's the soil that determines that issue. The sower sows the Word indiscriminately.

The second interesting thing about the parable is that there are both internal and external forces that can get in the way of producing the crop—it can be shallow or hard soil, but it can also be rocks in the way or birds that steal the seed. And then there is the most surprising thing of all. If this is a comment on Jesus's ministry, then Jesus is not like many bragging modern preachers—he admits there will be many failures, many who will not receive the Good News, or at least not for long. What he is saying is that the successes, however, are so astounding that they make it all worthwhile. It is not an exercise in futility but in fertility, at least in some cases. Thus, there are allegorical elements in the story, but the story is not symbolic in every detail.

Our second parable is perhaps an example of what happens when one becomes too familiar with a story—one misses a lot of the surprising elements. Luke is a master of the narrative parable whether you think of the parable of the prodigal son, the parable of the rich man and Lazarus, or the parable of the Pharisee and the tax collector—and we could go on. Our focus, however, will be on the most famous of all Lukan parables, the parable of the Good Samaritan. And here we will dig even deeper and go into more detail. What we will discover is that without a good understanding of the history of the relationship (or lack thereof) between Jews and Samaritans, we will miss the shocking character of the parable and its attempt at social commentary and social change. Here is the text (Luke 10:25–37):

> Just then a lawyer stood up to test Jesus. "Teacher," he said, "what must I do to inherit eternal life?" He said to him, "What is written in the law? What do you read there?" He answered, "You shall love the Lord your God with all your heart, and with all your soul, and with all your strength, and with all your mind; and your neighbor as yourself." And he said to him, "You have given the right answer; do this, and you will live." But wanting to justify himself, he asked Jesus, "And who is my neighbor?" Jesus replied, "A man was going down from Jerusalem to Jericho, and fell into the hands of robbers, who stripped him, beat him, and went away, leaving him half dead. Now by chance a priest was going down that road; and when he saw him, he passed by on the other side. So likewise a Levite, when he came to the place and saw him, passed by on the other side. But a Samaritan while traveling came near him; and when he saw him, he was moved with pity. He went to him and bandaged his wounds, having poured oil and wine on them. Then he put him on his own animal, brought him to an inn, and took care of him. The next day he took out two denarii, gave them to the innkeeper, and said, 'Take care of him; and when I come back, I will repay you whatever more you spend.' Which of these three, do you think, was a neighbor to the man who fell into the hands of the robbers?" He said, "The one who showed him mercy." Jesus said to him, "Go and do likewise."

The parable of the Good Samaritan is perhaps the most beloved and most belabored of all of Jesus's parables, along with the parable of the prodigal son found in Luke 15. It is one known to have been overread and overallegorized repeatedly by numerous church fathers such as Augustine. As Craig Evans warns,

> The man leaving Jerusalem does not represent fallen Adam's exit from Paradise (Gen. 3:22–24); the robbers do not represent Satan and his demons; "stripped him" does not refer to humanity's loss of immortality; the priest does not represent the Law nor the Levite the Prophets or some other part of the OT or Jewish practice; the Samaritan is not Jesus; the oil

and wine do not represent the Holy Spirit and/or gifts of the Holy Spirit; the inn is not the Church; the innkeeper is neither the apostle Paul nor the Holy Spirit; and the two silver coins refer neither to the sacraments of baptism and the Lord's Supper nor to anything else.[3]

The church fathers were not wrong that there are symbolic or allegorical elements in various of Jesus's parables; but the allegorical interpretation of the story in detail in a way that denudes it of its Jewish character and historical context and turns it into a story about later Christian ideas, institutions, and practices not only is anachronistic but also can be said to be anti-Semitic, anti-Jewish. Careful attention to the social context is required to avoid such mistakes.

The social context of this parable is especially important, so we have to be aware of the history of the debacle between Jews and Samaritans. Briefly, a great antipathy developed between Jews and Samaritans after the return of Judean Jews from the Babylonian exile sometime around 525 BC. Both Jews and Samaritans came to claim that their holy mountain was where the real temple was or should be built (Mt. Zion vs. Mt. Gerizim—see John 4). In Nehemiah 4:1–2 we are told that both the governor of Judea appointed by Darius (a man named Sanballat) and the "army" of Samaria were opposed to the rebuilding of the temple and the city walls in Jerusalem (cf. Ezra 4). A little over a century later (around 388 BC) the Samaritans did build their own temple on Mt. Gerizim, which in turn was destroyed by the Hellenized Jewish ruler John Hyrcanus in 128 BC (*Ant.* 13.254–256).

These two sets of actions only raised the level of antipathy between Jews and Samaritans. In fact, it is not too much to say that by Jesus's era there was racial hatred involved between these two groups. Most Jews would be likely to see the idea of a Good Samaritan as an oxymoron, a contradiction in terms. Josephus suggests that Samaritans were somewhat quixotic, claiming to be related to Jews when the latter group was prospering but claiming they were a separate race when things were not going well for Jews (*Ant.* 9.291). This is believable. Babylonian Talmud Sanhedrin 57a says that a Samaritan is one who is unworthy of receiving assistance from a Jew.

In short, the relationship between Jews and Samaritans was about as rancorous a situation as the modern Palestinian–Jewish conflict in Israel. Thus, we must realize that the Samaritan in this story is socially out of bounds, is in enemy territory,

---

3 See Craig A. Evans, *Luke* (Peabody, MA: Hendrickson, 1990), 178. On the many allegorical abuses of this story, see Robert H. Stein, *The Method and Message of Jesus' Teaching* (Philadelphia: Westminster, 1978), 45–55.

and is taking a considerable risk in helping a Jew on the road between Jericho and Jerusalem.

But there is another social factor to understand about this story. The lawyer who raised the question "who is my neighbor" is presumably an expert in Torah, and his associates, perhaps even his employers, would have been the priests and Levites mentioned in the story. The Temple complex had a host of scribal scholars or, as Luke calls them, "lawyers"; and they readily identified with and looked up to the priests and Levites. Thus, this parable is not a nice little generic lesson on being charitable or going the extra mile to help. It is actually a biting social commentary, with Jesus criticizing the views some of his fellow Jews have of Samaritans as a race or ethnic group, views that this lawyer himself may well have held.

Notice that the story begins in verse 25 with a question that is meant to "test" Jesus. The lawyer may not be hostile—he addresses Jesus in a respectful way as "teacher"—but nevertheless he is interested in justifying his own predilections and interpretations of these matters, as verse 29 suggests. The question at least initially is what must he, the lawyer, do to obtain everlasting life, and Jesus responds with a question, as was often his way—"what is written in the law?" Jesus treats the man as knowledgeable and literate, for he adds, "what do you *read* there?"

The lawyer in turn responds by reciting Deuteronomy 6:5 and Leviticus 19:28. This combination of texts already existed in early Judaism, as *Testament of Issachar* 5.2 and *Testament of Dan* 5.3 indicate. Indeed, we know from elsewhere that Jesus himself has cited the same OT texts and agrees with the lawyer's answer (cf. Mark 12:29–31; Matt. 22:37). Thus, it is unsurprising that verse 28 says that Jesus tells the man he answered correctly, to which Jesus adds "do this, and you will live" which is probably a quote from the same vicinity of the citation by the lawyer, namely, from Leviticus 18:5.

The story could have concluded at this juncture, but the lawyer wants to press a particular point, namely, the definition of *neighbor*; so he asks Jesus who qualifies. Verse 29 suggests that the lawyer wants to vindicate his own preconceived notions on this point. It needs to be realized that when someone asks the question "who is my neighbor?" he or she is surely asking for a boundary definition, or else he or she would not ask. It implies the question, "who is not my neighbor?" Notably, Jesus refuses to give a straight answer to that question; instead, he tells a story about how to be a neighbor to anyone and everyone.

The story begins at verse 30 with a man who presumably is a Jew since this is a story set in Judea and Jesus identifies the one person in the story who is not a Jew quite clearly. The man is going down the serpentine and dangerous road from Jerusalem to Jericho, a normal commuter route—in fact, a route that priests and

Levites regularly took because some of them, presumably those who could not afford to live in the high-rent district on Mt. Zion, actually lived in Jericho and commuted. This was not a short commute; it was some seventeen miles, but that was a journey that could certainly be made on foot in a day, especially since it was quite literally all downhill. The road drops some 3,300 feet in elevation as one travels from Jerusalem to Jericho; but the twists and turns and hills along the way made this journey perilous, for it was easy for bandits to lurk in one place or another and waylay someone on the road (as Josephus reminds us in *Jewish War*, 4.451–475). Such was the fate of the man mentioned at the beginning of the story. The man was stripped and left half-dead. Presumably we are meant to think that he appeared dead, though he was only comatose.

These sorts of narrative parables usually stick to the rule of having only three main characters and, more often than not, it is the third figure who is the hero. Verses 31 and 32 tell us that a priest and a Levite happened to be going down the road; they clearly see the man lying there, but both of them pass by on the other side of the road. The likely reason for this description ("passing by on the other side of the road") is that priests and Levites were, of course, very concerned to maintain ritual purity, and touching a corpse made them unclean for a week. They would be unable to do their job for a whole week if they touched this man. Now one can imagine the lawyer listening to this story, a lawyer who would identify with the priest and Levite and perhaps would be disappointed by their behavior; but then perhaps he would expect that some compassionate ordinary Jew would be spoken of next as one who stops and helps the man. If this is what he anticipated as the story went along, he was about to be thrown a world-class curveball.

Verse 33 indicates a surprising development—"but lo, a certain journeying Samaritan came near him and seeing, he had compassion."[4] Note the emphatic position of the word *Samaritan* in the Greek sentence. Notice as well how unlike the priest and Levite, the Samaritan, even though he is in dangerous territory (doubly dangerous since he is a Samaritan), is not self-protective or self-regarding. Instead, he slows his journey and puts himself at greater risk by helping this man. He bandages the man's wounds, using oil to sooth the hurt of the bruises and wine, with its alcohol, to clean the cuts.[5] But this is not all. He could have stopped at that, having done his good deed for the day; but he does not. He places the man on his own pack animal and carts him all the way to the inn in Jericho. Verse 34

---

4 Notice already the contrast with "passed by on the other side."
5 On these two things used as healing agents in this age and context, see Mishnah *Shabbat* 14:2 and 19:4.

indicates that he does not just dump the man in the lap of the Jewish innkeeper; rather, he takes care of him for the rest of the day.

The next day the man goes to the innkeeper, takes out two denarii, and pays the innkeeper to take care of the man until he can return; and he promises to pay whatever additional cost accrues while he was away. This was clearly above and beyond the call of normal neighborly duty, even between a Jew and a Jew. Since a normal day's room and board would have been about one-twelfth of a denarius, what he had given should have been plenty to last for a good number of days.

It is at this crucial juncture in the story that Jesus turns to the lawyer in verse 36 and asks him which man has been a neighbor to the man lying on the side of the road. The lawyer again answers correctly, "the one who showed him mercy," though perhaps he does so reluctantly, for he does not call the hero "the Samaritan." In a further shocking development, Jesus then says in verse 37, "Go and do likewise," which in essence meant go and be like this Samaritan, go and expand your understanding of neighbors and neighborliness. The great lesson about compassion and mercy is brought home in a vivid way. "Divine mercy does not ask the worth of the recipient. It only sees the need."[6]

It is quite probable that 2 Chronicles 28:8–15 was in Jesus's mind when he told this parable, for there we have the story of how Samaritans, after Samaria had defeated Judah and acting on the advice of a prophet, had treated their captives with mercy. In fact, the story says they clothed the naked, gave them food and drink, anointed them, carried the disabled on donkeys, and brought them to Jericho. Thus, even in the very book that the lawyer revered, there was an example of neighborly and compassionate behavior involving Samaritans and Jericho. Jesus believed that the coming of the eschatological saving reign involved the deconstruction of the old paradigms, prejudices, and boundaries. If this meant the annulling or treating as obsolete various of the Torah's rules about clean and unclean, so be it. The higher principles of the law of love and compassion were being upheld.

WHAT JUST HAPPENED?

In this chapter we learned a good deal of interesting things about Jesus as a wordsmith—whether operating in a prophetic or a wisdom mode. Jesus's teachings were not merely memorable; at least in the case of the parables, he put them into

---

6 Frederick W. Danker, *Jesus and the New Age. A Commentary on St. Luke's Gospel* (Fortress Press, 1988), 133.

a form that made them easily memorizable as well, especially in an oral culture where oral memory could be considerable. We also learned that looking at biblical texts in considerable detail and paying attention to the structure of the material (Mark 13) and the historical context of the material (Luke 10) can be crucial to not only avoiding a bad misinterpretation of the text (like Schweitzer's view that Jesus predicted the end of the world in his own lifetime) but in fact being on the right track to understanding clearly and precisely what the text means. Context always matters, especially when one is dealing with either very controversial or very familiar biblical texts that are prone to being misused and misinterpreted.

FOR FURTHER READING

On the subject of Jesus as an eschatological prophet, see my *Jesus, Paul, and the End of the World: A Comparative Study in New Testament Eschatology* (Downers Grove, IL: InterVarsity Press, 1992). On the subject of Jesus as a sage and teller of parables, see David Flusser, *The Sage from Galilee*, with R. Steven Notley (Grand Rapids, MI: Eerdmans, 2007).

DIGGING DEEPER—
PAUL: HIS
REFLECTIONS
on HYMNS
and HIM

*About midnight, Paul and Silas were praying and singing
hymns to God and the prisoners were listening to them.
Suddenly, there was an earthquake.*
—ACTS 16:25–26

Figure 14.1 The earliest image of Paul, with Thecla, found in a cave church above Ephesus. (© Mark R. Fairchild, PhD)

WHERE ARE WE GOING?

In this chapter we will explore what Paul said about Christ and what he said about himself. We find Paul using hymnic material to praise and explain Christ in Philippians 2 and biographical material to explain the before and after of his own conversion. Both the genre of poetic hymns and the genre of biography can be used to convey serious theological and ethical content even when figurative language may be used.[1]

Though we have talked about the songbook in the OT, the Psalms, we have not talked about the NT evidence of the use of hymns, new hymns, Christological hymns created by Christians for their worship. Most scholars are convinced we have such evidence within the NT itself, so before looking at a particular example of these hymns in Philippians 2:6–11, a little context or background information is in order.

One of the things that characterized early Christians was singing. We see this even in non-Christian sources like the letter of Pliny the Younger to the emperor where he tells about Christians in his province (in Turkey) who meet at sunrise on the first day of the week to sing "hymns to Christ as to a god" (*Epistle* 10.96.7).

---

1 This chapter, like the Pauline material in general, goes into a little more depth and will serve as a good test as to whether the student is ready to take the "next steps," which we will discuss in the following chapter.

There were, in fact, various early Jewish groups who composed hymns as part of their devotion to God. Philo, for instance, tells us about such a group in the first century AD in Egypt called the Therapeutae: "Then the President rises and sings a hymn composed as an address to God, either a new one of his own composition or an old one by poets of an earlier day who have left behind them in many measures and melodies. . . . They all lift up their voices, men and women alike . . . two choirs one of men and one of women. . . . After choric dancing they form a single choir and sing until dawn" (*Vit. Cont.* 28–29, 68–80).[2]

It is thus not a surprise that Paul tells us in Ephesians 5:19 that Christians would sing to each other using psalms (the OT hymnbook), hymns, and spiritual songs (presumably spontaneous songs inspired by the Spirit). What does the word *hymns* refer to? Perhaps it refers to the new Christological hymns that were being composed for worship in the early church. We have portions of several of these hymns embedded in a variety of places in the NT. The best examples are found in John 1:1–5, 9–14; Colossians 1:15–20; Hebrews 1:2–4; 1 Timothy 3:16; and finally Philippians 2:6–11, on which we will focus here. Some of these hymn quotes are just fragmentary or partial, for example, 1 Timothy 3:16; but all of them reflect a certain pattern, a *V* pattern, which refers to a preexistent person (a person who existed in heaven before the creation of the universe), in this case the Son of God, who takes on flesh and becomes a human being, dies, and then is exalted to God's right hand. The hymns do not refer to the second coming of Christ but do talk at length about his preexistence and earthly existence and how God vindicated him beyond death.

Some of these texts focus more on the downward slope of the *V*, so to speak. For instance, in John 1, the Christological hymn is used to introduce the whole story of Jesus, and thus, not surprisingly, it does not go much beyond "and the Word took on flesh and dwelt among us."[3] Contrast this with 1 Timothy 3:16, where the focus is on the upward slope of the *V*: "he appeared in flesh/was vindicated by the Spirit/was seen by angels/was preached among the nations/was believed on in the world/was taken up in glory."[4]

These hymns were, of course, tailored to the particular context in which they were used. We do not have simple quotations but rather adaptations of the hymn. S, for example, in Hebrews 1 the author, who is very concerned to present Christ

---

2 On the parallels to the writing of new hymns at Qumran, see my *Jesus the Sage: The Pilgrimage of Wisdom* (Minneapolis, MN: Augsburg Fortress, 1994), 250–251.

3 Though the phrase "we have seen his glory" may refer to the resurrected Jesus, note that there is really no account of the transfiguration in the Fourth Gospel.

4 The inserted lines represent the line breaks in the hymn.

Figure 14.2 It was in these sorts of arenas in Rome and elsewhere in the Greco–Roman world where Christians were sometimes martyred, beginning under the reign of Nero. (© Mark R. Fairchild, PhD)

as our heavenly high priest, will include the idea of a priest offering a sacrifice for purification from sins in his opening use of the hymnic material: "his Son, whom he appointed heir of all things/and through whom he made the universe/the Son is the radiance of God's glory/and the exact representation of his being/sustaining all things by his powerful word/*After he had provided purification for sins*/he sat down at the right hand of the Majesty in heaven" (Heb. 1:2–3, author's italics). One thing that characterizes these hymns in general is a very high Christology, even referring to how Christ was present with God and involved in creating the universe. This becomes especially clear in this much fuller Christological fragment in Colossians 1:15–20:

> He is the image of the invisible God/the firstborn of all creation/for in him all things in heaven and on earth were created/things visible and invisible/ whether thrones or dominions or rulers or powers/all things have been created through him and for him/He himself is before all things/and in him all things hold together/He is the head of the body, the church/he is the

beginning, the firstborn from the dead/so that he might come to have first place in everything/For in him all the fullness of God was pleased to dwell/ and through him God was pleased to reconcile to himself all things/whether on earth or in heaven/by making peace through the blood of his cross.

What we see here, also in Hebrews 1 and again in Philippians 2, is that the death on the cross is the bottom of the *V*, the nadir of the downward journey of the Son. Sometimes the elements in the hymn are rearranged a bit to suit the narrative context, as here in Colossians 1:15–20 where the cross is mentioned last in the hymn fragment. The word *firstborn*, found twice in this hymn fragment, is a little misleading because what the author is trying to say is that Christ is preeminent over creation and over the new creation by means of his resurrection. The author is not claiming that Jesus was the first creature made by God or the first person God raised from the dead. In these hymns, Christ is portrayed as on the God side of the ledger; in particular, he is the creator of all things, in him all things hang together, and he is the redeemer of all things. The Son is not just a demigod with some part of God in him; rather, the fullness of God dwells in the Son so that he too can be called God. This brings us to perhaps the most sublime of all these Christological hymns, in Philippians 2:5–11. We will look at it in considerable detail.

CHRIST THE PARADIGM

Verse 5—Have the same mindset in yourself which was also in Christ Jesus

Verse 6—Who being in the form of God

Did not consider taking advantage of being equal to God

Verse 7—But stripped/emptied himself

Taking the form of a slave

Verse 8—Being born in the likeness of human beings

And being found in appearance as a human being

Humbled himself

Being obedient to the point of death

But the death on the cross.

Verse 9—Therefore also God exalted him

And gave him the name which is above all names

Verse 10—In order that at the name of Jesus

Every knee might bend, heavenly and earthly and subterranean

Verse 11—And every tongue might confess publicly

That the Lord is Jesus Christ, unto the glory of God the Father.

THE DOWNWARD ARC

Philippians 2:5–11 consists of a transitional verse (verse 5) followed by a two-part structure involving self-humbling (verses 6–8), followed by divine exaltation (verses 9–11).[5] From a rhetorical point of view the hymn itself is an example of *epideictic* rhetoric, the rhetoric of effusive praise (Aristotle, *Rhet*. 1.33–34), but Paul has chosen to use the hymn for a deliberative purpose and in a deliberative argument, calling for imitation and like-mindedness. Indeed, Christ is the paragon of paradigms and provides a climax to the early arguments in Philippians that presents Paul, his coworkers, and then Christ as examples the Philippians should emulate.

Verse 5 is a crucial transitional verse that sets up how the hearer is to interpret the hymn that follows and the frame of reference in which it is to be understood. The "this" here ("have *this* mindset") could be either retrospective (the mindset already described in 2:1–4) or prospective (the mindset of Christ about to be described) or both, but it is most likely the former. Certainly, the reference to a mindset echoes what was said in verse 2, and he has already described briefly the sort of humble unitive mindset he has in mind in verses 1–4. Paul is drawing an analogy between Christ and believers or, better said, between Christian behavior and that of Christ, with Christ providing the leading example. He is asking them to strive to emulate Christ (2 Cor. 8:9; Rom. 15:1–3).

This, however, brings up a further point. Should we understand the Greek prepositional phrase to mean "within each one of you" or to mean "among you"? The former would provide us with a more exact parallel between Christ and believers, but the context favors the latter rendering because Paul is strengthening the

---

5 What follows in the rest of this chapter can be found in a much fuller form in my *Paul's Letter to the Philippians: A Socio-Rhetorical Commentary* (Grand Rapids, MI: Eerdmans 2011).

unity among the community members in Philippi in this discourse. If the discourse is trying to promote self-sacrificial interpersonal Christian behavior as a way to strengthen the community's unity and aid it to walk in a manner worthy of the gospel, which is to say in a manner like the story of Christ as depicted in Philippians 2:5–11, then the latter rendering clearly suits this largely rhetorical aim better. The mindset of Christ that led to a certain course of conduct that provides the pattern will then be explicated beginning with the relative clause in verse 6.

Verses 6–8 belong together and bristle with exegetical and theological issues, which have been debated almost since the time of Paul. It is important to see the structure of this material to get a sense of its flow, and here I offer a translation that is a bit less literal than the one at the beginning of this section.

> *Who,*[6] *being in very nature God*[7]
> *Did not consider equality with God something to be taken advantage of*
> *But emptied*[8] *himself*
> *Taking the very nature*[9] *of a slave*
> *Being made in human likeness*
> *And being found in appearance as a human being*
> *He humbled himself*[10]
> *And became obedient until death—*
> *Even death on a cross!*

It is useful at the outset to raise the question of what happens to social hierarchies in the Philippian church if the exhortation given here, to have the mindset of and follow the self-sacrificial practices of Christ, is followed. By this schema, leaders become head servants, though they still are leaders; and even the lowliest gain respect because Christ took on their station and hallowed it. In other words, while

---

6 One of the key signals that we are dealing with a quotation, in this case a quotation from a Christological hymn, is the use of "who" to introduce the material and link it to what came before (see also Col. 1:15).

7 The question about this clause is, Is it causal or concessive? I tend to think it is the latter—"even though he was in very nature God, he did not consider. . . ."

8 The Greek verb is reflexive, and its normal meaning is "to empty."

9 The parallel construction between verses 6 and 7 requires the same translation in each verse. If one goes with "form" for *morphē* in verse 6, one must do the same in verse 7. The problem with the translation "form" is that Paul does not want to say that Christ merely *appeared* to be or played the role of a servant any more than he wants to say Christ merely appeared to or had the form of God. God is spirit and has no form anyway.

10 Again, this is a reflexive verb. This was something freely taken on by the Son.

this passage should not be seen to deconstruct all hierarchy in the community (leaders are still leaders, and Paul will appeal to them as overseers, deacons, and coworkers), it does have a way of stressing the equality of being of all the members of the community and produce a certain leveling effect. After all, if the head of the body can renounce his privileges and prerogatives and take on the roles of a servant, indeed even die a slave's death, then no one should see the roles of servants as beneath their dignity ever again within the Christian community.

The key terms in this hymn need to be interpreted together as they have overlapping semantic ranges. Of the three terms, *schēmati* is the one that most clearly means the way something appears to human senses, its external and changeable appearance. Thus, for example, in 1 Corinthians 7:31 when Paul says the *schēma* of the world is passing away, what he does not mean is that the material substance of the world is vanishing; rather, its outward form is changing. By contrast, *morphē* normally connotes an outward form that fully expresses the real being or substance that underlies it. Thus, when applied to Christ, it most likely means he manifested a form that truly represents the very nature and being of God, hence the translation "being in very nature God." The terms *morphē* and *eikōn* should not be equated or seen as synonyms. The former connotes something more than the latter. That Adam was created in God's image (*eikōn*) does not mean he had God's form or essence. Whenever in the LXX humanity is referred to as having been created in God's image, it is always with the use of *eikōn* and never with *morphē*. These two terms are not synonymous.

As for the term *harpagmos* in verse 6, it occurs only here in the NT and never in the LXX, and it is rare in other Greek literature. Though it has been endlessly debated, this word, when in combination with the verb, involves an "idiomatic expression [which] refers to something already present and at one's disposal" and thus one should translate the much belabored phrase "he did not regard the being equal to God as something to be taken advantage of."[11]

This phrase then is not about Christ grasping after or attempting to grab or steal something (*harpagmos* in other contexts and with other verbs can refer to robbery or the booty obtained by robbery or even rape, for in such contexts it refers to an illegal action, i.e., stealing from or "ripping off" of someone else) but rather about his not taking advantage of, or using, something he already had. This verse is unique in revealing to us something that Christ refrained from or did not do but

---

11 R. W. Hoover, "The Harpagmos Enigma: A Philological Solution," *Harvard Theological Review* 64 (1971): 95–119, here 118. See the full discussion in N. T. Wright, "Harpagmos and the Meaning of Phil. 2.5–11," *Journal of Theological Studies* 37 (1986): 321–352.

could have done. This way of reading verse 6 comports perfectly with what came before in Philippians 2:4 so that Christ becomes the ultimate example of one who does not pursue his own interests or selfishly take advantage of rights, privileges, and status that were by rights his but rather one who "emptied himself." This allows one to give full weight to the contrast between verse 6b and verse 7a. As Karl Barth puts it, the Son "is so much God's Equal that he does not . . . have to make of his equality with God a thing to be asserted tooth and nail . . . it is beyond dispute."[12]

Verse 7 then tells us that Christ stripped or emptied himself. But of what? Some translations try to get around the straightforward implication of the verb here by rendering the text "he made himself nothing," but that does not convey the important idea that something was set aside, at least for a period of time. Notice, for example, other places where Paul uses this verb. In 1 Corinthians 1:17 it's about the cross of Christ being emptied of its power. In Romans 4:14 it's about faith being emptied of its value. Our text does not tell us directly what he emptied himself of, but clearly some kind of self-imposed limitations are implied. The position of the word *himself* is emphatic, anticipating that the audience will find this surprising. In a world full of glory grabbers and social climbers and robbers, someone who stripped or emptied himself of something valuable would be seen as strange at best.

I would suggest that the phrase "he did not consider the being equal to God something to be taken advantage of" provides the clue we need. There are privileges, powers, and prerogatives that a deity has. There is a status, a standing, a rank that a deity has above all others. In status-conscious Philippi, what Paul is stressing is that Christ stripped himself of his divine privileges and status and took on the responsibilities, limitations, and status of a human being, indeed of a servant among human beings, the lowest of the low. In other words, we should read this passage in a social way, in light of the given social order in Philippi.

Just as Paul is not asking the Philippians to give up their Roman citizenship and the identity that came with that in order to truly be a citizen of the heavenly commonwealth, so he is not suggesting that Christ gave up his heavenly identity in order to be a human being. What he gave up was his privileges and status in order to self-sacrificially serve others and even die for them. So, too, the Philippians are to take on the mindset of Christ and not to view their social status and privileges in the way they have in the past, which should lead to different and more self-sacrificial behavior. This is a discussion about mindset and social behavior and, thus, about the way one views one's self and one's status and how one heeds the exhortation to look not to one's own interests but rather to the interests of others.

12 Karl Barth, *Epistle to the Philippians* (Louisville, KY: Westminster/John Knox Press, 2002) 62.

What Paul is suggesting is a twofold condescension by the divine Son of God. He became a human being and not only so; he became a servant among and of human beings. A dramatic picture of just what this could entail is found in the foot-washing episode in John 13:5–17. Slaves, of course, had no rights at all; indeed, they were considered living property and were entirely under the authority of their masters.[13] The issue is self-limitation.

What then are the natural limitations of being human? They include limitations of time, space, knowledge, power, and mortality. Sin, in Paul's mind, is not a natural limitation, one with which Adam was created, but rather one that came by a bad choice and by inheritance. Paul is suggesting that for the Son to be truly human, he took on the limitations we all naturally face—of time, space, knowledge, power, and mortality (hence obedient until death). But this is not all. Paul also wants to suggest that the Son took on the limitations of the lowest of human beings—of persons bought with a price, persons sold in a market, persons who were the property of others, persons whose lives were not their own, persons who are under authority and go and do what they are told to go and do. The Son came not to be served but to serve and give his life a ransom for the many, to die the death of a rebellious slave in fact.

All too often lost in the theological debates about this passage is the social and ethical thrust and implications of what Paul is saying—the Philippians need to have the mind of a servant and, if need be, be prepared to give their lives self-sacrificially for others, thinking not of their own best interests but those of others. This should put an end to the vicious cycles of reciprocity, rivalry, preening, status-seeking, and the like. Honor is being redefined as following the example of Christ, and the self-sacrifice on the cross is no longer seen as shame (though it remained a scandal) but rather the ultimate example of self-sacrificial love.

Looked at from the perspective of social identity theory, one can say that at the incarnation the Son assumed a secondary identity, a human one, which became primary during his time on earth. It is interesting, however, that in this hymn there is no stress on his becoming a Jewish human being, unlike in Galatians 4:4. The focus here is more generic—on the Son's humanity in general and his assuming the limitations of that and of servants. This comports nicely with what Paul says in 2 Corinthians 8:9, on how Christ gave up riches in order that he might be poor so that through his poverty believers might become rich. The implication for the Philippians is that they need to see their secondary identity as citizens of

---

13 For a detailed look at what Paul has to say about slavery, see my *The Letters to Philemon, Colossians and Ephesians* (Grand Rapids, MI: Eerdmans, 2007).

a heavenly commonwealth as their primary identity now and so norm their mind-set and behavior accordingly, living lives worthy of the Good News, which is to say the story of Christ, the pattern of which is provided here. Just as the Philippians don't cease to be Philippians and human beings when they become new creatures in Christ but rather have a transvaluation of values and outlooks, so by analogy the same can be said when the Son takes on human identity.

Though the Adamic reading of this text has a long history (see, e.g., Irenaeus, *Haer.* 5.16.2–3; cf. 3.22.1–4), Adam never experienced existence which amounted to being equal to God or being in the form of God (form is not equal to image), nor was he ever asked to give it up. In fact, it is Eve, not Adam, who is tempted to "be like God"; and indeed, Eve and Adam obtained the knowledge of good and evil. They did not merely grasp after it (see Gen. 3:22). According to Philippians 2, the Son took the form of a human being. He did not already have it. It will not do to talk about an eternally preexistent human being since the verb *took* means there was a point in time before which the Son did not have the form of a human being. Adam, by contrast, was created in the image of God and before that event did not exist at all.

Verse 7 brings us to the point of asking whether Paul has in mind some sort of exchange. The Son exchanged the form of God for the form of a servant. First of all, we are not told anything which strongly supports such a notion. The "emptying of self" is not said to entail divestment of his divine nature, despite what those who are advocates of that sort of Christology might think. The Greek verb here can mean to empty or, in a metaphorical sense, to make of no effect or to deprive (cf. 1 Cor. 9:15; 2 Cor. 9:3; Rom. 4:14). What it does not mean is to exchange. And notice that it is *himself* that the Son emptied or deprived. The most obvious sense is that he emptied himself of the things which would have prevented him from being truly and fully human—his divine prerogatives and status, which can be contrasted in the extreme with the status and lack of choices and prerogatives of a servant.

Scholars have been about equally divided about whether and to what degree we have echoes of the Isaianic servant songs in this passage. On the one hand, the allusions to the Servant of Isaiah seem clear in some places. R. Bauckham, for example, suggests the following:

Phil. 2.7—emptied himself Isaiah 53.12—poured himself out
Form of a slave/human likeness Isaiah 52.14; 53.2—form/appearance
Phil. 2.8—humbled himself Isaiah 53.7—he was brought low
Obedient to death Isaiah 53.12—to death

Phil. 2.9—therefore God exalted Isaiah 53.12—Therefore I will allot him a
Him to the highest place a portion with the great/Is. 52.13—exalted
And lifted up and shall be very high
Phil. 2.10—every knee bow Isaiah 45.22–23—"to me every knee will bow
Every tongue confess every tongue swear"[14]

What is most interesting about this list of parallels is that in some cases the parallel is with the Servant in Isaiah, but in the last case the parallel is with Yahweh himself. Bauckham suggests this hymn amounts to a reinterpretation of Isaiah 45 and 52–53. But there are some places where the analogy breaks down. In Isaiah, but not in Philippians 2, there is emphasis on the suffering and marring of the servant. In Isaiah, but not in Philippians 2, the death is said to be atoning and is connected with the forgiveness of sins. Furthermore, as I have shown, some of the particulars of the language here reflect the language used to describe the personification of Wisdom in earlier Jewish sapiential material, particularly Wisdom of Solomon 5–11.[15] There is a further problem with the notion that Paul is solely drawing on Isaiah here: that the language of *doulos* ("slave" or "servant") is not the same as the language of *pais* (which can mean "son" or "servant") in the LXX of Isaiah 52–53 or 45. True, the language of *doulos* is used in other passages in Isaiah 40–55, but Bauckham is arguing on the basis of these particular passages and not, for example, Isaiah 42:19, 48:20, or 49:3–5. These passages are clearly not echoed here in Philippians 2, and the language of slavery, particularly because of the specific reference to the slave's death on a cross, seems important to the sense of Philippians 2. The title "my servant" in Isaiah 52:13 is used in a positive honorific sense (like calling other prophetic figures God's servants), but here in Philippians 2 it is doubtful *doulos* would be heard in that sense at all by the Philippians. But there are more problems. Isaiah 53:12 is about the death of the Servant. The language of pouring out of a life in death and thus being brought low is not comparable to the language about the Son emptying himself to become human. The Servant doesn't humble himself; he is taken away in humiliation, according to Isaiah 53:8. That is a very different matter.

Bauckham is right, however, that in both sets of texts we have the contrast between what the Servant did and then what God did on behalf of the Servant after his demise. It seems to me at the end of the day that the most that can be said is

---

14 Richard Bauckham, *God Crucified: Monotheism and Christology in the New Testament* (Grand Rapids, MI: Eerdmans, 1998), 59.
15 Witherington, *Jesus the Sage*, 257–263.

that there is a clear allusion to Isaiah 45 at the end of Philippians 2, where language previously applied to Yahweh is applied to Christ. I agree as well that the self-sacrifice contrasted with God's exalting the person is found in both Isaiah 53 and Philippians 2. My point is that the Servant in Isaiah does not preexist or take on human form or have equality with God any more than Adam does. So it is a mistake to overread Philippians 2 in light of Isaiah 52–53.

I would say that Isaiah is only one font of ideas and images from which the author has drawn to compose this Christ hymn, and the most important allusion to Isaiah, to Isaiah 45, goes to prove that Christ is God, not that Christ is the servant. In sum, Philippians 2:5–11 is rich with intertextual possibilities; but when it comes to the really most significant parallels, parallels that make clear the divinity of Christ, they come from Wisdom of Solomon, on the one hand, and Isaiah 45, which speaks of Yahweh, on the other hand. Thus, the beginning and ending of the hymn are about his divinity, and the middle is about his humanity and the form and focus it took.

The order of the clauses, "taking the form of a slave" and "being born in the likeness of human beings his appearance was found as human" suggests that the emphasis is on the former rather than the latter two clauses. Thus, the stress with the strongly adversative *but* in verse 7a is on the contrast between his being in the form or nature of God and being in the form of a slave/servant and on the way he got from the former to the latter by stripping or emptying himself in some fashion.

The latter two clauses are about his humanity in general, not about his status or assumed roles as a slave or servant. They do not say he was like *a* human but rather like human beings as a group. Both his birth and human nature are fully human. Thus, "being born in human likeness" does not imply he was in some respects unlike us; it means he assumed the very same human conditions as we experience—he was born, he lived as a human being and so was mortal, and he died. Again, the comparison with Galatians 4:4b is instructive—born of woman, born under the law.

Paul suggests that there was nothing extraordinary about the birth of Jesus itself; he came into the world the normal way all humans since Adam do, by being born of woman. In Philippians 2 there is a strong stress on the Son's humanity; in Galatians 4 the stress is on his Jewishness. Not only was Jesus fully human but this is how he was seen by, or appeared to, others. He did not look or appear any different from any other normal human being. No halo hovered slightly above his head. No angelic glow radiated from his face, except perhaps on the Mount of Transfiguration. Notice that the two clauses about his humanity aren't stressing some action he deliberately took—birth happened to him, and others saw he was a human being.

The choices came when he emptied himself and deliberately took on the "form" of a slave or servant.

It would not have been shocking to Gentiles to hear that their God had chosen to take on human form (they had heard such stories of Zeus and Hermes, among others), but to be told that their God had chosen to become a slave among humans was a very different story, a shocking story because it deconstructed everything they thought was written in stone about the hierarchical nature of reality and relationships and about all of their honor and shame codes. It was one thing to have a Saturnalia, when slaves became masters and vice versa for a day. It was another matter entirely to suggest that a person equal to God (and not just any God but the only true God) came in person to earth and chose to become a slave and live his whole life that way, including the way he died. This was an epic-making tale that outstripped all previous epics including *The Odyssey*, *The Iliad*, and *The Aeneid*.

In verse 8, after two clauses about what happened to the Son who came in recognizably human form, the author resumes the discussion of what Christ himself chose to do and did—he humbled himself, and he was obedient even up to death. It does not say someone humbled Christ, unlike the Servant who was "made low," humbled by others. The strong emphasis on the Son making choices all along the way and including in regard to his death should not be missed. His death was not an accident. It was an act of obedience, but obedience to whom or what?

There is certainly nothing in Torah that required a Jewish king or messianic figure to die on a cross. The emphasis here is clearly on a particular kind of death—death on the cross. The final clause "but death on the cross" is crucial. This was more than just humbling himself; this was submitting to humiliation in an honor-and-shame culture. The bottom of the *V* pattern has been reached. Not only did the Son stoop to conquer, not only did he take on a slave's role and even die a troublesome slave's death, but he even submitted to the most shameful way to die imaginable (see Cicero, *Pro Rab.* 5.10).

It is hard to miss the fact that Paul is not here, unlike elsewhere (see, e.g., Rom. 3), reflecting on a theology of atonement. Here, his rhetorical concern is that the language be couched in terms to show the lengths to which Christ was prepared to go to consider not his own interests but those of others. In other words, the language is deliberately extreme, to shock the audience into following the example of self-humbling and self-sacrificial service as a cure for party spirit, rivalry, or tensions in the community. Such attitudes or thoughts of status seeking or climbing the honor ladders of society are squelched here with great force. The call to obedience, even obedience unto death, even a humiliating death, is stark.

Notice that the Son was not inherently obedient or compliant with God's Word and will by nature. The text says he "became" obedient. This must be taken to mean that his willing it to be so was crucial and decisive (cf. Heb. 5:8 about Christ learning obedience; Rom. 5:19; even Luke 2:51–52). He was not automatically or inherently obedient. Choice was involved. "Jesus can serve as a moral example only if his obedient humility was voluntary rather than automatic or enforced."[16]

Though Paul does not elaborate, we must assume that he is alluding to Christ's obedience to God even until death on a cross (see Gal. 1:4). Much is implied by this, but nothing is more fully explicated. The phrases in a Christ hymn like this are charged and packed with meaning, but they are not unpacked here. The Greek phrase in this last clause of the first half of the hymn must mean "until death" not "unto death."

Paul only once elsewhere discusses the obedience of Christ, in Romans 5:9, where obedience is paralleled by "an act of righteousness." This suggests a reference not just to Christ's righteous life but to a particular act of righteousness, namely, his freely chosen death. It is interesting that in Philippians 3:18 Paul speaks of those who are enemies of the cross of Christ. There may be a subtle rhetorical anticipation here of the polemic there. Christ's obedience then was without limit and without regard to his own reputation. Jesus did not choose the honorable death of the zealot or the resistance fighter who dies in and for the struggle against oppression. He did not follow the Greek practice of honorable suicide either. Crucifixion was universally reviled as a horrible and shameful way to die, not a noble or honorable way to die.[17]

As Paul indicates in Galatians, some Jews could see it in the light of Deuteronomy 21:23 as a sign that the person had been cursed by God. For a Jew, the thought of the one expected to be most anointed and blessed by God, namely, God's messiah, being cursed by God was almost unthinkable. For a Gentile, the thought of their God willingly dying on a cross was equally unthinkable. Indeed, even the word *cross* was not welcome in polite company. Cicero says "The very word 'cross' should be far removed not only from the person of a Roman citizen, his thoughts, his eyes, and his ears" (*Rab. Perd.* 16). In short, it was obscene and should not be mentioned. The shock value of Paul's argument here should not be minimized for Gentiles, in general, and Roman citizens, in particular.

If we are wondering why it is that crosses seem to have only become popular Christian symbols much later, this is why—no one was likely to be turning crosses

---

16 Markus Bockmuehl, *The Epistle to the Philippians* (Peabody, MA: Hendrickson, 1998), 138.
17 See the still useful study of Martin Hengel, *Crucifixion in the Ancient World* (Philadelphia: Fortress Press, 1977).

into jewelry in the first century AD any more than American jewelers today make little electric chair replicas in gold or silver to wear around one's neck. The cross in the first century had an entirely negative and horrific connotation and didn't suggest salvation or redemption at all. It suggested "termination with extreme prejudice." This is precisely why, unless something positive happened to Jesus beyond crucifixion, like his arising, it is very difficult to explain historically how Christianity ever arose at all. Crucifixion should have ended once and for all any notions that Jesus was anyone special. Just as the cross was an abrupt end for some one, so the close of verse 8 is abrupt—the phrase "death on a cross" apparently intentionally breaks up the nice rhythmic pattern and rhetorical flow of the text. By the end all of the emphasis falls on the word *cross*, the unmentionable word. "Like the crescendo of a drum roll, the reverberation of the word 'death' brings the first half of the hymn to a deafening silence before the cross. The last word to be heard is 'cross.'"[18] The social question this first half of the hymn raises is, What does it mean and what sort of transvaluation of cultural values in Philippi does it take to praise and celebrate the death of a slave on a cross?

THE UPWARD ARC

The dramatic upward turn in the *V* pattern begins in verse 9, of course, with the word *therefore*. More precisely, we have two conjunctions here, *therefore* combined with *and*. Together they normally introduce a result. A conclusion is being drawn, not merely in the syllogistic sense but in the sense that God drew a conclusion about the Son and his birth, life as a servant and obedience even until death came. One could just as readily translate these two words here by the English phrase "that is why." Because the Son did *X*, God did *Y*. This comports with the notion that God vindicates righteousness and righteous behavior. One could even say God rewards it or at least always responds graciously to it.

One of the implications of this is that the Philippians are being urged to pursue a life like the Son's and so leave the exalting and glorifying in the hands of God, rather than engaging in a life of self-glorification and the taking on of honor challenges. One of the immediately noticeable differences between verses 6–8 and verses 9–11 is that while the Son is the actor in the former verses, in the latter verses he is the one acted upon—he is exalted and given a better name by God. Also, like what precedes them, verses 9–11 are one long sentence in the Greek. One can say

---

18 G. Walter Hansen, *The Letter to the Philippians* (Grand Rapids, MI: Eerdmans, 2009), 157.

that God vindicates the Son's obedience; in fact, one can say that his exaltation is precisely because of his obedient self-sacrifice.

If we compare Psalm 97:9, it reminds us that the main verb here means to "raise exceedingly high" or to "superexalt"; and it was used metaphorically of assigning a person to a high status so that the person would receive high honor, obedience, praise, and submission from people of lower status. The point is not that the Son was given a status higher than what he had when he preexisted, for there is no "up" from being equal to God, but that is he is given the highest position possible. Perhaps it is important to add that there is a difference between the Son who took on flesh and the Son after the resurrection, namely, that he existed in a resurrected, glorified body which he did not have before either the incarnation or initially after his earthly life ended in death. So there is an answer of sorts to "what more could be added to his previous divine status and identity."

The social implications of the hymn then continue to play out as it draws to a close, for if one's paradigm is a servant/slave who takes on servile ways and sets aside status and even honor (through dying on a cross), then the implication is that the Philippians should be prepared to engage in status-rejecting ways and even for public humiliation like Christ suffered. But Paul is also insisting strongly that one should evaluate such actions as God evaluates them, not as Greco–Roman culture would, and therefore, one may rightly expect vindication instead of vilification and glorification instead of condemnation by God on one's behalf at the eschaton. Christians, in short, are part of a commonwealth with very different sort of social codes about what counts as honorable, praiseworthy behavior and what status and rewards look like.[19]

It is right to compare 2 Corinthians 8:9, where we also find the language of Christ exchanging social status in the incarnation—he was rich, but for the believers' sake he became poor so that they too, in a different sense, could become rich and have a status change. John Chrysostom saw how Paul was emphasizing the paradigmatic nature of this material: "Nothing rouses a great and philosophic soul to the performance of good works so much as learning that as in this it is likened to God. What encouragement is equal to this? None!" (*Hom. Phil.* 6).

Just as God vindicated the Son, so too will he vindicate the believers if they will but be obedient until death. The Philippians are asked to see in the Christ hymn both a paradigm for their own behavior and the trajectory of what will happen if they are obedient—God will glorify them by means of conforming them to the image of his Son through resurrection. Of course, this does imply that the

---

19 See the helpful discussion in D. B. Martin, *Slavery as Salvation: The Metaphor of Slavery in Pauline Christianity* (New Haven, CT: Yale University Press, 1990), 130–131.

analogy applies in every way. Believers will not be given the divine name, nor will they be worshipped. But the point of the paradigm is to instill the mindset, life pattern of obedience, and vision of where this would lead in the Philippians.

The name which is above all names is, of course, the name of God; so Paul is not referring in verse 9 to the name *Jesus*, a name he was given at birth, but rather the name *Kyrios* ("Lord"), the LXX equivalent to *Yahweh* (see, e.g., Is. 42:8). The earliest Christian confession seems to have been "Jesus is [the risen] Lord," a title given to him, obviously enough, after his death and resurrection (see Rom. 10:9; 1 Cor. 12:3). The term *Kyrios* shows up an amazing 717 times in the NT, mostly in Luke–Acts and Paul's letters, which may tell us something of its popular provenance. Here, we are told of perhaps an unexpected outcome of God's vindicating him. Not only is he highly exalted and given the divine name but he will be universally worshipped as a result. In the biblical world a change of name connoted not only a change of status but often a new set of roles and functions and a new stage and direction of life (cf. Gen. 17:5; 32:28; John 1:42).

Verses 10 and 11 make clear the purpose of God's exalting and renaming the Son. What we have is a clause with two main verbs, *bow* and *confess/admit* introduced with the Greek word that means "in order that," indicating either purpose or result or perhaps both. The Son was given the divine name in order that every knee would bow and every tongue confess. The partial quotation of Isaiah 45:23 in verses 10 and 11 is important here, and the force of it must not be underestimated, for it comes from a portion of Isaiah where we hear, "I am the Lord, and there is none else . . . there is no other God besides me. . . . Turn to me and be saved all the ends of the earth . . . I have sworn by myself . . . that to me every knee will bow, every tongue will swear allegiance" (excerpts from vv. 18–25).

What is especially remarkable about the use of this partial quotation is that elsewhere Paul uses it of the Father (Rom. 14:11). Furthermore, we are now being told that it is Jesus to whom this worship will be directed at the eschaton, and far from subtracting from the glory of the Father, it will add to it. The Father hands over his throne name and the focus of the worship to the Son and suffers no diminution in the process. This, indeed, is what it means to be highly exalted by the Father. Even the Father, by doing this exalting and giving of a divine name to the Son, is in one sense modeling the role of a servant. Even more stunning is that in this same material in Isaiah 48:11 God says he will never give his glory to another. One can only conclude that Paul believed that the Son was not "another" in the sense that Isaiah had in mind, another order of being, someone less than God the Father.

Scholars have debated just how universal this recognition will be since it does say every knee will bow and every tongue acknowledge "Jesus is Lord." It may imply that even those who don't want to acknowledge Jesus is Lord will at the eschaton be forced to do so, willingly or unwillingly, simply because it will be such an obvious and unavoidable reality. The phrase "to bend the knee" means to acknowledge someone's authority, and it comes from a throne-room scene where someone or some group is submitting to the rule of some ruler (see Rev. 4–5). Furthermore, in the LXX the term regularly shows up in a context of worship. The partial quote of Isaiah 45 provides a clue as to Paul's thinking at this juncture, for Isaiah 45:24 refers not to universal salvation but rather to "all who have raged against him will come to him and be put to shame." Besides, Philippians 1:28 already referred to the destruction of those who oppose Christ.

To use an example where service is given but praise may be withheld, a person may well not want to swear allegiance to some particular president of the United States; but if, for example, he or she serves in the military, he or she will, one way or another, have to serve the commander in chief whether with a heavy heart or wholeheartedly. He or she cannot deny that the president is the president even if he or she is not pleased about it. The verb *confess* here need not imply praise with thanksgiving but rather "to admit" or "to acknowledge openly" (so 2 Macc. 7:37; cf. Rom. 14:10–12). Thus, I don't think we should see verses 9–11 as an example of pure rhetorical hyperbole, though that cannot be entirely ruled out, for it is clear enough that when throne names begin to be listed, hyperbole is often not far behind as one tries to exalt the person in question far above all others (see, e.g., the list of throne names in Is. 7:14 or 9:6; notice how a human-born child is named *Immanuel* or *Everlasting Father*).

Probably Paul has in view the eschatological scene where all sentient beings of the higher orders (angels, demons, humans) will make this confession. This need not mean they will all be converted, but it does mean they will not be able to avoid recognizing the truth about Jesus, like the demons in Mark 5:1–20. This view seems preferable to the suggestion that Jesus will have already banished all foes by the time this confession is made, though that is not impossible. This Christ hymn, unlike Colossians 1, does not focus on the *Christus Victor* theme or Christ's triumph over the principalities and power motif. Chrysostom was surely right that the categories "in heaven, on earth, and under the earth" do not specifically target angelic powers, whether malevolent or benevolent, but rather refer to the whole world of angels, humans, and demons (*Hom. Phil.* 7.2.9–11). The point is that nothing escapes or is outside of the lordship of Jesus. Indeed, some have suggested that all of creation is referred to here, not just the higher orders of sentient beings (cf. Ps. 148; Rev. 5:13).

None of this would make much sense if it were not the case that Paul thought of the Son as part of the Godhead, for if we were merely thinking of the exalting here of a human being, then Isaiah 45 would be a very poor choice of scriptural allusion. No, for Paul, Christ was equal to God from before the foundations of the world and would be recognized to be such at the eschaton. The language of high exaltation does not imply that the Father was acclaiming the Son to be something he wasn't before. Rather, he was bequeathing to him the role and title that were rightfully his, which he could resume after his period on earth in the form of a servant/slave. The language of exaltation here reflects the throne-room scene when the king is crowned and acclaimed to be the Lord, assuming new roles, duties, and authority.

Especially the stress on worship of the Lord makes clear that Paul believes the Son is also God and therefore may be worshipped as God. What we have here, as we also see at 1 Corinthians 8:6, is the Christological redefinition of monotheism to include more than one person.[20] In an important essay, R. Bauckham has reflected on the meaning of the phrase "God is One" in early Judaism. The declaration "the Lord our God, the Lord is one" in its original setting probably was a statement *against* polytheism. But that declaration, called the *Shĕma*, in which both the terms *God* and *Lord* applied to Yahweh, is in fact bifurcated in 1 Corinthians 8:6 so that God is said to apply to the Father and the Lord is said to be Jesus Christ. Would this have been a totally shocking and unbelievable development in early Judaism?

Bauckham's answer is no because what the oneness of God meant was a complex but unified being, or put another way, it was a way of referring to God's unique identity (hence the phrase could be rendered—"our God is unique") and so not a being that by nature could not express the Godhead in multiple persons. It was, in short, a statement about God's identity, not God's singularity. It seems obvious enough that the earliest Christians—all of whom were Jews, affirmed Jesus is Lord, and were prepared to talk about his being equal to God, indeed even calling him God (see Rom. 9:5)—did not find this stretching things too far.

But there are more social implications to this dramatic declaration than might seem apparent to us this far removed from first-century Philippi. All over the empire, especially in Roman colony cities, there were public inscriptions declaring the emperor as the ruler of all the world. The Philippians would have had to be tone-deaf to miss the resounding critique of such a view in this Christ hymn (cf. Acts 25:26). If Jesus is the one universal Lord, then the emperor certainly is not, whatever the imperial cult propaganda might say. This hymn then becomes a withering critique of the emperor cult. "That the one who was humiliated and crucified by Roman power is declared universally sovereign directly challenges the

---

20 See N. T. Wright, *The Climax of the Covenant: Christ and the Law in Pauline Theology* (London: T&T Clark, 1991), 121–136.

empire's version of how to achieve world rule. The story of a self-emptying Lord not only subverts Caesar's claims to universal dominion but also turns the whole Roman value system of what constitutes honor and power on its head." Indeed, Paul has just turned the *cursus honorum*, the honor ladder one had to climb to gain social status, upside down. The way up is not by social climbing or status seeking but by self-sacrifice and pursing the path of the Son who stepped down.[21]

In the end, the self-giving, the self-sacrifice, the servanthood belongs as much to the divine identity as does his glory and exaltation. As Stephen Fowl puts it, self-emptying is far from just a singular act of the Son. It is the basic disposition of the triune life of God (see above on the Father serving the Son).[22] This is why it is not a surprise that the cross and the sacrificed Lamb are seen elsewhere in the NT as the highest revelations of the character of God, for instance, in John 8:28 and 12:32–34 and in Revelation 5:6–14.

There is a paradox here, and it is well expressed by St. Augustine: "What greater mercy is there than this which . . . imposed 'the form of a servant' on the Master of the world—such that the Bread itself was hungry, Fullness itself was thirsty, Power itself was made weak, Health itself was wounded, and Life itself was mortal? . . . What greater mercy than that which presents to us the Creator created; the Master made a slave; the Redeemer sold; the One who exalts, humbled; the One who raised the dead, killed" (*Sermon* 207). Though Paul's letters are the earliest or some of the earliest Christian documents ever written, in the NT it is impossible to miss the high Christology of these documents. Jesus was being worshipped as God from the earliest days of the Christian movement, and what makes this especially shocking is that it was Jews like Paul leading the charge in that direction. Perhaps, as Richard Bauckham suggests, this is because they understood the confession "God is One" to mean God is unique, singular, not that God expresses the divine identity in only one person.

PAUL'S BIOGRAPHICAL REFLECTIONS

Paul was skilled not only at telling Christ's story but also at telling his own, and in both cases he is presenting his audience with something to imitate, a pattern of self-sacrificial life to follow. We will look at the relevant material in Philippians 3 here.

---

21 N. T. Wright, *Paul: In Fresh Perspective* (London: SPCK, 2005), 589; J. Hellerman, *Reconstructing Honor in Roman Philippi: Carmen Christi as* Cursus Pudorum (Cambridge: Cambridge University Press, 2005), 152–153.
22 Stephen E. Fowl, *Philippians* (Grand Rapids, MI: Eerdmans, 2005), 96–97.

What we should take note of at the outset is that narrative, or story, crops up and becomes crucial even in largely nonnarrative portions of the NT, in this case in Paul's deliberative rhetorical discourse in Philippians.

This reminds us once again that Paul does his theologizing and ethicizing out of his narrative thought world, not on the basis of a collection of abstract ideas or principles. This is why, earlier in this study, I cautioned about the process of abstracting such "theological" principles from the Bible, even though such a practice is inevitable and in some ways necessary. I warned about this because often what the text is teaching is theological ethics, not theology per se. This is the case with both of the examples being discussed in this chapter that come from Philippians.

In verses 4–6 Paul lists those traits of which he could well have boasted, if he were to evaluate them from a human and Jewish point of view.[23] If his opponents boast in circumcision, Paul was circumcised on the very day the Law required, something few, if any, in Paul's audience could claim. Paul was a Jew by birth ("of the gens Israel," as a Roman would put it), not through a process of conversion. *Israel* is not the term Jews tended to use with outsiders, but the point here is that Paul is using insider language of himself and his audience ("we are the circumcision"). This forestalls any arguments that the audience needs to do something to become a true Christian insider.

Furthermore, Paul was a "Hebrew of Hebrews." The meaning of this phrase can and has been debated, but it probably means a person who speaks Hebrew and came from a family where it was spoken (see Acts 6:11) as opposed to a **Diaspora** Jew who never learned to speak it. This likely tells us something about Paul's up-bringing and education, not merely in Tarsus, the place of his birth, but, as Acts 22 suggests, in Jerusalem. Acts 22:3 says Paul was brought up in Jerusalem and learned as a disciple of Gamaliel. There is good reason to accept this historical bit of information as accurate, as I have shown elsewhere.[24] Paul in addition was a Benjaminite, named Saul, after the first king of Israel, the most illustrious member of that tribe. The tribe itself was known for its faithfulness to Judah. The cumulative effect of the four phrases here is like that in 2 Corinthians 11:22, and its rhetorical function is to make clear that Paul could claim all the best there is to claim about being a Jew, both religiously and ethnically.

---

23 Obviously Greco–Roman persons would find these very odd things to boast about, especially circumcision which most Gentiles derided or despised from what we can tell.
24 See Witherington, *The Acts of the Apostles: A Socio-Rhetorical Commentary* (Grand Rapids, MI: Eerdmans, 1998), 666–670.

Paul turns from what he innately is by birth and upbringing to three phrases about what he once was and did, including his religious praxis: "according to Law a Pharisee, according to zeal, persecuting the church, according to righteousness from the Law, blameless." In terms of forensic righteousness, righteousness under some law (in this case, Mosaic Law), righteousness that consists in fulfilling legal expectations, Paul says he was blameless (spotless), by which is meant he could not be accused of breaking a Mosaic Law, committing a transgression, a willful violation of a known law. This should not be confused with a claim to be faultless, much less a claim to be perfect.

Paul is speaking here about his Pharisaic past and perhaps as a Pharisee. It is clear he was and is proud of this heritage. This makes all the more clear to the audience how much he was prepared to give up to be "found in Christ." The implication is that Paul is no longer a Pharisee, no longer an observant Jew in that sense. At the same time, a text like 1 Corinthians 15:9 makes perfectly clear that Paul the Christian knows in retrospect that Saul the Pharisee was certainly not without fault in God's eyes. How could he be when he had opposed God's Anointed One and had persecuted his followers? At the same time, the upshot of Philippians 3:6 is that prior to Paul's conversion to Christ, there is no evidence at all that Saul saw himself as the guilt-ridden individual described in Romans 7:13–25. "We do not have in this text [i.e., Phil. 3] a portrait of a man at war with himself, crucified between the sky of God's expectations and the earth of his own paltry performance. Paul is not in this scene a poor soul standing with a grade of ninety-nine before a God who counts one hundred as the lowest passing grade."[25]

Indeed, Paul, as described in Philippians 3, had a robust conscience as a Jew and saw himself as a law-keeper who could not be accused justly of being a law-breaker. It is only after the Damascus Road event in his life that Paul seems to have had and expressed remorse and regret about his behavior toward Christians and toward Christ while a Pharisee (see Gal. 1:13, 23; 1 Cor. 15:9; 1 Tim. 1:13). There is not a shred of evidence that Romans 7:14–25 describes Paul's mental outlook prior to his conversion to Christianity, and as Philippians 3 suggests, it hardly describes his views as a Christian looking back on his Jewish past; otherwise, he would hardly be bragging here about being faultless under the Mosaic Law.[26] Are the

---

25 Fred B. Craddock, *Philippians* (Atlanta: John Knox Press, 1985), 59.

26 I have shown at considerable length in Witherington, with Darlene Hyatt, *Paul's Letter to the Romans: A Socio-Rhetorical Commentary* (Grand Rapids, MI: Eerdmans, 2004), that Romans 7 is not Pauline autobiography of any sort. It is rather a textbook example of the rhetorical device called "impersonation."

Judaizers zealous? They could hardly outdo Paul for zeal since he persecuted the Jewish followers of Jesus as violators of the Law.

To make the contrast as bold and dramatic as possible, Paul in verses 7–11 says that he now counts all those "gains" as an observant Jew as loss, indeed as *skubalon* (defined in the next paragraph). In a deliberative argument it is normal to talk about benefits and gains past or future in order to persuade the audience to a particular course of behavior. We have accounting language here of "profit" and "loss" (cf. Matt. 25:16–17; Jas. 4:13). This is commercial rather than legal language, as is the language about "reckoning."

Notice that Paul does not say they are *skubalon* but that he now *reckons* them that way. The word *skubalon* can mean spoiled food, garbage (Sir. 27:4), or even dung. In Greek literature it is generally used of food (see Plutarch, *Moralia* 352D), and in Josephus it refers to human excrement (*Jewish War* 5.13.7). Occasionally, it can refer to food scraps left over from a meal and thrown to the dogs or other animals. The previous reference to dogs in Philippians 3:2 could even have prompted Paul to think of using this term here. Dogs ate scraps in antiquity (see Matt. 15:26–27 and par.). If the dog theme is still in play here, then the implication would be that these "dogs" are being contentious about things that Paul would consider just "scraps" at this point in time, compared to what he has in Christ. If, on the other hand, *skubalon* means "dung" here, then the reference would be to food the human body could not profitably use and so excreted.

In any event, Paul is saying that such earthly things have been totally eclipsed by the value of knowing Christ and the benefits one has in him. In fact, here alone in the whole Pauline corpus Paul talks about "gaining" Christ, using the mercantile language to which he adds the interesting phrase "and to be found in him." Found by whom? By God? When? At the final judgment? Or does Paul mean that he found his true self in Christ through union with Christ? It is probably a mistake to *underestimate* Paul's language about union with Christ and being "in Christ." This suggests something intimate, whether we want to call it mystical union or not; and Paul is prepared to press the language so far that he actually talks about participating in, and even filling up, the sufferings of Christ, sharing a death like his and being raised by the power of his resurrection.

The only thing now to place totally on the credit side is knowing Christ and the power of his resurrection. Paul considered and continues to consider all other things which were good before as a loss. Christ is the one thing of supreme value. Notice that in verse 8 Paul actually says he has lost everything. This certainly meant his status as a Pharisee, various Jewish friends, probably property, and perhaps even his wife and family. Because of the age at which Paul came to Christ, it is indeed likely he had a wife and family already.[27] The point is that Paul gave it all up or reckoned it all as a loss in order to follow Christ and be the apostle to the Gentiles. He even gave up "my righteousness," the kind that comes from the Law. This does not imply that Paul means some sort of self-righteousness in an egotistical or legalistic sense; "rather, it is a sense of accomplishing what the law expects and seeking forgiveness through prescribed means when the law is violated. This is not legalism, but faithful living in covenant. This was generally viewed as a good situation in which to find oneself [indeed, Paul once viewed it that way, saying he was "blameless"]; however Paul has found something superior"[28]—or, perhaps better said, something and someone superior has found Paul. What is being contrasted is "my righteousness," which came from keeping the law without blemish or committing a blameworthy error, as opposed to a righteousness that comes from God. Jerry Sumney puts it this way: "Paul contrasts the (spotless) righteousness that he attained through his own faithfulness to the Law with the righteousness achieved by Christ's faithfulness"[29] even unto death on the cross. But what exactly is the means by which this other righteousness comes to the believer?

In verse 9 we encounter the much debated phrase *dia pisteōs Christou*. A literal rendering of the phrase would be "through the faith/faithfulness of Christ." I have argued elsewhere that when one compares this verse to the close parallel in Romans 3:22, it leads to the conclusion that the reference here is not to faith *in* Christ but rather to the faithfulness *of* Christ even unto death on the cross. In fact, if one looks closely at Romans 3:22–24, one will notice a similar "through" clause in 3:24 there about the redemption that comes through Christ.

A variety of factors strongly favor this rendering here. Firstly, there are close verbal connections between Philippians 2, particularly with Philippians 2:5–11, and this discussion in Philippians 3. This phrase then would be yet another link between these two texts. Secondly, the phrase in verse 9b surely must mean "the righteousness that comes from God." In other words, Paul is talking about the objective means by which one has obtained this righteousness. Thirdly, the most natural rendering of the Greek preposition here is "through," not "in." Fourthly, there is a reference to faith in Christ at the end of this verse, where we hear that this

---

27 On Paul as a formerly married man, and possibly even a widower, see Witherington, *Women in the Earliest Churches* (Cambridge: Cambridge University Press, 1988), 30–35, and compare 1 Corinthians 7, where he seems to understand the plight of the formerly married.

28 Jerry L. Sumney, *Philippians: A Greek Student's Intermediate Reader* (Peabody, MA: Hendrickson, 2007), 80.

29 Ibid. This rendering suggests that we are not talking about a righteousness inherent to Christ's character but rather one achieved by the ultimate gracious action of self-sacrifice.

righteousness is bestowed upon those who have faith. An earlier reference to the subjective means of appropriating this right standing is unnecessary. The contrast is between what one obtains from two different objective sources—the Mosaic Law versus the faithful acts of Christ. Last but not least, this entire discourse is appealing to good examples of faithfulness and obedience even unto death, a life lived to the end in a manner worthy of the Good News, including the story about Jesus's life retold in Philippians 2:5–11. It is about sacrificial behavior that produces unity in the body. Philippians 3:9 should be seen as a further point supporting that larger argument.

In verse 10 Paul will list the things of real value to him—knowing Christ (*gnōsis* here meaning something more than "knowing about," closer to "understanding through experiencing") and the power of his resurrection, the latter of which Paul will stress is experienced later in full, but he may mean he experiences it in part now, which enables him to endure all that has happened to him and indeed to share in Christ's sufferings. Sharing in Christ's resurrection also entails sharing in his sufferings, as a text like Colossians 1:24 suggests. Paul then, in a lesser sense, is talking about the honor of suffering with Christ for the same ends and aims, the redemption of the world. This is in part what it means to be conformed to the image of Christ, being conformed to his death.

Here is where we note that the "imitation of Christ" is not just something the believer does through his or her own choices and actions. It is also about what happens to the believer, unavoidably, when God uses certain experiences to conform the person to the image of Christ. *Koinōnia* here means sharing in common or participating in common, and in either case it means experiencing some suffering. Probably Paul means that knowing Christ means experiencing the power of his resurrection and the sharing in common of his sufferings. Experiencing the power of the resurrection does not exclude experiencing the suffering or vice versa. Indeed, Paul speaks of taking on the same form of his sufferings as he suffered, which presumably means martyrdom ultimately, a suffering for the cause unto death.

Verse 11 states clearly the future hope—resurrection from out of the dead. Here, Paul clearly envisions what he speaks of more fully in 1 Corinthians 15, namely, a resurrection of Christians from among the dead. This comports well with the use of the phrase in Luke 20:35 and perhaps in Acts 4:2 to refer to a resurrection of the righteous dead alone, which makes good sense in light of the previous discussion in Philippians about righteousness and the need for it to be saved. This does not amount to a general resurrection of all persons, not least because what Paul is talking about is conformity to the image of the risen Christ in the body, and only Christ's followers get that.[30] In this regard, Paul is in continuity with previous resurrection discussion in early Judaism, which on the basis of texts like Daniel 12:1–3 distinguished between the resurrection to new life of the elect, shining like the stars, and the resurrection of everyone else which will be inglorious, rising to shame and contempt, a condition distinguishable from the "better resurrection" (see Rev. 20:4–6). The end of the apostate is destruction, a fate Paul says the Judaizers are heading for if they don't change their ways.

We can debate the implications of verse 11, but one of them seems to be that Paul does not count his own personal resurrection as a certainty or a predetermined foregone conclusion. The phrase "if possible" (cf. Rom. 1:10; 11:14; Acts 27:12) here may be used to counter some sort of guarantee of salvation offered by the Judaizers if the Law was fully kept, but we cannot be sure of this. Paul's own view, however, is made clear in a text like 1 Corinthians 9:27, where he indicates that even those who have preached Christ could be disqualified if they do not remain in Christ and obey him.

Paul's basic view of the matter is that while there is *assurance* of salvation, there is not "eternal security" until one is securely in eternity. I like the way Fred Craddock puts the matter: "Trust in God's grace did not make Paul less active than the Judaizers but rather set him free now to run without watching his feet, without counting his steps, without competing with other servants of Christ."[31] It is possible that we should take the verb here *attain* to be the future tense rather than a subjunctive, but in Romans the phrase "if perhaps" is followed in both cases by the future tense. In any case, the phrase does express some doubt or contingency about the outcome, and possibly being conformed to the image of Christ's death is seen as the contingency here.

In verse 13 Paul reiterates that he has not yet fully attained all God has for him, nor does he reckon he has done so; thus, he must press on to the goal, a point reiterated in a different way in the next verse. Paul in verse 14 amplifies one of his favorite metaphors, the running metaphor, to show how hard he is striving toward the goal marker. The *skopos* was the marker at the finish line on which the runner set his sight and toward which he ran with all his might.

In contrast to some, Paul does not claim to have reached the goal or perfection yet. Paul may be concerned that there are some in Philippi who think they have arrived at the goal, simply because they are in Christ and have begun the race.

---

30 See Witherington, *Jesus, Paul, and the End of the World: A Comparative Study in New Testament Eschatology* (Downers Grove, IL: InterVarsity Press, 1992), 186–188.
31 Craddock, *Philippians*, 61.

Paul disabuses the audience of such a notion by indicating that perfection or completion of salvation transpires only when one is fully conformed to the image of Christ, in the body as in the spirit. Paul thus insists that neither he himself nor the audience have yet reached the finish line called resurrection and full conformity to the image of the Risen One. One must be conformed to Christ not only in one's behavior or attitudes but even in one's physical form of existence. Only then has resurrection in the full sense happened to a believer (see 1 Cor. 15:42–50).

Thus, while Christ has indeed taken full possession of Paul and his converts, Paul tells his converts they must press on to take full possession of full conformity to the image of Christ. What Paul actually calls the goal in this verse is the "upward call of God in Christ," which seems to prepare us for verses 19 and 20, where Paul mentions the heavenly citizenship. In terms of the racing metaphor, Paul has spoken of a "prize" that seems to be explicated by the phrase "the upward call of God in Christ Jesus," and there is a possibility that this phrase continues the metaphor.

Paul thus sets the example of a forward-looking Christian, not only not dwelling in the past but forgetting all that is past, including the assets accrued while a Pharisee. Paul is not only not looking over his shoulder; he is not looking back in longing or even in anger. Rather, like the good runner, he is singularly focused on the goal and the prize that awaits. Paul explains that the reward or prize is the "upward" or "heavenly" calling of God. What is likely envisioned here is when the judge, who sits in a special box in the stands at the finish line, the judge's seat, calls out the name of the winner, calls him *up* into the stands, and presents him with the laurel wreath.

Thus, finishing the metaphor in verse 15, Paul says with some irony that Philippians who wish to be "perfect" in a sense in the present will think as Paul has been urging them to do, not as others with differing views of perfection might suggest. Here the term *teleioi* can certainly be translated "the mature." Thus, we have a play on words—the mature (*teleioi*) will realize they have not yet fully matured, not yet reached perfection (*teleios*), because they have not yet reached the goal (*telos*), the finish line marker, for "perfection" or the goal equals resurrection in the flesh. A perfect understanding of a believer entails knowing that he or she has not yet reached perfection in this life because he or she has not yet been fully conformed to Christ's image by resurrection. Perfection then does not come merely by or at death but by means of "obtaining the resurrection."

In verse 15 Paul includes himself among the mature but not among those who have obtained perfection or reached the finish line. As in any language, a word can have several different semantic nuances, and here Paul uses the *telos* language in two different ways in the same context. Paul is so confident he is right about this viewpoint that he says that if anyone thinks differently on this matter, God will eventually enlightened him or her about the truth of it. Right reasoning is knowing oneself well enough to know one has not yet obtained perfection in this life but at the same time knowing that one has been enabled to live up to the level of Christian maturity one has already obtained.

In verse 17 Paul makes evident, as he has already by his autobiographical remarks, that for the Philippians to begin keeping the Law would be a step backward, not forward, in their Christian lives. Paul does not want them to take up what he himself has reckoned as loss and left behind. Therefore, the autobiographical remarks serve to provide a basis for the appeal here to imitation. Indeed, he is not just appealing to the spiritual athletes among the audience or the "mature" but for all of them to become "coimitators" of Paul, making a collective effort. The term *coimitators* is found only here in the NT, and indeed in all of ancient Greek literature, and thus may be a term Paul coined as he likes to add the *co-* prefix to various words to emphasize sharing things in common with others (e.g., *coworkers, cosufferers*).

This is textbook pedagogy used by teachers and rhetoricians in antiquity. The teacher models for his students what they are to do. Such calls to imitation presuppose a close relationship between the mentor and the followers. From a rhetorical point of view, this sort of appeal was especially common in deliberative rhetoric, where the goal is to affect the course of the audience's actions in the near future. The appeal was urgent because of the limitations of the situation: "To show them how to walk, those first generation believers, with no precedent or history, with no NT, with few preachers and most of them itinerant, struggling as a minority in a pagan culture, no better textbook could be offered than the lives of those who stood before them as leaders."[32]

In verses 20 and 21 Paul is probably echoing the Christ hymn in 2:5–11, for in these two verses there are a whole series of striking echoes of that hymn. Notice the juxtaposition of *Lord* with *Jesus Christ* here and the pattern of transformation from the lowly to the exalted and glorious condition. Christ's history is the believer's destiny. It is interesting that here as well, apart from once in Ephesians, is the only place Paul calls Christ "Savior." He may be doing this to make clear that salvation is not complete until the Savior returns and raises the dead.

WHAT JUST HAPPENED?

You may know the famous lament about Paul's letters found in 2 Peter 3:15–16, which reads "So also our beloved brother Paul wrote to you according to the wisdom given him, speaking of this [i.e., of God's patience] as he does in all his letters.

---

32 Ibid., 68.

There are some things in them hard to understand, which the ignorant and unstable twist to their own destruction, as they do the other scriptures." Most of us could say "Amen" to the statement that some things in Paul's letters are heavy-going, hard to understand. No wonder that the great British cleric John Donne once said that wherever he opened the letters of Paul he heard thunder, a thunder that rolls throughout the earth. In this chapter we have dared to dig into some of the deeper things in Paul's discourses, deeper reflections about Christ and about himself.

What this exercise has shown us is that superficial, noncontextual study of something like Paul's letters is often bound to lead to misunderstanding and misuse of the text. Some things in Scripture could actually take a very long time to understand. We must resist the tendencies of our culture to demand not merely instant information but instant understanding of deep things. Reading and studying the Bible is not like reading a comic book or even an easy and breezy novel. This is in part why some, such as myself, have given a lifetime to its study. I find I always have more to learn each time I pick the Bible up and read and study it.

In our next chapter, we discuss how to take next steps after you have worked through this book and learned how to begin interpreting the Bible in a careful and responsible manner. Having begun on your odyssey of learning, I am hoping to tempt you to become lifelong studiers and learners of the Bible. I can promise this—such an educational journey will not be boring, and it has many rewards along the way.

FOR FURTHER READING

If you are interested in the biographical passages in Paul's letters, I would suggest you read through my *The Paul Quest: The Renewed Search for the Jew of Tarsus* (Downers Grove, IL: InterVarsity Press, 1998), which deals with them in great detail. On the issue of Christological hymns, and the one in Philippians 2 especially, see Richard Bauckham, *Jesus and the God of Israel: God Crucified and Other Studies on the New Testament's Christology of Divine Identity* (Grand Rapids, MI: Eerdmans, 2008).

CHAPTER

15

NEXT STEPS

The one thing the New Testament forbids us to do is to treat it as a static document to be used as a set of proof-texts for instant solutions to complex and controversial contemporary problems. To misuse the New Testament in this way is to deny its dynamic character and to fail to realize that the Word has to be applied in a specific context. . . . A static interpretation of the New Testament is dependent on a frozen Christology.
—KARL PAUL DONFRIED *THE DYNAMIC WORD. NEW TESTAMENT INSIGHTS FOR CONTEMPORARY CHRISTIANS* (HARPER COLLINS, 1981)

WHERE ARE WE GOING?

In this chapter we will discuss how to move from a beginning study of the Bible and an initial understanding of its content and intent to a more in-depth and systematic way of studying and learning the rich material in the Bible.

Figure 15.1 Steps in an ancient Greco–Roman theater. (© Mark R. Fairchild, PhD)

If you've gotten this far in this book, then you will have realized that understanding the Bible involves so much more than just opening the book and reading it. It's not like reading a modern novel or current news online. The universe of discourse, the culture, the history, and a host of other factors make it a book that requires help to read, if, that is, you want to go beyond a surface reading and understanding of the Bible. So, you may be saying, "How can I remedy this problem, since I clearly want to understand the Bible better?"

One answer, of course, would be to take some courses on the Bible, or at least audit them; and the good news is that there are plenty of places you can do this—colleges, universities, churches, and online. There is no lack of educational opportunity to improve your understanding of the Bible. Some courses are better than others, some schools are better than others for this purpose, some online resources are better than others; but anything that helps you do a better job of understanding both the text and the original contexts of the Bible is worthwhile. You can even get together with friends and study the Bible together, though I would encourage you to do it with at least one teacher who knows the Bible well, knows even the original languages and cultures, so that it won't be a matter of just pooling ignorance and speculating. As the most popular and important book ever written, the Bible deserves better than a casual or careless approach.

A second way to improve your Bible reading and understanding is to build a decent library of good commentaries and reference books. Here, the use of electronic resources can be a big help. There are now a plethora of good sources of online commentary packages, and many of them are good and useful commentaries. I would advise checking out the resources available through Logos or Bibleworks, especially the extra commentary packages offered by Logos. The goal would be to build a library with at least two good commentaries on each book of the Bible. Don't worry, many good commentaries cover more than one book of the Bible, so if you're doing the math, I'm not necessarily saying you will need 66 times 2 commentaries. For example, the Pastoral Epistles or the Johannine Epistles are almost always treated together in one commentary.

The level of commentary that you purchase depends on (1) your biblical language skills and (2) where you are in the process of your biblical education. And there are different kinds of commentaries as well—devotional, popular, semi-technical for the educated layperson and clergy, and full-dress technical scholarly commentaries. My advice to a pure beginner is to start with something like N. T. Wright's series of brief commentaries in *The New Testament For Everyone* series (e.g., *Luke for Everyone* [Louisville, KY: Westminster/John Knox Press, 2010ff]). This series was intended to replace the popular series by William Barclay, which is still good reading but very out of date and out of touch with current scholarship. There is also John Goldingay's series *The Old Testament for Everyone* (Louisville, KY: Westminster/John Knox Press , 2010ff). These are excellent points from which to start your deeper probing of the text.

For those who are more seasoned readers of the Bible, I would suggest you assemble a good collection of mid-level commentaries to use in your personal study and in teaching Bible studies or Sunday school. These will serve your own education well and will help you educate others. There is a good guide to such commentaries written by my colleague David Bauer entitled *An Annotated Guide to Biblical Resources for Ministry* (Eugene, OR: Wipf & Stock, 2011).[1] Don't be put off by the word *ministry* in the title; the book is not just for ministers and priests.

If you were to go as far as to do doctoral work, then highly technical commentaries like the *Hermeneia* series published by Fortress Press and the *International Critical Commentary* series published originally by T&T Clark and now by Bloomsbury are for such higher levels of academic study of the text. The Anchor

---

1 The second edition of this book will be emerging soon.

Bible commentaries, now published by Yale University Press, are often very good resources but still a bit too technical and language-based for those without a knowledge of the biblical languages.

The truth in any case about commentary series is that they are always a mixed phenomenon, by which I mean some volumes in the series are quite excellent but others not so much. This is why I do not necessarily recommend buying a whole series of commentaries but rather purchasing eclectically from a variety of series, following the Bauer guidebook. If you were to press me, I would say look at the series of socio-rhetorical commentaries published by Eerdmans, perhaps the series published by Hendrickson (now Baker), some of the commentaries in the Baker Academic series, the Smyth and Helwys series, or the InterVarsity Press commentaries series. You might especially profit from my three volumes entitled *Letters and Homilies for Hellenized Christians*, volumes 1 and 2, and *Letters and Homilies for Jewish Christians* (Downers Grove, IL: InterVarsity Press). If you are looking for a mid-level series that is consistently good and interesting and very readable, I would commend the *New Cambridge Bible Commentary* series (Cambridge: Cambridge University Press), of which I am the senior editor. Try the Genesis volume by Bill T. Arnold, and the Revelation volume, which I wrote.

It's not just commentaries that you will need however. You will need some reference books of a more general sort as well, and here I highly recommend the whole series of dictionaries published by InterVarsity Press, such as the *Dictionary of Jesus and the Gospels* (now in a new second edition), the *Dictionary of Paul and His Letters*, and various other volumes in the series. These dictionaries have been recently updated, unlike other series of this sort such as the *Anchor Bible Dictionary* series. And the further good news is that you can get all those dictionaries as a package in electronic form, with proper search engines.

There is another good reason to have commentaries to check as you seek to interpret this or that passage of Scripture. All of us come to the biblical text with certain assumptions and predispositions. That is to say, all of us to one degree or another are active readers and so apt to read things into the text which are not really there. Commentaries provide a check on such predispositions, an external control on interpretation run riot. We need to think of understanding the Bible as a group or community project, and fortunately we have millions of predecessors who studied the text long before we ever picked up a Bible. Having good commentaries amounts to having not merely checks and balances but also having dialogue partners, many of whom are much better informed about the meaning of the Bible than we likely are. A "common sense" individual reading of the Bible needs to be supplemented with a "community sense" reading that can confirm or correct our readings and encourage us to go down the right track either way.

In any case, one needs to keep in mind that our learning and teaching will only be as good as the resources we use to accomplish those aims; and frankly, there are lots of resources online which, while often free, are virtually worthless or, even worse, distort the meaning of the Bible. In general, until one can develop one's own skills at critically evaluating such resources including online resources, it is best to trust the judgment of good, reputable scholars who know the field well.

Let's say, however, that you have some language skills and would like to learn OT Hebrew or NT Greek. Again, there are a plethora of entry-level textbooks, but here are two you could start with—N. Clayton Croy's *A Primer of New Testament Greek* (Grand Rapids, MI: Eerdmans, 2011) and, for Hebrew, Bill T. Arnold and John Choi's *A Guide to Biblical Hebrew Syntax* (Cambridge: Cambridge University Press, 2003).

I would simply say, don't let the "foreignness" of these languages put you off from studying them. It is well worth the effort and the time, and the especially good news about learning the languages themselves is that as you develop skill with them, you also develop the ability to make your own judgments about what words, clauses, and sentences in the original language of the Bible mean. You no longer have to depend whole scale on the commentaries of others who are experts in the languages.

Let's say you've taken the steps suggested above to improve your reading and understanding of the Bible. What next? My suggestion would be that after you have gotten a decent grasp of the biblical language, you start to make your own translations of some of your favorite passages in the Bible. To do this you will need a basic lexicon or word dictionary for each testament. Start with F. Danker's *The Concise Greek–English Lexicon of the New Testament* (Chicago: University of Chicago Press, 2009). Here, I really can't recommend the electronic version because it is not really very searchable when you need to look up the meaning of a word. Buy the physical book instead. As for the Hebrew text of the OT, perhaps a good entry point would be Terry A. Armstrong, Douglas L. Busby, and Cyril F. Carr's *A Reader's Hebrew-English Lexicon of the Old Testament* (Grand Rapids, MI: Zondervan, 1989).

Perhaps the most important skill to learn in becoming a better reader and interpreter of the Bible involves developing your ability to think critically about what you are reading. By "critical thinking" I mean analytical thinking. I am not referring to developing a penchant for criticizing the Bible or criticizing commentaries on the Bible. So what does this look like?

In regard to reading commentaries, don't simply take the author's word for something. Read another commentary from another point of view. Let me illustrate. Suppose for a moment you come to a controversial issue. For example, you come to the ending of the Gospel of Mark, and some commentaries tell you "the original Greek text likely ended at Mark 16:8," while others tell you "the ending found in the older English translations such as the King James Version (KJV) which involved verses 9–20 is likely the original ending," and still others tell you "neither Mark 16:8 nor verses 9–20 are the original ending. The original ending is lost." How do you decide such an issue, thinking critically? Here are some steps you could take.

First of all, you would need to know something about textual analysis of the original Greek text. There are rules for this sort of analysis. For example, all other things being equal, the reading found in earlier Greek manuscripts of the text is more likely to be original. Mark 16:9–20 is not actually found in various of our earliest and best manuscripts of the last chapter of Mark. It is not found, for example, in the two great early codexes called Aleph and B. Immediately this is a red flag because Christian scribes tended to be conservative. They were more apt to include more than the original than delete part of the original Greek text.

A second important rule has to do with the quality of the manuscripts that do or do not include verses 9–20. Generally speaking, the better quality of manuscripts do not have these verses. And the geographical origins of a variety of manuscripts are important. For example, the witness for the omission includes manuscripts from Egypt, Syria, and the western part of the empire. Geographical spread is important because it shows independent copying of the original Greek text. It's like having the testimony of several witnesses instead of just one.

Another rule for deciding this issue is "the more difficult reading is to be preferred." This rule is based on the recognition that scribes, as the copying of the Bible went along, were more likely to smooth out bad grammar and infelicitous speech than to let it stand. Mark 16:8 ends oddly, with the Greek word *gar*, which means "for." This is not a normal way to end a paragraph in Greek, much less a book. This is precisely why Clayton Croy and other experts in the text of Mark have argued, persuasively in my mind, that 16:8 is not the original ending. Even just from a grammatical point of view it is quite unlikely that Mark 16:8 is the original ending of this gospel. Who ends a Good News story with "and they said nothing to anyone, for they were afraid"? Rather, the original ending is lost but probably can be reconstructed from Matthew 28 since that gospel so closely follows the text of Mark, taking over about 95% of Mark's content. The ending of Mark originally likely involved an appearance to the women at the tomb and an appearance of Jesus in Galilee to a large group of disciples.[2]

---

2 N. Clayton Croy, *The Mutilation of Mark's Gospel* (Nashville, TN: Abingdon, 2003).

This last paragraph shows the need to develop critical judgment especially about problem issues and problem passages in the Bible. Let's take one more example, from the OT. It will illustrate the dangers of putting too much stock in a particular English translation.

I once had a parishioner in North Carolina who was mentally challenged, but he loved to read his Bible. Indeed, it was about the only book he did read, and he read it in the version his mother used to teach him—the old KJV. He came to me puzzled one day. He had been learning Psalm 23, and the very first line had stumped him.

"Dr. Ben," he said, "it says 'the Lord is my shepherd I shall not want' but I want him! Why does it say 'I shall not want?'"

I responded as gently as I could: "Well, Ralph, what that verse means is 'if God is your shepherd, you shall lack for nothing essential.'"

With relief written all over his face, Ralph replied, "Oh, good. I just knew it couldn't mean I shouldn't want him!"

The problem in this case is with the archaic English language in the old KJV. The word *want* today doesn't really mean "lack" as it did in the seventeenth century. Because English is a living language, the use and even the meaning of words change over time.

One more example will be of use. I was once asked why the Psalms (in the KJV) say that God is "awful"—as in "God is a mighty God, an awful God is he." I explained that the word *awful* in the seventeenth century meant "awe-ful," that is, full of awe and wonder, deserving of our awe. But awful over time morphed from a word with a positive connotation to a word with a negative one. This is why we need ever-fresh English translations of the Bible. If English were a dead, no longer spoken, language, like Latin, where the meanings do not continue to evolve and change, then we would not have this issue.

Think of this process this way: interpreting the texts of the Bible in light of their original contexts is a way of showing respect to the original inspired authors of the Bible, acknowledging that we don't have the right to tell the author what he meant because proper interpretation is not a matter of putting words in an ancient author's mouth. Rather, interpretation that approaches the text with this sort of respect is seeking to uncover the inherent original meaning the author intended. It also involves giving the original author the benefit of the doubt. This should especially be our approach if we believe these biblical writers were inspired by God. And this brings up another point.

Let us take the posture assumed by believing Jews and Christians for centuries, namely, that God speaks in and through the Bible. It is this fundamental belief, that the Bible involves God's word to us all, not just human words about God, that leads to the further hermeneutical assumption or presumption that the Bible must be telling a consistent story, presenting us with a coherent portrait of God, ourselves, and the interrelationship between God and ourselves. Indeed, the assumption is that the Bible is telling us, and the many generations that have come before us, *the truth* about history, theology, ethics.

If we are not merely seeking understanding but seeking truth and not merely seeking truth but seeking God and the most important truths about God, what follows from this is that we will approach these as sacred texts, which can tell us all kinds of things about the meaning of life, even the meaning of our own individual lives. The Bible is not some old dusty historical tome of no relevance to persons in the twenty-first century. On the contrary, it is the very book that is capable of telling us the truths about ourselves, even when those truths are inconvenient, painful, difficult.

A PRACTICAL EXERCISE

Let's take a step-by-step walk through what good reading and good interpretation of the Bible looks like. Start by picking a passage of Scripture you are interested in understanding, say Psalm 23. If you can start with the original-language text, then the first step is to make your own translation of the text. Start with a rather literal word-for-word translation and then smooth it out. If you are not able to do that, then start by gathering three or four good translations, say the New International Version, the New Revised Standard Version, the Common English Bible, and the New KJV; and read through the passage you have picked in each translation, comparing and contrasting them. Write down questions that the differences in the translations raise in your mind—like, Why does one translation begin "If Yahweh is my shepherd," whereas another begins "The Lord is my shepherd"? You will probably not be able to answer such questions just by pondering the translations themselves. Here is where you need to pull out your two or three good commentaries.

The next step is to read your commentaries on the whole passage, not skipping around but getting a sense of the whole psalm. Once you do this and get a sense for the flow of meaning in the text, then it's time to go deeper.

The next step is perhaps to look up some key terms in the text in your lexicon or dictionaries. For instance, you might want to look up the term *hesed* from the last verse of Psalm 23 that is translated variously into English in your dictionary.

Is this the "loving kindness" elsewhere referred to in the OT as God's covenant love? At this stage as well you might want to read some social history about ancient shepherds and their flocks and how they operated. One useful way to do that would be to read Kenneth Bailey's *Jesus Through Middle Eastern Eyes* (Downers Grove, IL: InterVarsity Press, 2008). You could then ask, How far do we press the analogy between ancient shepherds and their ways of sheep herding and the way God leads his people? There will also be articles in the dictionaries I referred to before by InterVarsity Press that will be of use at this point.

Having done this, if you are going to not merely read and understand the Bible but in fact teach or preach this passage, there is a further step you can take. You can consult good books of illustrations or at least commentaries that provide such illustrations. The socio-rhetorical commentaries by Eerdmans have a "Bridging the Horizons" section with each major literary unit, and you might want to look at the New International Version "Application Commentaries" as well.

If you will go through this process of learning carefully and prayerfully, there will be many "Aha!" moments along the way. You will gain some skill in reading, interpreting, and applying the text and in critical thinking about all these things. Like most things, good reading and good teaching take practice, practice, practice.

WHAT JUST HAPPENED?

In this chapter we have outlined some clear steps which you can take from being a casual reader of the Bible, understanding it at the informational level, to studying it more deeply as part of a commitment to lifelong learning about and of the Bible and finally moving to a responsible application of the Bible to your own life and the lives of others. Skipping from step one all the way to the last step is rather like trying to assemble a bookcase by laying out and identifying all the parts and then skipping right to putting books on the shelves before you have even assembled the shelves into a whole bookcase. Not only does this leave a big mess on your floor; it does not allow the bookcase to function as it was intended to function—as an assembled whole unit. Similarly, the Bible, a library of books in itself, was intended to function as an assembled unit. But you need to know the nature of the individual pieces, how they fit together, and how to use them to build not merely your own understanding but even your life. In order to get from back then and back there to applying the Bible here and now, you need to work through the steps I have outlined in this book.

I have two more tasks to undertake in this study. In the next chapter I will have a complex story to tell you, the story of how we got our Bible as we have it today. Call it a short history of the Bible itself and its journey through the centuries. How did it come to have the books it has? When was it assembled? Why did the process stop with a certain number of books, and who stopped it? The story is complicated and will take some elaboration. If you want to understand how the OT and NT went from being ancient collections of writings to being our modern Bible, then the final main chapter will be of great interest to you.

FOR FURTHER READING

There are some wonderful guides for taking these next steps, and I would encourage you to look at Gordon D. Fee's classic study *New Testament Exegesis*, 3rd ed. (Louisville, KY: Westminster/John Knox Press, 2002), and Douglas Stuart's *Old Testament Exegesis*, 4th ed. (Louisville, KY: Westminster/John Knox Press, 2009).

16

DID the CANON MISFIRE? The BIBLE'S OWN STORY

It is the simple truth to say that the New Testament books became canonical because no one could stop them doing so.
—William Barclay[1]

Put another way, instead of suggesting that certain books were accidentally included and others were accidentally excluded from the New Testament canon—whether the exclusion be defined in terms of the activity of individuals, or synods, or councils—it is more accurate to say that certain books excluded themselves from the canon. . . . it is a clear case of survival of the fittest.
—Bruce M. Metzger[2]

---

1 W. Barclay, *The Making of the Bible* (London: SCM Press, 1961), 78.
2 B. M. Metzger, *The Canon of the New Testament* (Oxford: Oxford University Press, 1987), 286.

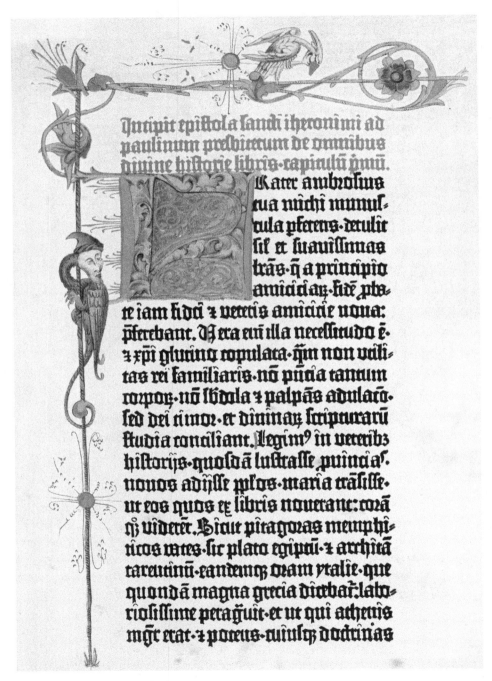

Figure 16.1 An illuminated manuscript in Latin.

WHERE ARE WE GOING?

The story of how the Bible came to be assembled, particularly in its present configuration and form, is a complex and long one; and here we can only hope to summarize some of the major highlights of how it all happened. As it turns out, not only the substance of the Bible but even the process of how we got the Bible has been and remains a subject of heated debate. This chapter can be said to be for more advanced readers or those prepared to go deeper than the previous ones, which is why I have placed it here.

THE FORMATION OF THE OT CANON: SOME ASSEMBLY REQUIRED

To begin with, we need to understand the meaning of the word **canon**. It refers to a measuring rod or rule by which something else can be measured. It came to have the sense of a collection of books which provides the litmus test or measuring device by which all other books, all doctrine, all ethics, all practices, all traditions, all experiences, all reasonings could be tested and measured. So when we talk about the formation of the canon of Scripture, we are talking about a limited or bounded collection of books that have such authority and inspiration that they provide the standard by which all beliefs and behaviors will be measured or tested.

After individual books were written, collected, and edited in places like the Temple in Jerusalem or the Jewish royal court, they began to be assembled into collections, the first of these being a collection of the books of the Law or Torah or, as we would call it, the Pentateuch (the first five books of the OT). After that, there were chronicles of historical events which provided the basis for 1–2 Samuel, 1–2 Kings, and 1–2 Chronicles, as well as the beginning of the collecting of actual prophetic oracles, a practice which continued throughout the period of the Jewish monarchy, beginning in about 1000 BC and continuing thereafter. The psalms were also likely collected and put into a collection of collections that we now have during the time there was actually a functioning Temple in Jerusalem. According to tradition, Solomon is the one who collected wisdom materials, like we find in Proverbs, Ecclesiastes, and Job. So the beginnings of the assembling of the OT date far back into the OT era itself, but it was not completed even by the time Jesus was born.

As I have just suggested, the canonizing process seems to have begun, in regard to what we call the OT, before the time of Jesus. This is reflected not only in the traditions surrounding the various stages of the translating of the Hebrew texts that became the LXX or Old Greek Scriptures[3] but also in the preface to Sirach (an important intertestamental Jewish text) written around 130 BC that counts the following as Jewish Scriptures: the Law, Prophets, and Writings, whatever the latter two categories may contain. The first clearly involved the Pentateuch. This means that at least in some quarters, particularly perhaps in the Diaspora, there was already the beginning of a canon consciousness and a concern about it. We must add to this the coming of Hillel from Babylon to Jerusalem, bringing with him his own version and vision of what the sacred texts were and were not. His collection as well seems to be rather less than may have been the case at Qumran.

Of course, the evidence at Qumran or the Dead Sea community needs to be sifted very carefully. We find every OT book, with the (probable) exception of Esther, among the Qumran scrolls. We also find books that may or may not have had scriptural authority, such as the well-attested books *Jubilees* and *Enoch*, which supported teachings very dear to the men of Qumran (involving law, calendar, antediluvian stories). But were these books "canonical," or were they auxiliary writings treasured because they supplemented and interpreted Genesis and the Law in ways amenable to Qumran beliefs? We find at Qumran other parallel versions of the Pentateuch (e.g., the so-called *Rewritten Pentateuch*, 4QRP), but there is no compelling reason to believe these writings were also regarded as Scripture. These writings creatively elaborated on the Law, as the men of Qumran understood it. *Jubilees* and *Enoch* may well have served a similar purpose.[4]

Sociological studies of sectarian groups ranging from ancient ones like the Essenes to the Christian sect or the later Gnostic sect have shown the propensity of such groups to have their own consciousness of what sacred texts were and to engage in the process of creating their own sacred texts to add to previous ones. This is particularly true of millenarian sects like the one at Qumran and the Jesus movement.[5] The degree to which a millenarian sect truly believes it is "the people of God" and that God is now intervening in human history affects the way they think about things like Scripture and its importance and fulfillment. Particularly the fulfillment mentality presses such a person to define what are true oracles or words of God, especially when they believe that such prophecies and other texts are

---

3 Those wanting a much more thorough discussion of the debate about how and when the canon was formed should see Witherington, *What's in the Word? Rethinking the Socio-Rhetorical Character of the New Testament* (Waco, TX: Baylor University Press, 2009), especially the chapter on the canonizing process.

4 My thanks to Craig Evans with helping me nuance this argument properly. See his *Ancient Texts for New Testament Studies: A Guide to the Background Literature* (Peabody, MA: Hendrickson, 2005).

5 See G. W. Trompf, ed., *Cargo Cults and Millenarian Movements* (Berlin: Mouton de Gruyter, 1990) for the general tendencies.

being fulfilled in their founder and his people. This clearly describes the mentality of the early Christians who wrote our NT books. They believed they were living in the age of fulfillment and that the end of the eschatological events might be close at hand. This sort of belief changes the way one looks at Scripture and, indeed, ups the ante when it comes to canon consciousness.

Clearly, the most prominent and influential of the subsets of early Judaism was Pharisaism, and we would expect their views on sacred texts to be the predominant ones, not only after the fall of the Temple but also before since they and their scribes were so influential in the synagogues and, as Josephus tells us, even the Sadducees followed the Pharisaic views of how the sacrifices should be done. But the dominant Pharisaic tradition in the time of Jesus was the Hillel/Gamaliel tradition, important because this is the tradition that Saul of Tarsus and many other Jews were trained in, in Jerusalem. It was a tradition that valued and used a wide array of ancient Jewish texts but treated as Scripture only a subset of the texts which eventually became fully codified as the First Testament, our Old Testament.

Whatever else one can say about Luke 24's reference to the Law, the Prophets, and Psalms, it must be noted that books like Wisdom of Solomon and Sirach were considered wisdom literature in their own time and thereafter, not prophetic literature, so it is highly unlikely such sources would be included under the rubric of "the prophets." And certainly they could not be called "the psalms." My point is that this Lukan phrase refers to some sort of bounded collection the author and audience already know. If it goes back to Jesus, which I suspect ultimately it does, it is quite telling.

Jesus himself suggests to his followers that there is a bounded collection of Scriptures they should study and that they will find the messianic story about him in them. And the interesting thing about this is that he mentions all three parts of what came to be called the Old Testament. Probably, however, the Greek of this verse in Luke 24.44 favors the notion that the Prophets and the Psalms are being placed under one heading, so this single bit of evidence should not be overpressed. In any case, it is typical of the eschatological mentality that it sees all the sacred texts as having prophetic potential. Even if we owe the reference in Luke 24 only to Luke himself, it still provides us with evidence of a canon consciousness that had at least begun to think in terms of definite boundaries.

What Jesus says in Luke 24 may be compared to what we find in Josephus, *Apion* 1.37–43, writing in the last decade of the first century, which says,

> We *do not have innumerable writings that disagree and contradict, but only 22 books which are truly reliable and contain the account of the whole period [i.e., of Jewish history].* Of these, the first five books of Moses contain the

laws in addition to the tradition of the origin of humanity up to Moses' death. This period encompasses almost 3,000 years. From Moses' death to Artaxerxes, the Persian king after Xerxes, the prophets have recorded the events of their times in thirteen books. The remaining four books contain hymns to God and didactic poems for human life. (italics added)

Here, we not only see the threefold division of the OT but have a specific number of books mentioned, which again bespeaks a closed or closing canon, according to the thinking of Josephus. His thinking on such subjects is likely to have been most informed by his connections with the Pharisees and his admiration of them. At *Apion* 1.42 he stresses that what is in these Scriptures are "the decrees of God." What would have been included in the thirteen books of prophets? This may be debated, and it is also not clear whether he would have considered 1–2 Samuel, 1–2 Kings, 1–2 Chronicles, and Ezra–Nehemiah as single books or not.

Were Esther, Ruth, and Daniel included as well since he is thinking of prophetic books that chronicle history? It is hard to say. What is not hard to say is that he thought there was a threefold division and a definite limit to the OT canon. It was a closed rather than an open collection for him and this well before the second-century list of OT books found in the Jewish source in Babylonian Talmud *Baba Batra*. Furthermore, Josephus never claimed to be a theologian or an expert in the Hebrew Scriptures. He must have gotten the notion of a twenty-two–book collection from someone else. My suggestion would be that it came from the Pharisees.

The list we find in Babylonian Talmud *Baba Batra* 14b–15a has traditionally been dated somewhere between AD 70 and 200. This list clearly identifies the twenty-four books that today make up the Hebrew Bible and presents us with the threefold division of the OT. That Christians did take some of their cues on what counted as OT canonical books from the rabbis is clear from the case of Melito of Sardis.

Melito of Sardis in about AD 180 (see Eusebius, *Hist. Eccl.* 4.26.13–14) made a pilgrimage from Asia to the Holy Land to find out for sure what were the books in the Hebrew Bible. He lists them clearly and completely, leaving out only Nehemiah (but that may be included under the mention of Ezra) and Esther and adding only Wisdom of Solomon. What is interesting about this is that if Nehemiah is included under the heading of Ezra, this list comports very nicely with the list in *Baba Batra* 14b–15a with the exception of Wisdom of Solomon. That is to say, both in Judaism and in the case of the Christian Bishop Melito we now have a canon identical with the Hebrew Bible we know today; and as things turned out it was accepted both by the rabbis of old (and new) and later by the Protestants, again with the exception of Wisdom of Solomon. This suggests that in the Holy Land and in some Christian quarters the canonical issues in regard to the OT canon were basically a resolved matter by the late second century AD. This must be taken quite seriously in view of the fact that seminal figures like Jerome and Eusebius, who both had much to do with the closing of the canon, spent their most important scholarly time in the fourth century, with efforts in the Holy Land itself and in consultation with the rabbis.

Let us say a bit more about the growing Christian movement of the first four centuries of the common era. Where did their ideas of what Scripture is come from? Why did they cite some books and not others? Since all such historical arguments are based on a weighing of probabilities, they fill in gaps in one way or another since the evidence is not exhaustive, sadly. Arguments from evidence are necessary as opposed to arguments from silence. But it is not an argument from silence to say that the threefold division we find in Sirach, and perhaps in the NT with Jesus and on into the second century in *Baba Batra*, is consistent with the hypothesis that there was a reasonably clearly defined and mostly bounded concept of what constituted the Scriptures and what did not for some Jews in that period. We have this threefold division in each of these three centuries. It does not crop up for the first time in the second century and after AD 70.

Therefore, it is not adequate to simply say we don't know what was in those groupings. Actually, we probably do know what was there for the most part. We simply catalog what was cited or used as scriptural authority. And lo and behold, in the NT, with one possible exception, there is no evidence of the "citation" of any extracanonical literature as Scripture (by which I mean no quoting of such texts as Scripture and no use of formulae like "Scripture says" or "God says" or "it is written"). This is truly remarkable, indeed I would say astounding, if the OT canon was wide open for debate and many things were in doubt and many extra books were in play, at least for the early Christian movement. In other words, the first-century evidence from the NT itself, which is after all the Christian starting point, reflects far less diversity than the next two centuries and far less diversity than was found at Qumran. Why is this?

One suggestion would be because all the writers of the NT were Jews, with the possible exceptions of Luke (whose knowledge of the LXX suggests he was at least a God-fearer) and the author of 2 Peter. I would suggest that there was a legacy from Jesus and from Paul in regard to what counted as sacred text—perhaps not an approved or exhaustive reading list but nonetheless a tradition. I would suggest the legacy reflects the influence of Hillel/Gamaliel and the Diaspora tradition. One has to explain the lack of diversity in what is used as Scripture in the NT, not merely the presence of more speculation later when the church was overwhelmingly Gentile.

At this point some scholars will object and say, What about the evidence of Jude verse 14? I am referring to the much-debated reference to a tradition from the book we now call *1 Enoch* in Jude. Doesn't this provide clear evidence of at least one early Christian who had a broader canon of Scripture than eventually made it into the Bible? Listen to how the quotation of the Enochian text reads: "Enoch, the seventh from Adam, prophesied about them: 'See the Lord is coming.'" This verse does not say it is quoting a sacred text but rather a holy prophet who, as the seventh from Adam, spoke a prophetic word. It is the person, not some text of *1 Enoch*, to whom authority is ascribed and presumed in this verse.

For all we know, Jude is quoting some oral tradition he knows. And notice that we do not find the formula here "it is written," which would refer to a sacred text. But even if he is quoting this line out of a copy of *1 Enoch*, this doesn't mean he sees the whole of 1 Enoch as having some scriptural authority any more than Paul's quoting of Greek poets from time to time does. It simply means that he thinks this bit of prophecy is true, but notice he is careful not to use a scriptural formula to introduce it. In other words, this single exception to the rule that NT writers only quote as Scripture books that were later viewed as part of the Hebrew canon proves not likely to be an exception to the rule. But what about what we will call NT canon consciousness?

THE FORMATION OF THE NT CANON

At least some NT authors, for example, Paul, were aware that they were both speaking and writing the Word of God, by which phrase they were referring to their tellings of the story of Jesus (see above on 1 Thess. 2:13). It is, however, one thing to have an awareness of writing God's Word; canon consciousness is something else. By "canon consciousness" I mean an awareness not only that what you say is God's Word but that it needs to be both written down and put together with other samples of the Word of God, thus forming a sacred corpus, a Scripture, a canon.

In a seminal essay my old mentor C. K. Barrett reflects on what it was that Luke, the author of Luke–Acts, saw himself as doing with his two-volume work. After ruling out various options, including the view that Acts should be seen as a stand-alone work of apologetics, Barrett suggests the following:

The author accepts the Old Testament, and provides, to accompany it, an explanatory and interpretive parallel book—we may call it, though Luke did not, a New Testament. It was the only New Testament Luke's church had, and this was the first church to have one. Throughout the development of the New Testament canon, New Testaments (including . . . Marcion's. His Gospel and Apostle must have made it very difficult for those who wished to beat him at his own game to use any other form. And it was intrinsically right) had the same basic form: Gospel and Apostle. In his first volume Luke supplied the teaching and action of Jesus which provided the foundation on which the whole Christian movement rested, and he was careful to show at the beginning of the book that Jesus was born within Judaism and in fulfillment of prophecy, and to underline the same point at the beginning of Jesus' ministry: "Today has this scripture been fulfilled in your ears" (Lk. 4.21). His second volume provides the guarantee that what followed was the intended and valid outcome of what had been narrated in the first and also contained specimens of the teaching of the apostles—sufficient to show (to the satisfaction of an author who was not a profound historian) the content of the Gospel and the unity of representative leaders in preaching it. What more did a church such as Luke's need? This was their New Testament; and as far as we know it was the first.[6]

From a historical point of view it would be hard to exaggerate the significance of these remarks, if Barrett is correct. It would mean that there was not only an awareness of writing the Word of God on the part of some NT writers but also a canon consciousness, not just about the OT but, in the case of Luke, about the beginnings of a New Testament as well. This development did not begin after, and in reaction to, Marcion, the second-century writer who suggested we ignore the OT altogether and use as sacred Scripture some version of the Gospel of Luke plus some of Paul's letters. Rather, the process of collecting and assembling the NT began in the first century AD even while some of the eyewitnesses and original apostles were still alive.

Let us turn to the end of the NT era. The discussion of the understanding of inspiration in early Judaism and early Christianity particularly in eschatological/prophetic/messianic sects should be broached at this point. What determined whether something should be seen as sacred text or not is whether it was believed

---

6 C. K. Barrett, "The First New Testament," *Novum Testamentum* 38, no. 2 (1996): 94–104, here 102–103. I have incorporated his note on Marcion into the text of the quote in a parenthesis.

to be an inscripturated form of the Word of God, in this case the Word of God proclaimed and then written down in the first century. This belief is crucial to understanding why there was so much emphasis on the apostolic source documents, viewing them in a more hallowed light than second-century figures like Bishop Papias and Bishop Ignatius viewed their own writings. They understood the crucial nature of apostolic and eyewitness testimony long before there were any canon lists at all, so far as we know.

But where do we find the origins of the idea that what the earliest Christians were proclaiming and writing was itself the Word of God and, thus, suitable to be viewed as Scripture if written down? Remember once more 1 Thessalonians 2:13 is in perhaps the earliest of all Christian documents, and it already presents us with evidence that Paul's proclamation of the Gospel was considered inspired, indeed considered the Word of God by Paul himself, and not merely the opinions of a human being.[7]

The issue was not just whether Paul had the Spirit, for that was true of all early Christians; the issue was whether he was an apostle of Jesus Christ commissioned for proclaiming the living Word of God to various people. Not all Christians were given such a gift or a task, as the gift lists in the Pauline epistles make clear. Apostles are seen as gifts to the church distinguishable from other inspired figures such as prophets (see 1 Cor. 12). 1 Corinthians 14:36–37 makes clear Paul's own thinking about this sort of matter, for in one and the same breath he affirms he has the Spirit, that he is authorized to give his converts the command of the Lord (which refers to what he is writing at that moment in 1 Cor. 14), and that he speaks the Word of God and it did not originate with the Corinthians.

In other words, we already see a mentality here that affirms not only that the apostle proclaimed the Word of God orally but that what he wrote as well was "the Lord's command" for that audience, not distinguishing his own teaching from that of Jesus in terms of inspiration or authority. In other words, we already see in our earliest Christian writer the beginnings not only of scriptural consciousness when it comes to Christian writings of the apostles and their coworkers but a connection between that idea and the apostolic proclamation.

The process of collecting and circulating apostolic documents in groupings had already begun by the end of the NT era if not before, as is evidenced by 2 Peter 3:15–16, which most commentators do think comes from the turn of the era, not

---

7 For more on this theme, see Witherington, *The Living Word of God* (Waco, TX: Baylor University Press, 2007), and Witherington, *What's in the Word?*, which provide a more detailed account of what we find in this chapter.

much later.[8] Not surprisingly, the earliest NT documents are the first ones to make it into a circulating collection—Paul's letters. More importantly, we learn from 2 Peter 3:16 that the letters of Paul could be ranked with "the other Scriptures." Now, this implies not only that the author is thinking of a collection of Paul's letters as a known entity but also that he assumes that the audience will know what "the other Scriptures" are. We are thus dealing with the beginnings of Christian canon consciousness here, and Paul's letters are already seen, despite their difficulties, as part of the collection of sacred texts for Christians. You don't refer to "the other Scriptures" unless you are implying that Paul's letters were considered as Scripture by at least this author and his Christian audience.

I agree with Graham Stanton and Martin Hengel that the label "according to Matthew" (et al.) did not become widely used until there was a grouping of these documents together, no later than early in the second century.[9] You don't need the label "according to" unless you have multiple volumes claiming to be gospels. If these documents had been previously anonymous, which is not clear, they certainly were not by Papias's day since he calls them by their canonical names already in AD 125 or so. It seems likely that there was already a codex or book of gospels, perhaps the canonical four, already early in the second century. We thus have already in play, perhaps as early as AD 125, collections of texts of the majority of what was to become the NT, collections made well before the end of the second century AD.

How were these texts viewed? Were they viewed as just like the writings of Ignatius, Justin Martyr, or Papias? There is absolutely no evidence they were. Those three writers all cite the earlier apostolic documents in ways that distinguish their own efforts from them, even when they see their own writings as in some sense inspired, as Ignatius seems to have done. Why? Because while there may not have been what could be called a full canon consciousness on their part, there was a strong apostolic writings consciousness as the source documents of the movement. In fact, we already see this in the 90s with Clement of Rome in the way he treats Paul's letters.

Thus, when we get to the Muratorian fragment and to Irenaeus at the end of the second century, they should not be seen as anomalies out of due season prior to the

---

8 While I would not go as far as he does, I do think that David Trobisch is on the right track in suggesting that apostles like Paul may well have already themselves reflected a sort of canon consciousness and so made collections of their writings for wider audiences than the originally intended one. See D. Trobisch, *Paul's Letter Collection: Tracing the Origins* (Bolivar, MO: Quiet Water Publications, 2001).

9 G. N. Stanton, "The Fourfold Gospel," *New Testament Studies* 43 (1997): 317–346; Martin Hengel, *The Four Gospels and the One Gospel of Jesus Christ* (Harrisburg, PA: Trinity Press, 2000). See also T. C. Skeat, "The Oldest Manuscript of the Four Gospels?" *New Testament Studies* 43 (1997), 1–34.

fourth century. They are rather reflecting this earlier apostolic tradition and even canon consciousness, if I can put it that way. The argument that the Muratorian list is anachronistic in the second century is questionable at best, especially when this list does not match up with later canon lists. The contents of the list (with excerpts from its comments), in its order, are[10]

- [Mark] ". . .
- Luke "the well-known physician"
- John "one of the disciples"
- 1 John
- Acts omits Paul's departure from Rome "when he journeyed to Spain"
- Corinthians "first" of Paul's letters
- Ephesians
- Philippians
- Colossians
- Galatians
- Thessalonians (2 Thess. is not excluded; cf. Corinthians)
- Romans "seventh" (compared to the seven letters of John in Revelation)
- Philemon
- Titus
- 1–2 Timothy
- Jude
- 2 John
- Revelation
- "There is current also one to the Laodiceans, another to the Alexandrians, forged in Paul's name to further the heresy of Marcion, and several others which cannot be received into the catholic church"

Were it a later list, we might expect it to be more like one or another of the fourth-century lists; and perhaps we have short-changed the impetus Marcion provided in the direction of composing such a list. Clearly, Irenaeus is reacting to Marcion and the Gnostics. There is no reason the composer of that Muratorian list might not have done so as well.

By the end of the second century, the church not only was overwhelmingly Gentile but it had largely begun to adopt the LXX as its OT Bible, for better or for

---

10 Note that the beginning of the document is missing, so it is probable it had Matthew listed first.

worse. As the Gnostic movement was to show, there was a growing anti-Semitism in early Christianity and in its fringe or split-off sects, witnessed both by Marcion and by the Gnostic literature.

This brings us to the so-called canon debate in the third and fourth centuries about the Catholic epistles and Revelation. The real problem with documents like Jude or James is that they were far too Jewish and too unlike the favored Pauline collection. The same was especially the case with Revelation. Eusebius can hardly contain his animus against the "chilasts" and Judaizers within Christianity. The same is sadly true of other church fathers. Because it cites so much of Jude, 2 Peter comes under the same rubric. And even Hebrews is suspected by some, not merely because it is anonymous but because it is too Jewish. Probably 2–3 John, especially if bundled with some of these other documents, raised problems for the same reason.

If we ask why it was so difficult to see these documents as genuine and apostolic in the third and fourth centuries (and even beyond), the answer is not hard to figure out. They are too unlike the more "Gentile" documents. They thus had an uphill climb into the hearts of many Christians in those centuries. In other words, it is not hard to figure out why the church of postapostolic times took so long to figure out what was already known by some in the first century—the general apostolic limits of their sacred texts. The truth is, the church had a different character and mentality, a largely non-Jewish one, by the end of the second century. This is why the recognition of some of the apostolic documents took so long in various quarters in the church.

We do not need here to retell the tale of Athanasius and his Festal Letter mentioning just twenty-seven NT books or the concurrence of Pope Innocent with that limitation or the Africa councils of the late fourth century in Africa who also said it was these twenty-seven books only which should be viewed as Scripture. Nor do we need to rehearse the canon lists themselves. What we need to note is that from at least three very different segments of the church the word went out that there were definite boundaries not only to the OT but to the NT also at that point in time. That the lists composed are not identical is not surprising since the church was not united. What is remarkable is that both in the east and in the west there was an ecclesiastical voice that said the NT had these twenty-seven books and not others.

What all such lists were saying is that the canon was closed, even if different segments of the church had a slightly different contents list for the closed canon of the Bible as a whole. In all of this, it was not a matter of the church *defining* but rather of the church *recognizing* what were and weren't the early apostolic books. This process of recognition inherently ruled out Gnostic and other later books, even books written by orthodox postapostolic Christian figures.

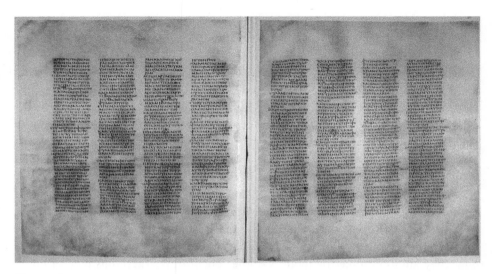

Figure 16.2

In my judgment it is a mistake to take the great **codex** (ancient manuscripts done in book, rather than roll, form), for instance, Sinaiticus (see Fig. 16.3) or Alexandrinus, and what is included in them as canon lists. Nowhere in those documents is there a preface or addendum that says "these are our Christian Scriptures." What we may assume is that the books present in the great codexes were all viewed as important and valuable Christian texts, and thus, where there was room in the codex more might be included than just the apostolic ones. Indeed, they might even go backward and include favorite earlier works like the Wisdom of Solomon. These were approved books for Christian study. We do not know that such codexes were taken out of the scriptorium and used as pulpit Bibles, so to speak.

What closed the canon was not the church but rather the dying out of the apostolic and eyewitness figures whose pens were laid down once and for all at that juncture, and this happened in the first century. It took a growing and increasingly Gentile church a further three centuries to fully recognize the importance of what had happened in the first century, in terms not just of what counted as orthodoxy but also of what counted as "the Bible" for Christians. The issue was not merely whether a writer had the Spirit. The church continued to have the Spirit. This was not the sole or whole basis for what was to be considered Scripture. What was also required was proximity to the Christ-event and its first eyewitnesses and apostles.

What was required was being part of the earliest and most ancient apostolic circles of Peter, Paul, James, and others.[11]

Even secondary figures, like Luke or Mark, who had direct contact with and had learned from the apostles and eyewitnesses were able to write these new Christian source documents, something later generations, not privy to interviewing or being eyewitnesses, could not do. Luke 1:1–4 makes quite clear what the mentality was, particularly of those in the wider apostolic circle. The eyewitnesses and original preachers of the Word had to be sought out and consulted. If earlier accounts had been written, they had to be consulted by the likes of a Luke. Papias reflects this whole attitude very clearly. He wanted to hear what the apostles had said, at least from those of the second and third generations who had met and heard them. The apostolic testimony was all-important, and in the end its pedigree would be the decisive issue. Why?

Christianity, like early Judaism, was a historical religion; and in historical matters antiquity, eyewitness testimony, and authoritative original witnesses were crucial. Even in Paul's day this was understood. He tells us, writing in about AD 52, that he passed on to his Corinthian converts what he had already received of the gospel story of the passion, burial, and resurrection that had happened "according to the Scriptures" (1 Cor. 15:1–4)—not, mind you, according to one or another text of Scripture, one or another prophetic scroll, but all the Scriptures. Paul had received this testimony as a sacred trust and tradition handed on to him probably, as Galatians 1–2 suggests, from Peter himself, who helped him get the history straight. Early Jews handled their sacred traditions with care and reverence. Paul was no different in handing on the gospel tradition.

Margaret Mitchell, in the seminal essay "The Emergence of the Written Record," says this:

> The earliest gospel message had texts in it as central to it—in this case the holy scriptures of Israel. The first followers of Jesus of Nazareth had turned to their "scriptures," the sacred texts of Judaism in the Hebrew and Greek languages, and sought to explain the Jesus whom they had come to know by what they found there. Paul could only have confidently summarized the message that these things were "according to the scriptures" if he was certain his audience was already familiar with the key supporting texts.[12]

---

11 See my *What Have They Done with Jesus?* (San Francisco: Harper, 2006).
12 Margaret Mitchell, "The Emergence of the Written Record," in *The Cambridge History of Christianity*, ed. Margaret M. Mitchell and Frances M. Young (Cambridge: Cambridge University Press), 178.

Just so, and this implies there was an enormous reason for the earliest Christians to have in hand and be sure about what their sacred texts were and what they contained. They, after all, had to demonstrate some remarkable things from Scripture, including the idea of a crucified messiah that would have seemed sheer folly to early Jews not expecting such a thing.

I am thus understandably dubious that there was not considerable clarity about the general boundaries of the sacred Scriptures of Israel for early Christians like Paul. If even texts like Job, Malachi, Ezekiel, Zechariah, Jeremiah, Isaiah, and Daniel could be seen as crucial sources for explaining the Christ-event, then it is clear that the corpus of sacred texts was viewed as much more than the Torah alone or even the Torah plus the former prophets and the later preexilic ones. And most remarkably neither those who relied on the Hebrew text nor those who relied on the Greek text cite as Scripture anything that doesn't eventually end up in the Hebrew canon—not once. This speaks volumes, and it needs to be taken into account by those who want to see the earliest period of the canonizing process as nothing but flux and great uncertainty.

What did the author of 2 Timothy 3:16 mean when he said "every passage of Scripture [or all Scripture] is God-breathed and profitable"? Notice the use of the singular for *Scripture*. It reflects an assumption of a bounded collection that has plenary inspiration. There was already in the NT era a reasonably clear sense on the part of some Christians of what counted as the OT Scriptures and what did not. Not only did the canonizing process begin before the first century for the OT and in the first century for the NT (as witnessed by Luke and 2 Pet. 3) but its limits were de facto defined by the nature of the historical reality of early Christianity in the first century, with its reliance on the apostolic and eyewitness testimony to provide it with its sacred tradition.

Canon consciousness is not, of course, the same as apostolic consciousness or awareness of writing Scripture. Canon consciousness when it comes to the NT as a full collection is something that was a matter of the later recognition by the church of final limitations or hard boundaries of the whole collection.

It is, of course, possible—many would say probable—that some of the writers of the NT may well have been unaware they were writing "canonical" documents, documents meant for a specific collection; but to judge from the case of our earliest Christian writer, Paul, they were aware that they were speaking "the Word of God" when they spoke the gospel and not merely the words of human beings, as that very early document 1 Thessalonians already tells us (1 Thess. 2:11–13).

They were aware of speaking inspired speech, and the written residue of such speech was likewise seen as inspired, authoritative, important, true. In the case of Luke, they were also aware that a "new testament" would include some combination of gospel plus apostle—the stories and teachings of Jesus and of his immediate apostolic followers and successors. Of course, there was no reality, or cognizance, of a full NT in the NT era as a collection. Such a full collection would come at a later time. For the very earliest Christians there was the OT (see 2 Tim. 3:16) and the apostolic tradition. As things turned out in regard to the NT books, apostolic documents were all that were to end up in the Christian canon as well, three hundred years later.[13]

The recognition and final definition of the canon took centuries. It is thus all the more remarkable that only apostolic books, and not those of the worthies of later centuries, were included in the NT canon. In the end, even the highly Gentile fourth-century church did not want to break faith with their Jewish Christian apostolic forebears, so both orthodoxy and the boundaries of the Bible were grounded in the earliest apostolic testimonies, which became our NT. Canon lists are only the after-the-fact residue of this affirmation of faith in the original apostolic witness. The Bible we have today was the product of many human hands, assembled over many centuries; but the same God who inspired it all guided this whole process so that God's people would have God's Word then and now. Let us consider these matters from a slightly different angle for a bit.

Paul Achtemeier stresses "the formation of the canon represented the working out of forces that were already present in the primitive Christian community and that would have made some form of canon virtually inevitable."[14] It was not a matter of fourth-century politics or another case of "history is written (or, in this case, the canon is formed) by the winners." It was never a matter of a group of old men sitting down in the fourth century AD and deciding these issues, nor was it a matter of ruling a bunch of books out which had previously been on somebody's canon list.

There was never any positive buzz for inclusion of any of the Gnostics texts in the NT canon; indeed, there was only negative press all along about those books. They were seen as heresy in their own day and long afterward. And you can't be said to exclude something that was never included on anyone's sacred text list in the first place. Not even perhaps the earliest of the Gnostic texts, the Gospel of Thomas, was ever on a canon list or seriously considered for inclusion as a sacred text for Christians, suitable for study and to be read in worship.

Often lost in the discussion of NT canonization is the fact that the early church had to also decide what form of the OT it would accept as Scripture, the

---

13 By "apostolic" I mean those written by apostles or their coworkers. The author of 2 Peter seems to have had some contact with apostles and certainly draws on apostolic documents like Jude.
14 P. Achtemeier, J. B. Green, and Marianne Meye Thompson, *Introducing the New Testament: Its Literature and Theology* (Grand Rapids, MI: Eerdmans, 2001), 589.

Hebrew text or the LXX in some form. De facto the Greek LXX seems to have become the church's OT, for the most part, in the second century AD.[15] This is interesting for our discussion because it meant that they thought a translation of the Bible could be viewed as the Scripture, the Word of God. Of course, this is good news for all those who are monolingual and whose spoken language does not include any of the biblical ones. It is interesting, however, that the church fathers were uncertain whether to include all the material found in the LXX or only the books found in the Hebrew Bible; and the question of order in regard to the last collection in the OT, the Writings, was an issue since the Hebrew OT does not end with Malachi.

Eusebius, the father of church history, informs us that it was actually some of the books which did make it into the NT canon that got debated and were sometimes disputed, books like Hebrews, because it was anonymous, or the more obviously Jewish documents like the letters and sermons of James or Jude, or the only NT prophetic book that made the cut, Revelation. There was no debate about whether to include any of the four earliest gospels—Matthew, Mark, Luke, and John—nor was there a debate about the Pauline corpus, with the exception of Hebrews.

Before the late fourth century when these matters were mostly settled, there had also been some debate about other orthodox books, including those of the Shepherd of Hermas, *1 Clement*, the Epistle of Barnabas, and even a Jewish book like Wisdom of Solomon, which was greatly loved by many early Christians and, indeed, had influenced Jesus himself. But there was no consensus on such books. There seems to have been some suspicion that Hermas tried to correct the author of Hebrews in Hebrews 6 who was (wrongly) understood by some to argue that sins committed after baptism were not to be forgiven and the person could not be restored. But orthodoxy was not deemed enough to recognize a book as Scripture—it needed to be an early witness, a first-century witness, one that went back directly or indirectly to the original eyewitnesses and apostles and their coworkers or an early prophet like John of Patmos.

The criteria discussed then involved things like apostolicity in some sense (from either an apostle or one of his cohorts writing in the apostolic tradition), orthodoxy, truth telling, whether the document was profitable for training in Christian righteousness, and the like. And recognizing these criteria, it then becomes interesting and remarkable that both the eastern part of the church represented by Athanasius

---

15 See Martin Hengel, *The Septuagint as Christian Scripture: Its Prehistory and the Problem of Its Canon* (Grand Rapids, MI: Baker, 2002).

(in his Festal Letter in AD 367), the African part of the church in 397 which listed only these twenty-seven books, and the Western part of the church represented by the pope, with the help of figures like Jerome, concluded that it was these twenty-seven books that should be recognized as the Christian Scriptures. And notice again that there was no one gathering of all the church fathers in one time or place to settle this issue by Constantine or anyone else. Rather, the process of discernment and discrimination was going on throughout the second through fourth centuries, and there was a settled agreement on the twenty-seven NT books by the end of the fourth century.

So, properly speaking, from a historical point of view, a book had to be widely recognized as true and orthodox and even apostolic in some sense before it could ever be recognized as Scripture, not the other way around. Canonizing a book didn't make it true or the Word of God, though it gave it added clout or authority after the fact. The Word of God was a much larger category than the written Scriptures and even referred to oral proclamation in its Christian form before there ever were any written Christian Scriptures. But once the canon was in place, of course, it became the main litmus test of truth or error thereafter.

There were both positive and negative historical developments that led toward canonization. For example, the dying off of the apostles and eyewitnesses and therefore the need to have things not only written down but collected and kept in safe places became crucial already in the second century AD. Then there was the wake-up call when you have figures like Marcion who came to Rome in about AD 144 and suggested a very truncated canon list—Luke's Gospel and Paul's letters minus the Pastorals. He entirely rejected the OT, on the grounds of its proclaiming a vengeful God. Against this limited canon list the church continued to say no. There was a wider corpus of writings, including more gospels and more letters, that the church would use as its sacred texts as well as the OT. It is interesting that Justin Martyr said that the fourfold gospel collection, which circulated in a single codex already in the second century, plus a collection of OT books were the Christian Scriptures. As we have mentioned, the earliest fuller canon list is the Muratorian one, which probably dates to the end of the second century and probably included Matthew, Mark, Luke, John, Acts, the letters of Paul including the Pastorals, 1 and 2 John, Jude, and Revelation. Notice that only James, Hebrews, 1–2 Peter, and 3 John are missing.

But another interesting criterion arises when we study this part of the story of the process of canonization. As Luke Timothy Johnson says, it becomes clear when it is decided that the Shepherd of Hermas would not be included, and the instructions are given that it is fine to read privately but ought not to be read in public worship, that a "key factor for canonization is not whether documents can be read or used by individuals but whether they are to be read publicly in worship."[16] It is understandable then that when we get to Eusebius of Caesarea (AD 320–330) he enunciates three criteria for acceptance of such writings—use in the church, apostolic origins, and theological consistency with the clearly apostolic documents (*Hist. Eccl.* 3.25.1–7). What he seems to be focusing on here is the criteria to be used to make decisions about the books still being disputed, namely, James, Jude, 2 Peter and 2–3 John, and whether they also can be included along with the universally recognized books, namely, the four canonical gospels, Acts, the letters of Paul, 1 John, 1 Peter, and Revelation.

It is remarkable that the various parts of the church, without political or ecclesiastical coercion and under the guidance of the Holy Spirit, all came to the same conclusion about the twenty-seven books. It was not a matter of the church sitting down in a big meeting and forming the canon. Rather, it was a matter of the church recognizing the canon which had been developing since one of the first letters of Paul was written and spoke of the living Word of God, oral and then written, as something synonymous with the Christian message about Jesus.

This is why Achtemeier is able to say,

> One can say then that the formation of the canon was conterminous with the life of the Christian community during its first three centuries of existence. It is not the case that some synod or council of bishops decided which books should be normative and thereafter required for Christians to accept. Rather the books that were finally included in the canon were included because over the centuries Christians had come to use them in their worship and instruction and to revere them for the power they displayed in engendering, enriching and correcting Christian faith. The canon thus represents the *collective experience of the Christian community during its formative centuries.*[17]

How then did we get from the fourth century until now, with the huge proliferation of translations of the Bible? What happened in between?

---

16 Luke Timothy Johnson, *The Writings of the New Testament*, 3rd ed. (Minneapolis, MN: Fortress Press), 601.

17 Achtemeier, Green, and Thompson, *Introducing the New Testament*, 608 (emphasis added).

Figure 16-3 The Bible is the most read book in all of human history and in almost all countries in the world. (Shutterstock/Damon Yancy)

THE BIBLE IN TRANSITION AND TRANSLATION

Sometimes missed in the discussion of the NT as Scripture and canon and the like is the fact that while the church was busy recognizing the Greek NT, it was also very busy translating it into numerous other languages. One of the earliest translations was the one into Coptic for Egyptians, which seems to date from as early as AD 270. Then too one must mention the translation into Ethiopic at least as early as the fifth century AD.

Just to cite a few examples, we have found fragments of a Syriac version from about AD 300—not a surprise since one of the major early ethnic churches was the

Syrian church. Somewhere between AD 350 and 439 the Bible was translated into Armenian for those in the area of the Caucasus Mountains and beyond, and for that same general vicinity there was a translation into Georgian about AD 450.

Of course, Latin was the official language of the Roman Empire, so not surprisingly there was already a translation in old Latin of the Bible in North Africa, perhaps as early as AD 195. This is not to be confused with the translation that became the classic and the standard, the so-called Latin Vulgate (*vulgatus* referring to the common tongue, from which we oddly enough get the word *vulgar*, which originally meant "common") undertaken by Jerome. Jerome began his work in about AD 390, finishing about 404; and what distinguished his work from that of others and earlier efforts is that he compared the LXX to a text of the Hebrew Scriptures in doing his Latin translation. This particular translation was to dominate the landscape through the Middle Ages and unfortunately, in the western part of the church, led to the neglect of the LXX and in many places even of the Greek NT itself. It was not until the Renaissance, with figures like Petrarch who sparked a renewed interest in Greek and ancient Roman literature, that there began a renewed interest in having the Bible in the West in its original languages again.

Looking eastward, we know that the Bible was translated into Arabic from Coptic and Syriac versions at least as early as the sixth century AD. Sometime in the ninth century the Orthodox church's missionary work going into the southern part of Russia led to a Slavonic translation of the Bible as well. Because of the dominance of Latin as the continued language of the church, even after the Roman Empire was long gone, it was not until the twelfth century AD that there were translations into the vernacular for French-, Italian-, and Spanish-speaking persons. Not surprisingly, the Roman Catholic Church prohibited the use of these versions other than as aids to persons who could not read the Latin, and so as a supplement to the Latin Bible, which impeded progress.

It took the invention of the printing press in the mid-fifteenth century (the first book was, of course, the Latin Vulgate rendering of the Bible printed by Johannes Gutenberg); the rise of Martin Luther, who provided his own translation into German (1522); the Reformation in general; and figures like Erasmus, who produced a Greek NT (1516) to move things along more rapidly toward the proliferation of translations and translations that would take into account the Greek and Hebrew texts, as Luther had done, using Erasmus's text. The important point is that the vernacular versions that began to appear after Gutenberg would increasingly go back and consult the original-language texts of the Bible.

Before we begin to talk about the English Bible, which requires a longer discussion, it is important to notice four things about the translation of the Bible into all these languages. (1) It was a function of and reflected that Christianity was an evangelistic religion throughout this period, and the assumption was that people could not be saved unless they heard the Bible message in their own languages. (2) Once again, this whole process happened in fits and starts and not under some central authority's efforts. It happened for the most part because the need arose for all these translations as the missions went forward. (3) It was assumed that a translation of the Bible could be called Scripture or the Word of God for this language group or that language group. (4) Yet, thank goodness some figures, such as Jerome and much later Erasmus and Luther, realized that these vernacular translations needed to be in touch with the original Hebrew and Greek texts of the Bible.

Since Erasmus's day we have not turned back from that principle when it comes to translation. And look where it has led. Today, the whole Bible is available in more than 340 languages and the NT in over 800 languages, and furthermore, at least one book of the Bible had been translated into more than 2,000 languages as of 1995. There is certainly no other book of comparable antiquity or even from the modern age about which one could claim this.

Without question, after the Latin Vulgate, no vernacular translation of the Bible has had more impact on Christian life and culture in general than the King James Version (KJV). What is seldom noted, while the KJV has been praised to the skies for its various qualities, is that it was a translation that owed an enormous amount of its diction and memorable phrasing to its English predecessor versions, especially the partial OT and the entire NT that William Tyndale finished; and at the other end of the discussion, the KJV went through various revised editions.

It was one of the key principles of the Reformation that the Bible should be placed in the hands of ordinary persons, not kept in the scholar's study or chained to a pulpit in some church. This revolution was made possible by the rise of the printing press, which reduced enormously the laborious process of hand-copying the Bible that had gone on since the first century AD and, in fact, well before then, counting the various books of the OT.

Yet our discussion in this section must start with John Wycliffe (ca. 1330–1384), who argued at length, and in both Latin and English no less, for an English translation of the Bible. Of course, there was great fear by the church hierarchy that if the Bible was placed into the hands of the laity, it might cause the breakdown of authority or even have a leveling effect on society. It might break the clerical monopoly over the church as well. It is not surprising then that when Wycliffe did his translation from the Latin Vulgate, or at least aided and abetted those who made the translation for him, he was roundly criticized. A certain Henry Knighton put it this way: "Wycliffe translated it from Latin into the English—not the anglic [*sic*]—language.

As a result, what was previously known only by learned clerics and those of good understanding has become common, and available to the laity—in fact, even to women who can read. As a result, the pearls of the Gospel have been scattered before swine."[18]

The efforts of Wycliffe opened the proverbial Pandora's box, and it is no surprise that the response was not only swift in his day but consistent thereafter. The archbishop of Canterbury in 1407, Thomas Arundel, banned anyone from translating the Bible on their own initiative and authority into English. He also took the second step to ban the reading in private or public of any such English translation. Clearly enough, he was worried that things were getting out of hand. The issue was sensitive well into the sixteenth century, for John Colet, then dean of St. Paul's Cathedral, was suspended in 1513 from his post for translating the Lord's Prayer into English. Just when the clerics thought they were getting things under control, along came Martin Luther, who published his German translation in 1522; and he had English admirers, notably William Tyndale (ca. 1494–1536).

Tyndale was no ordinary layperson. Indeed, he studied at Magdalen College, University of Oxford. Tyndale was later to complain that the Oxford dons would not allow him to study the Scriptures until after he had had many years of studying the Greek and Latin pagan classics. But, in fact, there was a rise in both Oxford and Cambridge of interest in and scholars competent in both Greek and Hebrew during the course of the fifteenth and sixteenth centuries, a good thing too since they would be needed on the translation committee for the KJV in the early seventeenth century.

This rise in the interest in biblical languages happened in spite of the scholarly prejudice that only Latin was really worth knowing as the language of academia. Just how much and how long this Latin influence continued to be true can be seen from the fact that even in the first half of the eighteenth century we have the story from John Wesley that when he wanted to have conversations with the Moravian Peter Boehler, since Boehler's spoken English was poor and the same could be said for Wesley's German, they spoke to each other in the other language they were both fluent in—Latin, even though the subject matter was Protestant theology. If we need further testimony to the enduring impact of Latin and the Vulgate, we need only mention the fact that Catholic services were still being conducted mostly in Latin when I was born. Vaticans I and II changed all that.

---

18 This quotation is found in the very fine study of my friend Alistair McGrath, *In the Beginning: The Story of the King James Bible and How It Changed a Nation, a Language, and a Culture* (New York: Doubleday, 2001), 20. In what follows in this section I will largely be following his lead.

Tyndale was smart enough to realize that England was too volatile a place for him to translate the Bible into English, so we must picture the poor man moving to Cologne, Germany, and translating the NT during the period 1524–1525. After some difficulties, the first edition finally came out in book form in 1526 in Worms.

The high degree of Luther's influence on Tyndale can be seen from the table of contents of his NT; as Luther had done with his translation, he listed Hebrews, James, Jude, and Revelation as being of dubious authenticity, and they were placed at the end of the book and not even numbered like the other books. It was the 1526 edition of Tyndale's translation that was smuggled into England. It was this event that produced irreversible pressure for an English Bible to be produced and controlled in England. Despite the fact that Tyndale's name never appeared on a copy of his translation, he was to pay a heavy price for his efforts—he was hanged and then burned at the stake on October 6, 1536, having been betrayed by those who opposed his efforts. This in turn earned him a place in John Foxe's *Book of Martyrs*.

Bishop Tunstall of London had gone on something of a personal crusade against Tyndale and his translation (both sad and ironic since Tyndale first came to Tunstall to ask if he would patronize the translation effort). One of the most amazing parts of this story is that Tunstall went all the way to Antwerp to stop the printing of the Tyndale translation in 1529. Through a merchant named Augustine Packington he was offered an opportunity to buy as many copies as he liked of the translation for a price. The bishop agreed. Unbeknownst to the bishop, Packington went straight to Tyndale and told him about the deal. Tyndale was thrilled because suddenly he would have a lot more money to produce more copies, even if Tunstall took all of them that he bought and burned them. And so it was that the deal was struck, and unwittingly the bishop funded the continuing publication of Tyndale's translation.

Tyndale, in fact, had a very great and rare gift of being able not only to translate the Bible but to translate it into beautiful and memorable English prose. It is to him we owe phrases like "my brother's keeper" (Gen. 4), "the salt of the earth" (Matt. 5), "a law unto themselves" (Rom. 2), and "the powers that be" (Rom. 13). It was Tyndale who came up with the hybrid term *Jehovah*, which combines two different Hebrew names for God. He invented the English word *Passover* for the Hebrew *pesakh*. It is also to Tyndale that we owe the use of terms like *scapegoat* and *atonement* to translate Hebrew terms that had no good direct English equivalents.

Tyndale unfortunately had not finished his translation of the OT. Only the Pentateuch had been really completed, so it was left to a far less skilled translator, Miles Coverdale (ca. 1488–1569), who almost entirely took over Tyndale's work and incorporated it into his own, adding a fresh translation of the rest of the OT depending mostly on Luther's German translation, it would appear. It first went to print in 1535, shortly before Tyndale was executed in England. One could call the Coverdale Bible really a compilation of earlier translations, mostly Tyndale's.

With the help of Thomas Cromwell, an entrepreneur named Richard Grafton printed another English Bible shortly thereafter called Matthew's Bible. The text was edited by John Rogers, who had been a close associate of Tyndale. It not only followed the Tyndale translation very closely but had the additional benefit of being printed in Antwerp where additional pages of Tyndale's OT translation had turned up which had never made it into Tyndale's own book.

In 1539 the Great Bible came out and really became the first authorized English translation, a good sixty plus years before the KJV. It actually was simply a revision of Matthew's Bible done by none other than Miles Coverdale himself but with a table of contents that did not reflect Luther's biases against various books including Hebrews and James. The reason it was called the Great Bible was its size because in addition to the OT and NT it included the apocryphal intertestamental books. This translation is mostly a retread of Tyndale, with some Coverdale blended in, especially where there was no Tyndale text to follow.

The next translation of note and influence was the famous Geneva Bible, which was largely the work of William Whittingham (ca. 1524–1579). His NT version was printed first in 1557, and once more it was heavily indebted to Tyndale, the real progenitor of all these later English versions. Whittingham's one real innovation is that he changed the nomenclature of those books Luther was largely unhappy with from the "Catholic Epistles" to the "General Epistles," which made Protestants, of course, feel much better. The Geneva Bible was widely read and accepted in the latter part of the sixteenth century, but when James of Scotland came to the throne of England upon Elizabeth's death in 1603, there still had not been a decision taken on what Bible might become the official Bible of the English realm. As it turned out, James disliked the Geneva Bible because its marginal notes did not support the notion that the Bible upholds the divine right of kings, a doctrine about which James was passionate.

In 1604 there was a conference held at Hampton Court Palace convened by James in which he proposed to listen to the laments and complaints of both Puritans and Anglicans about church life in that period. Some of the complaints had to do with the Prayer Book, which the Puritans wanted abolished, something James was not prepared to do. Could he make a concession on another matter, which he saw as less crucial, that would placate the Puritans? The answer turned out to be yes, and it led to the KJV.

John Reynolds, the leader of the Puritan delegation, proposed a new Bible translation. James saw this as the concession that would ease the religious tensions, so the decree was made that "a translation be made of the whole Bible, *as consonant as can be to the original Hebrew and Greek*; and this to be set out and printed without any marginal notes, and only to be used in all churches in England in time of divine service."[19] It is not clear whether after the translation was finished there was an official authorization of it by the king as the records of the period 1600–1613 were lost in a fire. The translation was to be done by scholars from both Oxford and Cambridge (the only two English universities at the time), and the team of fifty-four scholars was to be led by Lancelot Andrewes, Regius Professor of Greek and Hebrew at Oxford; however, it is perfectly clear that James's close ally Bishop Richard Bancroft is the person who laid down the translation rules for this English Bible.

Rule one read, "The ordinary Bible read in the Church, commonly called the Bishop's Bible, to be followed and as little altered as the Truth of the original will permit." Now the Bishop's Bible of 1568 was simply a smaller version of the Great Bible, meant to compete with the Geneva Bible, though it never eclipsed the latter. Notice that this rule makes clear that the scholars on the translation team were to do their best to follow an earlier English translation, and they are further instructed to stick with the most commonly used renderings in this and other earlier English versions. Their process was to compare these earlier translations to the Hebrew and Greek texts and do their best to follow the lead of the earlier English versions. Rule fourteen adds that they should consult Tyndale's, Matthew's, Coverdale's, and Geneva's translations and follow them where they agree better with the original-language text. *The KJV translators did not attempt, nor did they see it as their duty, to produce an entirely fresh translation based just on the Greek and Hebrew texts of the Bible.* As McGrath makes abundantly clear, they saw themselves as standing on the shoulders of giants like Tyndale. They were not trying to be innovators, nor were they mere copiers of earlier versions, particularly in spots where there had been advances in original-language study.[20] And they were only as good as the original-language manuscripts they had would allow them to be.

Erasmus's Greek NT was based on five or six Greek manuscripts, none of which was any earlier than the tenth century AD. Nevertheless, this allowed Erasmus to make some corrections of errors found in the Vulgate. The next edition of the Greek NT, the so-called Bezan text (compiled by Theodore Beza in Geneva), has the same liabilities of not having any really early Greek manuscripts to follow. The Bezan text of the Greek NT came to be called the Textus Receptus, but this

19 See McGrath, *In the Beginning, 164.*
20 Ibid., 176–177.

was not because there was any church that ever officially pronounced it to be the best Greek NT text. It was simply the best available to scholars at that time, and the KJV team used it in their translation work. One other more technical point needs to be made. The Textus Receptus is not simply identical with the so-called Byzantine text that became so important in the eastern part of the Roman Empire from the fourth century onward. It is, however, close to it at many points. The vast majority of scholars today do not think that the Bezan Greek text reflects our earliest and best text of the Greek NT.

Not surprisingly, considering where the universities were in England and taking into account Tyndale's own Oxford pedigree, the English that we find in the KJV is basically the English of southeastern England, not the English of the northern part of the country (much less the king's English as he was a Scot). It took from 1604 to 1610 for the six different teams of scholars to finish their work. From the start, strong consideration was given to the aural dimension to the text as it was primarily a translation to be used in public services. The teams undoubtedly read their translations aloud and tried them out on each other, something we could use more of with modern translations. In the original preface to the KJV the translators state plainly, "Truly (Good Christian Reader) we never thought from the beginning, that we should need to make a new Translation, nor yet to make of a bad one a good one . . . but to make a good one better, or out of many good ones, one principal good one . . . that hath been our endeavor."[21]

It is interesting at this remove to also hear what Miles Smith, one of the translators of the KJV, says about the authority and inspiration of the Bible. "The original thereof being from God, not man; the inditer, the holy spirit, not the wit of Apostles or Prophets; the Penmen such as were sanctified from the womb, and endued with a principle portion of God's spirit; the matter, verity, piety, purity, uprightness; the form, God's word, God's testimony, God's oracle, the word of truth, the word of salvation."[22] Notice that he is not referring to his and his colleagues' translation work; he is referring to "the original thereof."

There is no evidence that the KJV translators ever saw themselves as uniquely inspired to do what they did. Instead, they saw themselves as those who followed in the human footsteps of their predecessors wherever possible, making changes cautiously. They were under no delusions that they had created a perfect translation; but they thought it to be the best yet available in English, and so it was. They also

---

21 Ibid., 189.
22 Ibid., 190.

freely admitted that there were many words, especially in the Hebrew text, for instance, names of birds, that they were very unsure how to render into English. The preface is commendably modest about the difficulties and imperfections of all translations including their own. The translators realized, of course, that there is great difficulty in managing a balance between faithfulness and elegance.

Smith was both passionate and eloquent about how important it was for the translators to do their best to render the Bible into good common English, and he adds in that first preface, "Translation it is that openeth the window to let the light it; that breaketh the shell, that we may eat the kernel; that putteth aside the curtain, that we might look into the Most Holy place, that removeth the cover of the well, that we might come by the water. . . . Indeed without translation into the vulgar tongue, the unlearned are but like children at Jacob's well (which is deep) . . . without a bucket or something to draw with."[23]

Unfortunately, there were many printer's errors in the first edition of 1611, which led to a second edition only shortly thereafter, in 1613, where most of the errors were corrected. It was the decision of Bishop Bancroft that the original editions of the KJV would include the translation of the Apocrypha, to the chagrin of some; and not surprisingly, in due course the Puritans lobbied to have it removed in later editions. Not surprisingly as well, various Puritans when they moved to America did not bring a KJV with them. Their Bible of choice was the Geneva Bible.

We have in a short span here gone on a long odyssey, taking us from the process that led up to the canonization of the OT and NT to the historical process that led to its translation into many languages, most importantly of all into English. There are many twists and turns to this story, but at every step of the way two things are clear. Those involved in these many labors believed the written down Bible was itself one expression of the Word of God. They also believed that foreign-language translations that were careful and faithful could reasonably approximate the original-language texts and so deserve to be called the Word of God in a secondary or derivative sense. But, as Miles Smith pointed out, only the original thereof deserves that title in the full and complete sense.

In the end, it was not necessary for God to drop the whole Bible from the sky on golden tablets to willing recipients among his people. Instead, the Word of God written was to have the same character as the Word of God incarnate, a fully human character, and a fully human history. So it was that the Bible came to us at a particular point in history, through particular cultures, and in particular

---

23 Ibid., 192.

languages. The God who created all things chose also to be involved personally in that human history, and part of that involvement entailed God's guidance of faithful persons to write down and preserve his Word for all future generations.

We are the beneficiaries of all this, and whenever we pick up a Bible, we should be thankful that God and his people of previous generations cared enough to make sure we got this book. It is the most important book, the most published book, the most read book, the most understood and the most misunderstood book in all human history. It is my hope that *this book* has provided some stimulus for you to study the Bible in more depth and commit yourself to a lifetime of exploration of a book whose meaning cannot be exhausted or replaced and is never out of date.

WHAT JUST HAPPENED?

In a short span of pages we have tried to tell the story of the canonization of the Bible, followed by the story of its translation and spread through many cultures, including its translation into hundreds of English versions. We stressed that the church did not create the canon but came to recognize which books could appropriately be called Scripture or sacred texts, through a process of discernment that lasted several centuries. We also explained that it was the evangelistic nature of Christianity that gave the impetus to the translation of the original Hebrew and Greek of the Bible into many languages. No other religion has had its source documents translated and disseminated so widely in all of human history.

FOR FURTHER READING

For much more on the material in this chapter, please see my *The Living Word of God: Rethinking the Theology of the Bible* (Waco, TX: Baylor University Press, 2009). There is no better or more readable account of the translation of the Bible into English, including especially the story of the King James Version, than that of Alistair McGrath, *In the Beginning: The Story of the King James Bible and How It Changed a Nation, a Language, and a Culture* (New York: Doubleday, 2001).

EPILOGUE: FOUND in TRANSLATION

One obvious starting point on a quest to understand and properly interpret the Bible is picking a translation of the Bible. But which translation? There are hundreds and hundreds of English translations of the Bible, both old and new. In fact, there have been about 900 translations of the Bible into English done since the sixteenth century. And I am referring just to the ones that made it into print. For example, here is a list of just some of the translations done of the Bible in the twentieth and twenty-first centuries.

TWENTIETH CENTURY

- American Standard
- Rotherham's Emphasized
- Ferrar Fenton
- Worrell New Testament
- Knox
- Philips
- Basic English
- Revised Standard
- Anchor
- New World
- New English Bible
- New American Standard
- Good News
- Jerusalem

- New American
- Living
- New International
- New Century
- Bethel
- New King James
- New Jerusalem
- Recovery
- New Revised Standard
- Revised English
- Contemporary English
- The Message
- Clear Word
- New Life
- 21st Century King James
- Third Millennium
- New International Reader's
- New International Inclusive Language
- God's Word
- New Living
- Complete Jewish Bible
- International Standard
- Holman Christian Standard

TWENTY-FIRST CENTURY

- World English
- English Standard
- Today's New International
- New English Translation (NET Bible)
- New English Translation of the Septuagint
- Orthodox Study Bible
- The Voice
- Common English Bible
- WGC Illustrated
- Apostolic Bible Polyglot
- Open English Bible

- Eastern Orthodox Bible
- New American Bible Revised Edition
- Lexham English Bible

No wonder the beginning student of the Bible becomes confused right from the start. It's like picking out your first car on www.cars.com. There is a bewildering array from which to choose. If you can't decide which one of a myriad of cars is best for you, you'll never make a purchase or take it for a test drive. Thus, a little guidance on picking a translation is in order at this point. Your teacher may well require you to buy a particular translation if you are beginning to study the Bible as part of a college course, but in this case I am talking about a translation that you can use on an ongoing basis as you begin to study the Bible on your own.

The truth is, there are many good English translations of the Bible, but no one translation is suited to every possible use. Indeed, most translations were intended for specific purposes and specific audiences. Furthermore, *every translation of the Bible is already an interpretation of the Bible*. This is so because the translators must make decisions about what English words or phrases best render the ancient Hebrew or Aramaic or Greek words in which the Bible was originally written. And not infrequently there is not an exact English equivalent for this or that ancient foreign-language word or phrase, especially when it comes to idioms. Let me illustrate.

In Numbers 22:22 (and elsewhere) we have a phrase in the Hebrew that if translated literally would read "and God's nose burned." This conjures up images of God having actual physical features and someone having set fire to his face! But that is not what the idiomatic phrase means at all. It simply means God was very angry or, as we might say, he got red in the face. Idiomatic phrases that are figurative in nature cannot simply be rendered literally without making the job of understanding the text more difficult.

But why are there so many English translations of the Bible? In part this is because English is a living and rapidly evolving language (who would have known that the word *tweet* or *texting* could refer to an electronic communication of words only twenty years ago?), and in part it is because we continue to make new discoveries of older and older manuscripts of the Bible, which are closer and closer to the original wording of the original copies. In short, because the English language is a moving target and because there are always more archaeological discoveries of ancient manuscripts, we continue to need new translations of the Bible.

SOME BASIC GUIDELINES

Bibles range from more periphrastic to more literal to somewhere in between in the way they render the ancient languages. *In general, the more periphrastic, the more the translator has tried to interpret the text for you to make it intelligible.* For example, Eugene Peterson's The Message is very readable, but it has many more words in it than a more literal rendering of the text. At the opposite end of the spectrum would be something like the New American Standard Bible, which strives to be as literal as possible, while recognizing that you can't simply follow the word order in the ancient language and make good English sentences. I would suggest, however, that one choose a translation that doesn't come from either end of the spectrum but from somewhere in between. It needs to be in good contemporary English so that the English itself does not become a barrier to understanding, and it needs to have some literary finesse so that idioms will be rendered as idioms, figurative phrases as figures, prose as prose, poetry as poetry, and so on. In fact, most popular good translations fall into this "in between" category of rendering the original text. Each translation has its strengths and weaknesses, but I would suggest that a good place to start would be with the New International Version or the New Revised Standard Version or, if one wants a translation with no more than an eighth-grade vocabulary, the Common English Version. These translations are all done in the main by Protestant scholars. If you are a Catholic, you may prefer the Jerusalem Bible.

I would say actually that none of these translations really reflects any sort of particular denominational or even theological bias, so the fact that they were done mainly by Protestants or mainly by Catholics is not necessarily relevant. The question is whether the text has been fairly and accurately translated, however one may interpret it. The virtue of a translation like the New Revised Standard Version is that it had both Catholic and Protestant scholars on the translation team and the translators reflected a spectrum of theological views, thus preventing some particular theological bias from being a guiding principle for the translation.

One of the possible inhibitors to reading through the narrative of the Bible is all those chapter and verse divisions and headings and distracting notes in the margins and in the footnotes and sometimes right in the text. If you find chapter and verse divisions distracting and would like to read the Bible primarily as a story, the new The Voice Bible is perhaps a good place to start, to get an overall sense of the flow of the biblical narrative.

Pick a translation done by a team of scholars, not a particular individual. This not only eliminates the possibility of individual bias in translation but is also advisable since no single person on earth can be an expert in the translation of every verse of the Bible. The translations recommended above are all team translations done by experts in the field.

Do not pick an e-book version of a Bible. Why not? Because it is difficult, even with the latest electronic technology, to be able to flip back and forth between "pages" of the text and compare and contrast things quickly. With an electronic book, if you are just reading it straight through, the e-book works well enough. But if you are studying, which sometimes requires jumping all over the place, and comparing say Isaiah 40–66 and the use and quotations of some of those chapters and verses in the New Testament, you really need a hard copy of the Bible to do this. In short, when buying your first Bible for studying, you need a good old-fashioned book you can hold in your hand, readily flip through, put several bookmarkers in, and, yes, even use a highlighter on. There is nothing sacrilegious about marking in your Bible. It is the words and their meaning that are sacred, not the paper and the print on it.

Pick a text with a size and character of print that makes it easy for you to read. The Bible is a complex enough book to read without having to overcome minuscule print, fonts that present a challenge to easy reading and study, pages that stick together because they are of poor quality, and so on. This means that you should not buy a "pocket"-sized Bible as your first study Bible. The print will necessarily be too tiny. The Bible is a big book, rather like a dictionary or another reference book; and as such, you should avoid miniature editions. *You should also avoid cheap paperback editions.* You want something that will last and stand up to a lot of reading and a lot of ongoing use. This means a good hardback or leather-bound edition. Make practical decisions about size and shape that will serve you well for a long time. The Good News, of all of the translations recommended above, comes in very affordable study editions in hardback. I myself regularly use the Wesley Study Bible that has the New Revised Standard Version, but there are many other good ones.

Choose a Bible that has useful footnotes and maps but does not overwhelm you with commentary in the margins or at the bottom of the page. While I recommend a good study Bible, I am not referring to the sort that is also a full-scale commentary on the Bible. It is important that your first in-depth reading of the Bible does not involve a lot of distractions, diversions, or left turns. You need to read the text carefully and prayerfully and think through what you are reading before consulting commentaries, dictionaries, and the like. Don't get me wrong: you will definitely need the commentaries before long but not at the outset of your journey of understanding.

For example, a study Bible that looks like this is not too busy to constantly distract you from reading the text. (See pages 248–249 for examples.)

MATTHEW 18.28—19.22   22

forgave him the debt. 28But that same slave, as he went out, came upon one of his fellow slaves who owed him a hundred denarii;*a* and seizing him by the throat, he said, 'Pay what you owe.' 29Then his fellow slave fell down and pleaded with him, 'Have patience with me, and I will pay you.' 30But he refused; then he went and threw him into prison until he would pay the debt. 31When his fellow slaves saw what had happened, they were greatly distressed, and they went and reported to their lord all that had taken place. 32Then his lord summoned him and said to him, 'You wicked slave! I forgave you all that debt because you pleaded with me. 33Should you not have had mercy on your fellow slave, as I had mercy on you?' 34And in anger his lord handed him over to be tortured until he would pay his entire debt. 35So my heavenly Father will also do to every one of you, if you do not forgive your brother or sister*b* from your heart."

Teaching about Divorce

19 When Jesus had finished saying these things, he left Galilee and went to the region of Judea beyond the Jordan. 2Large crowds followed him, and he cured them there.

3 Some Pharisees came to him, and to test him they asked, "Is it lawful for a man to divorce his wife for any cause?" 4He answered, "Have you not read that the one who made them at the beginning 'made them male and female,' 5and said, 'For this reason a man shall leave his father and mother and be joined to his wife, and the two shall become one flesh'? 6So they are no longer two, but one flesh. Therefore what God has joined together, let no one separate." 7They said to him, "Why then did Moses command us to give a certificate of dismissal and to divorce her?" 8He said to them, "It was because you were so hard-hearted that Moses allowed you to divorce your wives, but from the beginning it was not so. 9And I say to you, whoever divorces his wife, except for unchastity, and marries another commits adultery."*c*

10 His disciples said to him, "If such is the case of a man with his wife, it is better not to marry." 11But he said to them, "Not everyone can accept this teaching, but only those to whom it is given. 12For there are eunuchs who have been so from birth, and there are eunuchs who have been made eunuchs by others, and there are eunuchs who have made themselves eunuchs for the sake of the kingdom of heaven. Let anyone accept this who can."

Jesus Blesses Little Children

13 Then little children were being brought to him in order that he might lay his hands on them and pray. The disciples spoke sternly to those who brought them; 14but Jesus said, "Let the little children come to me, and do not stop them; for it is to such as these that the kingdom of heaven belongs." 15And he laid his hands on them and went on his way.

The Rich Young Man

16 Then someone came to him and said, "Teacher, what good deed must I do to have eternal life?" 17And he said to him, "Why do you ask me about what is good? There is only one who is good. If you wish to enter into life, keep the commandments." 18He said to him, "Which ones?" And Jesus said, "You shall not murder; You shall not commit adultery; You shall not steal; You shall not bear false witness; 19Honor your father and mother; also, You shall love your neighbor as yourself." 20The young man said to him, "I have kept all these;*d* what do I still lack?" 21Jesus said to him, "If you wish to be perfect, go, sell your possessions, and give the money*e* to the poor, and you will have treasure in heaven; then come, follow me." 22When the young man heard this word, he

a The denarius was the usual day's wage for a laborer   *b* Gk *brother*   *c* Other ancient authorities read *except on the ground of unchastity, causes her to commit adultery;* others add at the end of the verse *and he who marries a divorced woman commits adultery*   *d* Other ancient authorities add *from my youth*   *e* Gk lacks *the money*

went away grieving, for he had many possessions.

23 Then Jesus said to his disciples, "Truly I tell you, it will be hard for a rich person to enter the kingdom of heaven. 24Again I tell you, it is easier for a camel to go through the eye of a needle than for someone who is rich to enter the kingdom of God." 25When the disciples heard this, they were greatly astounded and said, "Then who can be saved?" 26But Jesus looked at them and said, "For mortals it is impossible, but for God all things are possible."

27 Then Peter said in reply, "Look, we have left everything and followed you. What then will we have?" 28Jesus said to them, "Truly I tell you, at the renewal of all things, when the Son of Man is seated on the throne of his glory, you who have followed me will also sit on twelve thrones, judging the twelve tribes of Israel. 29And everyone who has left houses or brothers or sisters or father or mother or children or fields, for my name's sake, will receive a hundredfold, *a* and will inherit eternal life. 30But many who are first will be last, and the last will be first.

The Laborers in the Vineyard

20 "For the kingdom of heaven is like a landowner who went out early in the morning to hire laborers for his vineyard. 2After agreeing with the laborers for the usual daily wage, *b* he sent them into his vineyard. 3When he went out about nine o'clock, he saw others standing idle in the marketplace; 4and he said to them, 'You also go into the vineyard, and I will pay you whatever is right.' So they went. 5When he went out again about noon and about three o'clock, he did the same. 6And about five o'clock he went out and found others standing around; and he said to them, 'Why are you standing here idle all day?' 7They said to him, 'Because no one has hired us.' He said to them, 'You also go into the vineyard.' 8When evening came, the owner of the vine-

yard said to his manager, 'Call the laborers and give them their pay, beginning with the last and then going to the first.' 9When those hired about five o'clock came, each of them received the usual daily wage. *b* 10Now when the first came, they thought they would receive more; but each of them also received the usual daily wage. *b* 11And when they received it, they grumbled against the landowner, 12saying, 'These last worked only one hour, and you have made them equal to us who have borne the burden of the day and the scorching heat.' 13But he replied to one of them, 'Friend, I am doing you no wrong; did you not agree with me for the usual daily wage? *b* 14Take what belongs to you and go; I choose to give to this last the same as I give to you. 15Am I not allowed to do what I choose with what belongs to me? Or are you envious because I am generous?' *c* 16So the last will be first, and the first will be last." *d*

A Third Time Jesus Foretells His Death and Resurrection

17 While Jesus was going up to Jerusalem, he took the twelve disciples aside by themselves, and said to them on the way, 18"See, we are going up to Jerusalem, and the Son of Man will be handed over to the chief priests and scribes, and they will condemn him to death; 19then they will hand him over to the Gentiles to be mocked and flogged and crucified; and on the third day he will be raised."

The Request of the Mother of James and John

20 Then the mother of the sons of Zebedee came to him with her sons, and kneeling before him, she asked a favor of him. 21And he said to her, "What do you want?" She said to him, "Declare that these two sons of mine will sit, one at your right hand and one at your left, in your kingdom." 22But Jesus answered, "You do not know what you are asking. Are you able to drink the cup that I am about to drink?" *e* They said to him,

But a study Bible that looks like this may well prevent you from being focused on reading and understanding the text. (Notice on pages 251–252 how there are probably too many annotations and comments at the bottom of these pages to keep one focused on the text.)

Let me be clear that I am not suggesting you take the anti-intellectual approach that says "I don't need any human help in reading the Bible. I have the Holy Spirit and a good brain, and that is enough." To a student who once said words to this effect to me when I was requiring him to read commentaries on the biblical text, I replied, "You need to give the Holy Spirit more to work with." You should not use the Holy Spirit as a labor-saving device.[1]

The journey to understanding the Bible begins with reading the Bible and not just any sort of reading but careful, prayerful, analytical reading. Armed with a good translation, the good will to study hard, and good guidance from teachers and written sources, you will be well on the way not only to exploring the Bible but also to understanding it and hopefully allowing it to enrich and enlighten your life the way it has done for literally billions of people before you. May you hear the same call that St. Augustine once heard which changed his life, namely, "pick it up and read, pick it up and read."

---

1 For much more about how to pick a proper translation and the problems of what gets lost in translation, see Witherington, *The Living Word of God: Rethinking the Theology of the Bible* (Waco, TX: Baylor University Press, 2007), pp. 137–149.

MATTHEW 19

on your fellow slave, as I had mercy on you?' [34] And in anger his lord handed him over to be tortured until he would pay his entire debt. [35] So my heavenly Father will also do to every one of you, if you do not forgive your brother or sister[a] from your heart."

19 When Jesus had finished saying these things, he left Galilee and went to the region of Judea beyond the Jordan. [2] Large crowds followed him, and he cured them there.

[3] Some Pharisees came to him, and to test him they asked, "Is it lawful for a man to divorce his wife for any cause?" [4] He answered, "Have you not read that the one who made them at the beginning 'made them male and female,' [5] and said, 'For this reason a man shall leave his father and mother and be joined to his wife, and the two shall become one flesh'? [6] So they are no longer two, but one flesh. Therefore what God has joined together, let no one separate." [7] They said to him, "Why then did Moses command us to give a certificate of dismissal and to divorce her?" [8] He said to them, "It was because you were so hard-hearted that Moses allowed you to divorce your wives, but from the beginning it was not so. [9] And I say to you, whoever divorces his wife, except for unchastity, and marries another commits adultery."[b]

[10] His disciples said to him, "If such is the case of a man with his wife, it is better not to marry." [11] But he said to them, "Not everyone can accept this teaching, but only those to whom it is given. [12] For there are eunuchs who have been so from birth, and there are eunuchs who have been made eunuchs by others, and there are eunuchs who have made themselves eunuchs for the sake of the kingdom of heaven. Let anyone accept this who can."

[13] Then little children were being brought to him in order that he might lay his hands on them and pray. The disciples spoke sternly to those who brought them; [14] but Jesus said, "Let the little children come to me, and do not stop them; for it is to such as these that the kingdom of heaven belongs." [15] And he laid his hands on them and went on his way.

[16] Then someone came to him and said, "Teacher, what good deed must I do to have eternal life?" [17] And he said to him, "Why do you ask me about what is good? There is only one who is good. If you wish to enter into life, keep the commandments." [18] He said to him, "Which ones?" And Jesus said, "You shall not murder; You shall not commit adultery; You shall not steal; You shall not bear false witness; [19] Honor your father and mother; also, You shall love your neighbor as yourself." [20] The young man said to him, "I have kept all these;[c] what do I still lack?" [21] Jesus said to him, "If you wish to be perfect, go, sell your possessions, and give the money[d] to the poor, and you will have treasure in heaven; then come, follow me." [22] When the young man heard this word, he went away grieving, for he had many possessions.

[23] Then Jesus said to his disciples, "Truly I tell you, it will be hard for a rich person to enter the kingdom of heaven. [24] Again I tell

a Gk *brother*
b Other ancient authorities read *except on the ground of unchastity, causes her to commit adultery*; others add at the end of the verse *and he who marries a divorced woman commits adultery*
c Other ancient authorities add *from my youth*
d Gk lacks *the money*

wages. **30:** 5.25n. **34:** *Tortured*, to ascertain the location of the slave's money or to coerce money from his family.

19.1–20.34: Jesus moves from Galilee to Judea. In Matthew, this transition marks Jesus' first (and final) trip to Judea.

19.1–12: Teaching about divorce (Mk 10.1–12). **1:** *Beyond the Jordan*, the Transjordan or Perea, regions on the east side of the Jordan river. Galileans traveling to Jerusalem for Passover would often cross over the Jordan to bypass Samaria (Lk 9.51–56). **2:** *Large crowds*, 4.25n. **3:** The Pharisaic schools of Hillel and Shammai both permitted divorce but differed over the appropriate grounds. **4–5:** Gen 1.27; 2.24. **7:** *Moses*, Deut 24.1–4. **9:** *Except for unchastity*, this exception clause has been added by Matthew. **12:** *Made themselves eunuchs*, hyperbole for the voluntary practice of celibacy; a eunuch is a castrated male.

19.13–30: Little children and the rich young man (Mk 10.13–31; Lk 18.15–30). **13–15:** Cf. 18.1–5. **17:** *Only one*, God; Mk 10.18. To *enter into life* means both "to enter the kingdom" and "to gain eternal life" (vv. 16,23,24). **19:** Ex 20.12–16; Deut 5.16–20; Matthew adds the love commandment from Lev 19.18 (cf. 22.39). **21:** *Perfect*, 5.48. **22:**

you, it is easier for a camel to go through the eye of a needle than for someone who is rich to enter the kingdom of God." [25] When the disciples heard this, they were greatly astounded and said, "Then who can be saved?" [26] But Jesus looked at them and said, "For mortals it is impossible, but for God all things are possible."

[27] Then Peter said in reply, "Look, we have left everything and followed you. What then will we have?" [28] Jesus said to them, "Truly I tell you, at the renewal of all things, when the Son of Man is seated on the throne of his glory, you who have followed me will also sit on twelve thrones, judging the twelve tribes of Israel. [29] And everyone who has left houses or brothers or sisters or father or mother or children or fields, for my name's sake, will receive a hundredfold,[a] and will inherit eternal life. [30] But many who are first will be last, and the last will be first.

20 "For the kingdom of heaven is like a landowner who went out early in the morning to hire laborers for his vineyard. [2] After agreeing with the laborers for the usual daily wage,[b] he sent them into his vineyard. [3] When he went out about nine o'clock, he saw others standing idle in the marketplace; [4] and he said to them, 'You also go into the vineyard, and I will pay you whatever is right.' So they went. [5] When he went out again about noon and about three o'clock, he did the same. [6] And about five o'clock he went out and found others standing around; and he said to them, 'Why are you standing here idle all day?' [7] They said to him, 'Because no one has hired us.' He said to them, 'You also go into the vineyard.' [8] When evening came, the owner of the vineyard said to his manager, 'Call the laborers and give them their pay, beginning with the last and then going to the first.' [9] When those hired about five o'clock came, each of them received the usual

daily wage.[b] [10] Now when the first came, they thought they would receive more; but each of them also received the usual daily wage.[b] [11] And when they received it, they grumbled against the landowner, [12] saying, 'These last worked only one hour, and you have made them equal to us who have borne the burden of the day and the scorching heat.' [13] But he replied to one of them, 'Friend, I am doing you no wrong; did you not agree with me for the usual daily wage?[b] [14] Take what belongs to you and go; I choose to give to this last the same as I give to you. [15] Am I not allowed to do what I choose with what belongs to me? Or are you envious because I am generous?'[c] [16] So the last will be first, and the first will be last."[d]

[17] While Jesus was going up to Jerusalem, he took the twelve disciples aside by themselves, and said to them on the way, [18] "See, we are going up to Jerusalem, and the Son of Man will be handed over to the chief priests and scribes, and they will condemn him to death; [19] then they will hand him over to the Gentiles to be mocked and flogged and crucified; and on the third day he will be raised."

[20] Then the mother of the sons of Zebedee came to him with her sons, and kneeling before him, she asked a favor of him. [21] And he said to her, "What do you want?" She said to him, "Declare that these two sons of mine will sit, one at your right hand and one at your left, in your kingdom." [22] But Jesus answered, "You do not know what you are asking. Are you able to drink the cup that I

a Other ancient authorities read *manifold*
b Gk *a denarius*
c Gk *is your eye evil because I am good?*
d Other ancient authorities add *for many are called but few are chosen*

Young, only found in Matthew. **24:** *Camel*, the largest animal in the region (23.24). **28:** *Renewal*, the new age on earth, featuring a general resurrection. *Thrones*, Dan 7.9–14. **30:** 20.16.

    20.1–16: The workers in the vineyard. 2: 18.28n. **15:** *Envious*, lit., "Is your eye evil?" (cf. 6.22–23n.). **16:** See 19.30.

    20.17–19: A third time Jesus foretells his death and resurrection (Mk 10.32–34; Lk 18.31–34). **17–19:** Cf. 16.21–28; 17.22–23. This prediction explicitly indicts the Gentiles in Jesus' death.

    20.20–28: The request of James and John (Mk 10.35–45). In contrast to Mark, the request here originates with their mother. **21:** *Right . . . left*, indicates those figures who, flanking a monarch, would rank as second and

GLOSSARY of TERMS

adiaphora Literally it means "things indifferent," referring to things that are morally indifferent, for example, the color of shirt a person wears or the model of car one chooses to drive. What was controversial in the NT era is that after the coming of Christ, some things which had previously been prohibited for the people of God, for example, eating nonkosher meat, were no longer considered prohibited for the followers of Christ.

apocalyptic "A genre of revelatory prophetic literature with a narrative framework in which revelation is mediated by an otherworldly being [i.e., an angel] to a human recipient." It "discloses a transcendent reality which is both temporal, insofar as it envisages eschatological salvation and spatial insofar as it involves another, supernatural world . . . intended for a group in crisis with the intent of exhortation or consolation by means of divine authority" (definition of the Society of Biblical Literature Seminar on Apocalyptic).

Aramaic A Semitic language that is a sister language to Hebrew. It became the spoken language of many Jews during the period of the exile (see the Aramaic portions of Daniel and then Ezra–Nehemiah) and continued to be the spoken language of many Jews after the return from exile. It was the spoken language of Jesus.

canon A transliteration of a Greek word which refers to a measuring rod or a rule by which something else can be measured. It came to refer to the Bible as the measuring rod by which all true theology, ethics, and practice should be normed or evaluated.

codex The ancient precursor to the modern book because, instead of being a papyrus roll, it had leaves or pages cut and sewn together. The Bible began to be copied in codexes as well as on rolls probably in the later first or early second century AD, although the great codexes that we have date to the fourth century AD.

covenant A treaty, agreement, or contract between two persons, two groups, or a group and a single person which is binding on both parties and has both promises and commandments, both blessings and curses involved.

deliberative The rhetoric of deliberation, or of advice and consent, typical of what was heard in the Greek assembly or Roman Senate.

Diaspora A term referring to the "dispersion" of Jews throughout the world, beginning with the periods of exile to Assyria and Babylon. It came to refer to any Jews living outside the Holy Land.

epideictic The rhetoric of praise or blame used to commend a person, idea, or virtue or alternately to condemn a person, idea, or vice. It was typically heard in the forum or at a funeral.

exegesis The interpreting of a text in its proper context so as to derive the inherent meaning.

forensic Legal or judicial rhetoric, in this context referring to the rhetoric of the law court, the rhetoric of attack and defense.

gematria Jewish term used for symbolic numbers.

genre A type or kind of literature which has specific recognizable traits.

hermeneutics The art of interpreting (and applying) texts and the rules used to make sure interpretation is done properly.

lector Someone who is a professional reader of texts, particularly important or sacred texts.

multivalent Generic, and often figurative, but referential language that could refer to a variety of persons or things precisely because it is so universal in character. It may be debated whether the human author realized the language had multiple possible referents.

patriarchal	Referring to male-dominated societies and societies where the "patriarch," or male head of the family, is the ultimate authority over women, children, slaves, and extended family members.
prophecy	It involves inspired speech intended to speak God's truth into some situation where it is needed. Sometimes it involves revealing the truth about the past or, more often, the present; and sometimes it involves foretelling some things about the future.
proverb	A short saying founded on long experience containing a truth.
rhetoric	The ancient art of persuasion. In NT times the writers of the Greek NT frequently used Greco–Roman rhetoric to persuade their audiences about Christ.
salvation history	The story of how God redeemed human beings and created the people of God, a community called "Israel" in the OT and "the assembly or holy ones of God" or "those who are in Christ" in the NT.
Sheol	Hebrew term referring to the land of the dead, the underworld, not to the later Christian concept of hell.
strophe	A rhythmic structure of two or more lines used in poetry and lyrics.
theophany	From two Greek words, *theos* ("God") and *epiphania* ("appearance"), it refers to when God shows up on the human scene in some way.
typology	A way of reading history which suggests that there are certain historical figures or institutions that provide previews or foreshadowing of later persons or institutions. Thus, for example, Melchizedek is seen as a "type" or foreshadowing of Christ the heavenly high priest in the book of Hebrews. The basic assumption behind typology is that there is a divine plan and purpose to human history.

BIBLIOGRAPHY

Ad Graecas literas totum animum applicui; statimque, ut pecuniam acceptero, Graecos primum autores, deinde vestes emam. —D. Erasmus (1500)

A literal translation of this would be "I have turned my entire attention to Greek. The first thing I shall do, as soon as the money arrives, is to buy some Greek authors; after that, I shall buy clothes." The more popular rendering that you see frequently, even on seminary T-shirts, is "When I get a little money I buy books; and if any is left I buy food and clothes."

I have already provided some initial guidance on building a good library through the books listed at the end of each chapter of this textbook. And I have stressed that the student will do well to obtain the new edition of David Bauer's guide to good commentaries and follow its recommendations. A comparable, and recently updated, volume (only on the NT) is D. A. Carson, *New Testament Commentary Survey*, 7th ed. (Grand Rapids, MI: Baker Academic, 2013). Here, I simply want to provide some additional very valuable resources.

Two major resources, if you are looking for one-volume resources, on context are John Walton, Victor H. Matthews, and Mark W. Chavals, *The IVP Bible Background Commentary: Old Testament* (Downers Grove, IL: InterVarsity Press, 2000) and the companion volume for the NT by Craig S. Keener, *The IVP Bible Background Commentary: New Testament*, 2nd ed. (Downers Grove, IL: InterVarsity Press, 2014). Although more expensive, one might also consider the multivolume sets of Clinton E. Arnold, ed., *Zondervan Illustrated Bible Backgrounds Commentary: New Testament*, 4 vols. (Grand Rapids, MI: Zondervan, 2002) and John H. Walton, ed., *Zondervan Illustrated Bible Backgrounds Commentary: Old Testament*, 5 vols. (Grand Rapids, MI: Zondervan, 2009). These are similar to the IVP volumes just mentioned, but the benefits of these are as follows: (1) illustrations; (2) they are written by multiple scholars, experts on each of the books covered; and (3) they are slightly more recent than the original editions of the IVP series.

It is well to read these volumes in tandem with John Drane's two very readable general introductions, *Introducing the Old Testament*, 3rd ed. (Minneapolis, MN: Fortress Press, 2011), and *Introducing the New Testament*, 3rd ed. (Minneapolis, MN: Fortress Press, 2010). I can also recommend a few other worthwhile general introductions on the OT and NT: Tremper Longman III and Raymond B. Dillard, *An Introduction to the Old Testament*, 2nd ed. (Grand Rapids, MI: Zondervan, 2006) and D. A. Carson and Douglas J. Moo, *An Introduction to the New Testament* (Grand Rapids, MI: Zondervan, 2005). Both thoroughly, but concisely, cover the important issues. T. Desmond Alexander, *From Paradise to the Promised Land: An Introduction to the Pentateuch*, 2nd ed. (Grand Rapids, MI: Baker Academic, 2002), provides a good thematic introduction to the Pentateuch. A brief, stimulating introduction to the OT which treats the interrelationship between Sinai (the mountain of covenant) and Zion (the mountain of Temple) is Jon D. Levenson, *Sinai and Zion* (New York: HarperOne, 1987). An introduction to the NT that demonstrates particular sensitivity to social and cultural background issues, as well as presenting a variety of approaches (18 to be exact) to the study of the NT, is David A. deSilva, *An Introduction to the New Testament: Contexts, Methods & Ministry Formation* (Downers Grove, IL: InterVarsity Press, 2004). For an excellent treatment of the theology of each of the NT documents, see I. Howard Marshall, *New Testament Theology: Many Witnesses, One Gospel* (Downers Grove, IL: InterVarsity Press, 2004), or his abridged *A Concise New Testament Theology* (Downers Grove, IL: InterVarsity Press, 2008).

Another very valuable general resource for studying the OT is John Walton's *Ancient Near Eastern Thought and the Old Testament* (Grand Rapids, MI: Baker Academic, 2006). I have already mentioned Robert Alter's work on narrative, and his work on Hebrew poetry is just as important: *The Art of Biblical Poetry*, rev. ed. (New York: Basic Books, 2011). If you are interested in the texts themselves from the ANE that relate to the OT in some way, I would recommend James B. Pritchard, ed., *The Ancient Near East: An Anthology of Texts and Pictures* (Princeton, NJ: Princeton University Press, 2010). Additionally, there is Martti Nissinen, *Prophets and Prophecy in the Ancient Near East* (Atlanta, GA: Society of Biblical Literature, 2003), which provides primary source translations in English of ANE prophetic texts. Obviously, there are many, many books on intertestamental Jewish literature, but one of the most accessible and helpful is D. deSilva's *Introducing the Apocrypha* (Grand Rapids, MI: Baker Academic, 2002). If one has interest in the intertestamental period, one should not pass up the single volume by John J. Collins and Daniel C. Harlow, eds., *The Eerdmans Dictionary of Early Judaism* (Grand Rapids, MI: Eerdmans, 2010). There are also many introductory guides to the Dead Sea Scrolls, but one of the most helpful is *The Meaning of the Dead Sea Scrolls* by two experts in this field, James VanderKam and Peter Flint (New York: HarperOne, 2013). Craig Evans's fine collection of texts entitled *Ancient Texts for New Testament Studies* (Peabody, MA: Hendrickson, 2005) is to be commended as well.

I cannot stress enough the usefulness of the InterVarsity dictionaries on both the OT and the NT. The whole set is worth having, and *The Dictionary of Jesus and the Gospels*, edited by Joel Green, Jeannine K. Brown, and Nicholas Perrin, has gone into a second expanded edition (Downers Grove, IL: InterVarsity Press, 2013). In addition, these resources are available in software packages. Check out what Logos Bible Software or Accordance offers in this regard (and note that Logos offers as a package my socio-rhetorical commentary series done with Eerdmans). An important volume that treats significant NT texts making use of the OT is G. K. Beale and D. A. Carson, eds., *Commentary on the New Testament Use of the Old Testament* (Grand Rapids, MI: Baker Academic, 2007). A very practical and must-have handbook on hermeneutics is Grant R. Osborne, *The Hermeneutical Spiral: A Comprehensive Introduction to Biblical Interpretation* (Downers Grove, IL: InterVarsity Press, 2006). Another standard text for the study of biblical hermeneutics is Kevin J. Vanhoozer, *Is There a Meaning in This Text? The Bible, the Reader, and the Morality of Literary Knowledge* (Grand Rapids, MI: Zondervan, 2009). One should also consider Richard B. Hays, *The Moral Vision of the New Testament: Community, Cross, New Creation, A Contemporary Introduction to New Testament Ethics* (New York: HarperOne, 1996), a good introduction to ethical issues that does not shy away from the complex questions of our time.

For a recent general introduction to the social and historical setting of the NT, see Joel B. Green and Lee Martin MacDonald, eds., *The World of the New Testament: Cultural, Social, and Historical Contexts* (Grand Rapids, MI: Baker Academic, 2013). I can also highly recommend two further studies that will expose you to more primary Jewish and Greco–Roman and early Christian sources: Moyer V. Hubbard, *Christianity in the Greco–Roman World: A Narrative Introduction* (Peabody, MA: Hendrickson, 2010) is simply excellent and, for even more on background issues and the NT, Everett Ferguson, *Backgrounds of Early Christianity*, 3rd ed. (Grand Rapids, MI: Eerdmans, 2003), has not been eclipsed. A slightly briefer but comparable work is James S. Jeffers, *The Greco–Roman World of the New Testament Era: Exploring the Background of Early Christianity* (Downers Grove, IL: InterVarsity Press, 1999). Specific to Greco–Roman background is Luke Timothy Johnson, *Among the Gentiles: Greco–Roman Religion and Christianity* (New Haven, CT: Yale University Press, 2010). Specific to Jewish background are J. Julius Scott, Jr., *Jewish Backgrounds of the New Testament* (Grand Rapids, MI: Baker Academic, 1995), and Marvin R. Wilson, *Our Father Abraham: Jewish Roots of the Christian Faith* (Grand Rapids, MI: Eerdmans, 1990). Specific to Paul is Wayne A. Meeks, *The First Urban Christians: The Social World of the Apostle Paul*, 2nd ed. (New Haven, CT: Yale University Press, 2003). While reading these studies on background it would be beneficial to begin reading the ancient primary sources. A collection of a variety of primary sources from Greco–Roman and Jewish sources which are translated into English with brief introductory commentary is Charles K. Barrett, *New Testament Background: Selected Documents*, rev. ed. (New York: HarperOne, 1995).

For those interested in the historical Jesus, there is no more entertaining and yet informative small introduction for college students than Bruce N. Fisk, *A Hitchhiker's Guide to Jesus: Reading the Gospels on the Ground* (Grand Rapids, MI: Baker Academic, 2011). For Jesus's parables, perhaps the best work written is Klyne R. Snodgrass, *Stories with Intent: A Comprehensive Guide to the Parables of Jesus* (Grand Rapids, MI: Eerdmans, 2008).

On the history and development of the Jesus movement (gospels) and the church (Acts), the somewhat lengthy two-volume work Eckhard J. Schnabel, *Early Christian Mission*, 2 vols. (Downers Grove, IL: InterVarsity Press, 2004), is worth considering. His slightly shorter single-volume work on Paul also demonstrates particular expertise on historical and geographical issues and is an alternative, *Paul the Missionary: Realities, Strategies and Methods* (Downers Grove, IL: InterVarsity Press, 2008). Also on Pauline theology is James Dunn, *The Theology of Paul the Apostle* (Grand Rapids, MI: Eerdmans, 2006).

For both OT and NT studies, familiarity with the geography in which the events took place cannot be overstressed. Several good atlases are worth considering, each having its own strengths and weaknesses. Barry J. Beitzel, *The New Moody Atlas of the Bible* (Chicago: Moody, 2009), is a moderately sized atlas produced by a solid OT scholar. For a smaller atlas, consider Carl G. Rasmussen, *Zondervan Atlas of the Bible* (Grand Rapids, MI: Zondervan, 2010). One of the best is Anson F. Rainey and R. Steven Notley, *The Sacred Bridge: Carta's Atlas of the Biblical World* (Jerusalem: Carta, 2005). As a complement to any of these atlases, consider Jerome Murphy-O'Connor, *The Holy Land: An Oxford Archaeological Guide*, 5th ed. (Oxford and New York: Oxford University Press, 2008). This very accessible single volume on archaeology will serve you well, whether in Israel or studying scripture thousands of miles away; and it does not require prior knowledge of archaeology.

If you want to begin to understand the impact of early Christianity and its literature from after the time of the apostles, see Robert M. Grant, *Second-Century Christianity: A Collection of Fragments*, 2nd ed. (Louisville, KY: Westminster John Knox Press, 2003), which includes selections from both the relevant pagan and early Christian texts. Even more useful is Michael W. Holmes's recent critical edition of *The Apostolic Fathers: Greek Texts and English Translations*, 3rd ed. (Grand Rapids, MI: Baker Academic, 2007). Also important for patristic literature is Frances M. Young, *Biblical Exegesis and the Formation of Christian Culture* (Grand Rapids, MI: Baker Academic, 2002), which deals with the post-NT development of Christian culture and exegetical practices in the Patristic period. It would be a great complement to Harry Y. Gamble, *Books and Readers in the Early Church: A History of Early Christian Texts* (New Haven, CT: Yale University Press, 1995). Finally, David L. Baker, *Two Testaments, One Bible: The Theological Relationship Between the Old and New Testaments*, 3rd ed. (Downers Grove, IL: InterVarsity Press, 2010), examines the church's historical struggle to understand the relationship between the OT and the NT while (1) recounting the history of research on the issue, (2) examining four modern proposals, and (3) considering four key themes related to this relationship.

INDEX OF SCRIPTURAL QUOTATIONS

GENERAL INDEX

Printed in the USA/Agawam, MA
January 25, 2018

668383.014